Language, Mind, and Power

Language is a natural resource: Power and vulnerability are associated with access to language, just as to food and water. In this new book, a linguist and a philosopher elucidate why language is so powerful, illuminate its very real social and political implications, and make the case for linguistic equality—equality among languages and equality in access to/knowledge of language and its use—as a human right and tool to prevent violence and oppression. Students and instructors will find this accessible, interdisciplinary text invaluable for courses that explore how language reflects power structures in linguistics, philosophy/ethics, and cognitive science/psychology.

Daniel R. Boisvert is Senior Lecturer of Philosophy at the University of North Carolina at Charlotte. His main areas of research are philosophy of language and ethics, especially their intersections and relations to broader issues in philosophy of mind and logic. He has authored or co-authored articles that have appeared in outlets such as *Pacific Philosophical Quarterly*, *The Philosophical Quarterly*, and *The Oxford Handbook of Philosophy of Language*.

Ralf Thiede is Associate Professor of Applied Linguistics at the University of North Carolina at Charlotte. His research interests include interfacing formal linguistics and cognition, including brain development. His book *Children's Literature, Brain Development, and Language Acquisition* appeared with Routledge (2019).

Language, Mind, and Power

Why We Need Linguistic Equality

Daniel R. Boisvert and Ralf Thiede

Routledge
Taylor & Francis Group

NEW YORK AND LONDON

First published 2020
by Routledge
52 Vanderbilt Avenue, New York, NY 10017

and by Routledge
2 Park Square, Milton Park, Abingdon, Oxon, OX14 4RN

Routledge is an imprint of the Taylor & Francis Group, an informa business

© 2020 Taylor & Francis

The right of Daniel R. Boisvert and Ralf Thiede to be identified as authors
of this work has been asserted by them in accordance with sections 77 and 78
of the Copyright, Designs and Patents Act 1988.

Library of Congress Cataloging-in-Publication Data
A catalog record for this title has been requested

ISBN: [978-0-367-22437-0] (hbk)
ISBN: [978-0-367-22440-0] (pbk)
ISBN: [978-0-429-27487-9] (ebk)

Typeset in Times New Roman
by Newgen Publishing UK

Contents

Figures

Tables

Permission

We acknowledge permission to reproduce the following material:

Excerpt from *Oh, Say Can You Say* by Dr. Seuss, TM and copyright © by Dr. Seuss Enterprises, L.P. 1979. Used by permission of Random House Children's Books, a division of Penguin Random House LLC. All rights reserved. For the UK and Commonwealth (excluding Canada): Reprinted by permission of HarperCollins Ltd. © Dr. Seuss 1979.

Acknowledgments

The idea for this book grew out of a course co-taught by the authors for the Liberal Studies program at the University of North Carolina at Charlotte in the fall semesters of 2014, 2015, and 2016. The course was part of a first-semester program called 'Prospect for Success,' designed to promote intentionality, curiosity, and awareness. We thank UNC Charlotte's College of Liberal Arts and Sciences and University College for encouraging the creation of team-taught, interdisciplinary courses and for offering us this opportunity to fine tune our ideas. We especially thank our extraordinary graduate and undergraduate assistants—Jibril Al-Sadat, Kevin Chauncey, Athina Hinson, Stephanie Holt, Nicole Jones, Rozie Khashmanian, Codie Maddox, Zoe Moore, Jason R. Rines, and Kailan Smith Sindelar—for helping us convey those ideas to our intelligent, curious, diverse students. Five anonymous reviewers provided an extraordinary number of insightful comments, suggestions, and questions, and we thank them as well.

We also learned, both in our research and from colleagues and friends. Daniel Boisvert learned from Kirk Ludwig, mentor and, now, friend just how fascinating and powerful human languages are and to always keep one's research eye firmly on the theoretical and practical problems one is trying to solve. He learned from Michele Boisvert, more than from anyone else, that human lives go best when people love each other. Ralf Thiede learned about the social responsibility and obligation of being a linguist in his many years with the SouthEastern Conference on Linguistics, and from the personal examples of Barbara Thiede, Erik Thiede, and Serafina Ha, who all are, in different ways, actively engaged with—and for—those who are 'othered' because of who they are and how they speak.

Introduction

A World without Words? Language and Linguistic Equality

> Learning how and why languages are so powerful can be fun and is morally, socially, and politically important.

Human beings use languages to do many things—analyze, bicker, categorize, define, dehumanize, elaborate, exclude, fudge, generalize, generate consensus, hunt, identify, insinuate, inspire, ... How and why we can use languages to do all of this—and much (much)—more is the subject of this book. And how and why we can use languages to do all of this is fascinating! Consequently, learning how it works can be fun. We wrote this book to share our joy of language, and we welcome those who wish to read it solely for this intrinsically good reason: enjoyment.

Language is fascinating, though, in large part because it is powerful. Human languages—like Chinese, English, and Spanish—do not just describe the world; they help create it. We use languages to decide—and thereby make it a fact—how much one can buy for two hundred dollars. For we use languages to decide—and thereby make as facts—exchange rates, the worth of products, the value of labor, and what a currency is. No 'real money' has to be in the wallet to exist, because currency exists linguistically as a social construct: An employer communicates numbers to a bank, and we pledge numbers ('200.00,' in the present example) via a rectangular piece of plastic and via the Internet. We expect cooperation: The number in our bank account will have to diminish by that amount to even out the *negative* amount (think about that one) on the credit card account, so that currency and anti-currency can cancel each other out. And not to stop here: A bank exists because of verbal guarantees and licenses, creditworthiness is a matter of judgment using idiosyncratic 'credit scores,' and a purchase is a renaming of ownership. A human society is created with language; language defines laws, contracts, deeds, power, duties, institutions, comparative values, penalties, memberships.

Powerful, too, are those who can use languages well, for good or ill. Linguistic power thus implies vulnerability of those less

> **social construct**
> A shared conceptualization creating a social reality. For example, sex is biological (based on how X and Y chromosomes combine), whereas gender identity is a social construct. Other examples of social constructs are race, class, privacy, citizenship, and news.

linguistically powerful and the need for trustworthiness of those who are more so. For as some become more linguistically powerful, others become more vulnerable to the former's potential abuse and harm. Thus the more linguistically powerful must be worthy of the trust required of them to wield their power in ways that empower others, or at least in ways that do no harm. Consequently, learning how and why language is so powerful is morally, socially, and politically important. We also wrote this book to renew—and to broaden—the call for linguistic equality.

'Linguistic equality' is used by sociolinguists to refer to two distinct theses, one about human languages, the other about the individuals who acquire them. Each thesis has a connected goal. The first thesis is that all human languages, and all varieties within a language, have a structure sufficiently flexible to enable its speakers to adapt it to meet new cognitive and communicative demands. In other words, no human language or variety within it is "primitive," "backward," or "inferior," nor is any community thereby linguistically or cognitively inferior. The widespread consensus is that this thesis is true, and the goal—the call for linguistic equality in this sense—is to have this thesis widely acknowledged, since its rejection has historically been used to exclude citizens from social and natural resources based on how they speak and, presumably, (cannot) think. We accept the thesis and, accordingly, share the goal, to both of which we will return in, especially, the conclusion.

Most of our focus, however, is on a second thesis, that all speakers, in virtue of having acquired a language, are equally well-equipped with sufficient linguistic skill to cope with new cognitive and communicative demands. The widespread consensus is that this thesis is *false*, and the goal—the call for linguistic equality in this sense—has been widespread linguistic immersion. Morality and justice, on this view, require that all babies, toddlers, and young children have equal opportunity to be sufficiently immersed in language's various modes (e.g. speaking, listening, reading, writing, singing), methods (e.g. rhyme, poetry, music), and aims (e.g. soothe, calm, play, fantasize, communicate facts, deride). It is in this latter sense that many have advocated in the last half-century for Head Start programs, parent–child reading time, summer reading plans, and similar immersion initiatives. Some "of a certain age" may nostalgically and gratefully recall RIF (Reading is Fundamental) trucks, in addition to ice cream trucks, driving through their neighborhoods. (Unlike the ice cream, the books were free! Please visit www.rif.org.) The ultimate objective of such immersion initiatives is individual linguistic skill and intuition—knowing how to use languages powerfully and developing one's intuitive sense of what is happening cognitively and socially in a particular conversational context.

There is no question that the number and variety of immersion initiatives has increased in the last half-century and that some, such as Head Start programs, have positively impacted the children who have been immersed in those programs. Less certain, as we'll see, has been their overall effect, especially for those from low-income families. Linguistic 'malnutrition' remains widespread 50 years on. In the chapters to follow, we produce and marshal research and evidence—most of it produced in just the last decade—to more deeply *explain* why language can be so powerful. By explaining why language can be so powerful, we strengthen the argument and hereby renew the call for linguistic equality, in the sense of opportunity for sufficient immersion.

Explaining why language can be so powerful also grounds our aim to broaden the concept and call for linguistic equality. For one can use and understand languages competently without knowing that human languages create and maintain relations of power and vulnerability. Simply knowing the various ways in which languages create such power relations can go some way toward alleviating linguistic vulnerability. Thus we broaden the call for linguistic equality in the sense of opportunity for sufficient *knowledge*. Older children, teens, and adults require factual knowledge of the ways in which language is powerful and, thereby, can be and is used to create and maintain relations of power and vulnerability. Still, one can know the various ways languages are powerful without understanding why they are so powerful—without understanding how language works. Understanding *why* language is so powerful nearly compels one to appreciate the moral imperative for linguistic vigilance— for remaining steadfast in identifying how someone's linguistic power may be taking advantage of another's vulnerability and in empowering the latter by helping to improve linguistic skill, knowledge, and understanding.

We therefore aim to strengthen the case for linguistic equality in the sense of opportunity, for babies, toddlers, and young children, for (1) sufficient immersion in languages' modes, methods, and aims. We also aim to broaden the call for linguistic equality in the sense of opportunity, for teens and adults, for (2) sufficient immersion in factual knowledge of the ways in which languages are used to create and maintain relations of power and vulnerability; and (3) sufficient understanding of why language is so powerful. The desirable outcome of the first aim is to improve individuals' respective linguistic skills and intuitive sense of what is happening cognitively and socially in any particular conversational context. The desirable outcome of the second is to increase one's stock of factual knowledge of a variety of ways in which languages can be and are used to empower and, all too often, to exploit. The desirable outcome of the third is to deepen one's understanding of why language is so powerful and, consequently, to foster and deepen one's appreciation of the need for moral and political vigilance with respect to the power of language and its potential to empower or exploit.

Distinguishing these three types of linguistic equality helps to carve the niche into which we believe this books fits. As we mentioned, the need for sufficient immersion for babies, toddlers, and young children is today (fortunately) largely uncontroversial. And again, there are reasons to be optimistic about the quantity and variety of immersion initiatives. But there are also reasons to think that their overall effect has been inadequately effective. By bringing together research and evidence from the last half-century—most of it from the last decade, and most of it dedicated to explaining why language is so powerful—we believe this book strengthens and renews the call for equality of sufficient immersion.

As the number and variety of immersion initiatives has increased in the last 50 years, so too has there been some improvement of opportunities for sufficient knowledge and sufficient understanding. Work in these areas has been of two kinds, which we'll call the 'power of language' and the 'language of power.' Work on the power of language includes resources to help increase one's vocabulary or stock of helpful phrases with the intention to bolster one's employment opportunities or social reputation. This body of self-help work largely assumes that language is powerful and provides tips on how to use it to be more successful. Its main value, from our perspective, is to raise awareness of just how powerful language can be and its intention to help empower individuals. Work on the power of language rarely deals with the social-political issues of power (mainly the power of language to create and maintain relations of vulnerability and domination) and fails to explain why language is so powerful in the first place.

Work on the language of power partially fills this void by increasing factual knowledge of a variety of ways that language has been used to establish and maintain power at the expense of the vulnerable—even to manufacture consent among the vulnerable to their own disenfranchisement! To that extent, work on the language of power implies, but often fails to explicitly argue, that the case for linguistic equality needs to be broadened to include sufficient factual knowledge and understanding. Moreover, much of this body of work fails to explain why language is so powerful, in the ways described, in the first place. Without sufficient understanding of why language is so powerful (why language can be used in certain ways to gain and maintain power), we cannot appreciate as deeply why we need to broaden the call for sufficient knowledge or understanding. Nor can we properly appreciate that its management (its uses and misuses, its accessibility and inaccessibility, etc.) requires moral vigilance. We believe this book fills these voids. *We explain the power of language to explain the language of power.* By doing so, we explicitly argue that we need linguistic equality not just in the senses of sufficient immersion and sufficient factual knowledge of its power, but also in the sense of sufficient understanding of why it can be used with such power and of sufficient appreciation that its management requires moral vigilance.

Having explained how we see this book fitting into the existing literature, we wish to say, again, that there is no incompatibility between the moral, social, and political importance of learning how language works and how fascinating and enjoyable such learning can be—just as there is no incompatibility between the moral, social, and political importance of learning how, say, DNA works and how fascinating and enjoyable such learning can be.

The job of explaining *why* language can be so powerful falls mainly, but not exclusively, to Part 1: *Language and Mind*. The central theme is that language is powerful because of its symbiotic, triadic relationship with brains and minds. Here are the short versions, on which we'll expand in due course: Human languages are powerful because (ironically) their most basic elements (such as consonants and vowels) are meaningless. Human languages convey information in a way that has, as we will call it, high unpredictability—high *informational entropy*—and they thus require their users to trust each other and cooperate (Chapter 1). Human languages are powerful because their very use exercises and thereby enhances—individually and evolutionarily—the very mental capacities that make language possible in the first place. The evolution of human languages requires, for example, a mental capacity to compare (among a whole host of other mental capacities). But with language, we not only can compare, say, dark to light, as many animals can do; we can compare thee to a summer's day (Chapter 2). And human languages are powerful because with them we can and, indeed, need to tell stories to ourselves and others to enhance informational organization and emotional impact (Chapter 3).

entropy
Here, the decrease of information *per signal* as meaning is created through layer upon layer of combinations of combinations of speech signals. See Chapter 1 for a more detailed definition.

The job of explaining *how* language can be so powerful—or some of the various ways it can be so—falls mainly, but not exclusively, to Part 2: *Language and Power*. The central theme is that we use words to do things. It begins by providing some theoretical tools to help us understand in general how we do things with words, much of which we do unaware (Chapter 4). This work continues by explaining a variety of ways we use languages to cooperate altruistically (Chapter 5) and violently (Chapter 6). It ends on a more uplifting note by returning to the language of cooperation, this time by exploring the cooperative dance between authors and their readers (Chapter 7). Each chapter begins with a point-by-point summary of its train of thought and ends with a set of questions whose aims are to help personalize the material, to draw attention to other important issues or controversies in the literature that the chapter does not directly address, and to foreshadow issues that will emerge in later chapters.

Language, Mind, and Power

We are writing this book for an intelligent, general audience who may be fascinated by how language works, who may want to understand the moral, social, and political implications of the power of language, or both. Our intended audience, therefore, includes linguistic students and scholars from different fields and highly interested non-scholars. We wish to respect the intelligence of both groups by using some terminology that scholars are using, since often there is good reason for such terminology (for example, when a more common word or phrase fails to capture important distinctions). We also want to keep the reading enjoyable. Our aim is to use scholarly terminology when necessary or helpful or when we believe a term or phrase is one that interested non-scholars, for personal enrichment, would likely wish to know, and to do so only after explaining as clearly as we can how we are using such terminology and turns of phrase. We ask that scholars give some leeway when they believe that a more scholarly term or phrase ought to be used or that a term or phrase ought to be used somewhat differently. We believe that, in most cases at least, it should be clear from the context what concept is intended. We also believe that giving such leeway is the collegial and charitable thing to do when reading work from different fields, since the same term is often used differently from field to field.

Very briefly, here is the most important terminology that will be used throughout, with more to come as it arises:

> *Brain/mind.* A brain is the biological organ in one's head, which consists of neurons, glial cells, etc. Mind is the set of mental capacities, or faculties—comparing, envisioning, dreaming, believing, doubting, fearing, planning, etc.—that are sometimes possible when a brain is working properly. As we'll see, many non-human animals have a brain that confers on them some of these mental capacities. In that sense, many non-human animals have minds.

> *Languages/Language.* By 'languages' or 'language' (uncapitalized) we will mean the various human languages around the world, such as English, Spanish, and Chinese, or perhaps artificial or formal languages, such as computer languages or various logical or mathematical languages, which are complex systems of communication. In what sense these are complex will be discussed in Chapter 1. Language (singular and capitalized) is the set of mental faculties, shared by individuals across a species, that allow them to create, use, maintain, and modify various languages. Although there are a variety of human languages, it is almost certain that all such languages are made possible by a single subset of mental capacities that are shared by all human beings. That is, it is almost certain that all human languages are made possible by a single human Language, which we metaphorically call the mind's *information management system.*

> *Power/empowerment.* By 'power,' we mean the capacity to produce an effect. Chainsaws and languages are powerful tools, because their uses have enormous capacities to affect other things. Individuals and groups are powerful when they have the capacity to affect others, and they become linguistically powerful when they can use languages to do so. An individual or group becomes more empowered when they accrue certain powerful resources, and they become more linguistically empowered when they accrue certain linguistic resources.

> *Linguistic (in)equality.* We've already touched on this, but we include this again here for the sake of completeness.

By 'linguistic (in)equality' we mean (in)equality of sufficient opportunity to access linguistic resources. Since there are various types of linguistic resources—immersion (into modes, methods, and aims of language use), knowledge, and understanding—there are various types of linguistic (in)equality. The most important for our purposes will be (in)equality of sufficient opportunity for immersion in factual knowledge of the ways in which languages are used to create and maintain relations of power, and in understanding why languages can be so used—all with the aim to grow one's appreciation of the consequent need for moral and political vigilance.

Language as a Natural Resource

> Drinking a glass of water from the tap presumes trust in hundreds of unknown individuals. Language presumes the same trust. Sometimes, the trust is misplaced.

To put into perspective how essential language is to society, let us engage in another thought experiment: Assume that language is a natural resource like water. (Of course water, like language, is also a social resource, as baptisms and community swimming holes attest.) In fact, English already makes the comparison idiomatically. English uses water images to describe language (*immersion, fluency, soaking up, mainstream, brainwashing, floating an idea*) and language images to describe water (for example, *a murmuring / babbling / chattering brook*). Human words can be *deep* or *shallow*, *clear / transparent* or *muddled*, *cleansing*, *cold*, *icy*, *meandering*, *streaming*, *flowing*, *spewing*, or *gushing*. We *drink in* someone's words when they are *watered down*.

Water covers almost three-fourths of the planet and more than half of us consists of it, so we take water for given. But in a society, we *have* to take it for given, because it is a managed resource. The overriding principle on which all water management is based is trust. There are literally hundreds of people unknown to us who negotiate water rights, protect reservoirs and areas, maintain infrastructure such as water towers, pumps, pipelines. The City of Houston, for instance, employs some 600 experts in its Drinking Water Operations (www.publicworks.houstontx.gov/pud/drinkingwater.html). Every glass of water consumed from the tap is a testimony to their trustworthiness.

Language covers the remainder of the planet. But in a society, it is similarly a managed resource. Since institutions of a society and their control are verbal constructs, stewardship of language should require as much cooperative trust as water management. Bylaws and policies and contracts and deeds and liens must use words that have an agreed-upon definition. Just as does water, so does the language of a literate society have a Great Cycle. Recall that water evaporates, condenses, falls as precipitation, and finds its way back into flowing bodies of water and reservoirs. Words, too, rise to new uses, are gathered up by dictionary makers, condensed into clearly defined entries from where they come back to the language user who looks them up for agreement's sake. That agreement rests on trust: the assumption that the word is correctly defined and appropriately used for the benefit of all.

As we have seen, however, trust can be abused. Recall how misplaced the trust was in the water supply of the City of Flint, Michigan. An article in the *Washington Times* outlined what happened ('A timeline' 2016). The City of Flint had changed their water supply from Lake Huron and the Detroit River to cheaper water from the Flint River. The Flint River water was more corrosive, however. Nonetheless, no corrosion inhibitor was added. As a result, the new water leeched out considerably more lead from the existing water pipes than the less corrosive water had in the past. In April 2014, residents complained that the water was discolored, tasted bad, and caused health problems. It was only then that the City issued a communication: It recommended boiling the water (!) before consuming it. But the City made no changes. In October, a local GM plant discovered just how corrosive the Flint River water was: It caused metal parts on their machines to rust. GM switched to another supply, but the City continued delivering the Flint River water. In March 2015, an announcement was made reassuring residents that the water had improved and that it met all state and federal mandates. Even when, on September 24, a group of doctors documented that the water was causing elevated lead levels in children's blood, state regulators still claimed that the water was safe and within federal guidelines. It was the governor who eventually admitted otherwise. The citizens of Flint's trust had been exploited.

The City of Flint example illustrates also our trust in what officials are telling us. If a statement says that the water meets federal mandates, we assume that the mandates in question apply to drinking water. Knowing the power of language entails a social obligation, which is why many linguists and philosophers—perhaps most famously, Noam Chomsky, Bertrand Russell, and John Dewey—have also been social advocates and activists. They work on behalf of Native American tribes who seek federal recognition, involve themselves in 'plain language' initiatives (ensuring that contracts, laws, etc. are written in a way that does not prevent the end user from understanding them), expose deceitful language from public officials or those who seek to become them, serve on ethics panels, etc.

Depletion and Preservation

Humankind has repeatedly come to a place where a natural resource had been depleted—all the trees were felled to build ships, all the nutrients were extracted from the soil to grow crops, all the water was contaminated or used up. There was always the option to move on to exploit new resources elsewhere. Humankind is now facing the end of "moving elsewhere," because we seem to have affected and

> Resources need to be guarded or they become depleted. This is true of water as it is of language(s). The expertise in the study of these resources is ever more sophisticated.

diminished resources on this planet everywhere. The 'Aral Sea,' once the largest lake in the world, is now the Aralkum Desert. The concept of 'natural resource' is beginning to add preservation to exploitation, 'inconvenient truth' to 'drill, baby, drill.' It is also adding an unsettling dimension of control. Nations are beginning to force other nations into dependency when they divert, store, and manage entire rivers such as the Euphrates, the Tigris, the Jordan, and, soon, the Congo and the Blue Nile (Fergusson 2015). Ethiopia's gigantic Grand Ethiopian Renaissance Dam is expected to be completed in 2022; as it fills, the Blue Nile will no longer carry sufficient water for Egypt's Aswan Dam to produce enough electricity for the region (Titz 2019).

In this book, we look at language as a natural resource with the same scope of exploitation and preservation. Certainly, language can be used to exploit. There is also a need to preserve languages, as many of them are disappearing like dried-up lakes, leaving only a name and a sense of loss behind. On a global scale, language management is as important as water management: The language industry is the world's third-largest employer after military and government. Ever more sophisticated knowledge of how language manages people is being applied by experts, often in ways so subtle that we are unaware of their control. It is not all negative: Language is used to educate, comfort, heal, empower, and liberate. Then again, it is also used to deceive, mislead, incite, and brainwash. Often, the latter comes in the guise of the former. George Orwell's 1946 essay 'Politics and the English Language' described the use of euphemisms in political discourse. After World War II, Orwell understood what was meant when a village was reported "pacified": A village counts as pacified after it is 'bombarded from the air, the inhabitants driven out into the countryside, the cattle machine-gunned, the huts set on fire with incendiary bullets.'

Orwell's 'euphemism' is today's 'framing'; his 'political discourse' is today's 'spin.' Subliminal advertising has morphed into 'localization' and 'semantic priming.' Desires and reactions can be elicited without ever being named, erroneous conclusions encouraged with legal impunity. A manufacturer can legally call a product 'Stevia' when the first listed ingredient is sucralose. With the right metaphors, a political campaign can make an entire population enthusiastic about voting against its own interests. Crest could legally proclaim 'Crest is best' so long as they did not claim that their product was *better* than other toothpastes (on the premise that toothpastes are 'parity products,' i.e. all of the same quality).

The following chapters explain how language works, how it became a natural resource with unbounded benefits and destructive power, and what happens when it links brains together. We explain both the techniques and the levels of mastery with which humans

localization
Adapting the language of advertising to local preferences, terminology, and sensitivities, e.g. finding the best language to market credit cards to particular segments of a population.

semantic priming
Presenting a word to speed up access to another word later, or to influence which sense a later word should have. For example, using the word *butterfly* will sway the interpretation of 'I have *bugs* in my apartment' in favor of insects rather than listening devices.

are able to put language to use. We will encounter some intriguing paradoxes on the way:

- The richness of human language results from a decrease of information in the communication signal.
- Speech is highly effective both in excluding others and in cooperating.
- Language enables large-scale violence through superior cooperation.
- We have no concept of how language forms concepts.
- Predictive processing can make us more powerful than a super-computer and highly vulnerable to suggestion.
- Speech can create reality.
- Good and clear writing achieves a state of managed confusion in the reader.

We will integrate current knowledge from the fields of linguistics, philosophy, psychology, evolution, cognitive science, and other disciplines to present an interdisciplinary look at the overwhelming beauty and power of language.

Please be moral and just with the superpower we are sharing with you. There is responsibility that comes with this level of knowledge.

References

A timeline of the water crisis in Flint, Michigan. 2016. The Washington Times (January 21). Online: www.washingtontimes.com/news/2016/jan/21/a-timeline-of-the-water-crisis-in-flint-michigan.

Fergusson, James. 2015. The world will soon be at war over water. *Newsweek* (May 1). Online: www.newsweek.com/2015/05/01/world-will-soon-be-war-over-water-324328.html.

Titz, Christoph. 2019. Zoff am Nil: Gigantischer Staudamm in Äthiopien. *SpiegelOnline* (July 8). Online: www.spiegel.de/politik/ausland/gerd-staudamm-in-aethiopien-der-streit-um-afrikas-groesstes-wasserkraftwerk-a-1275170.html.

Part I Language and Mind

Why is language so powerful? Answering this question is the primary job, but not the sole job, of the first three chapters. The central theme is that language is powerful because of its triadic relationship with brains and minds.

Chapter 1, 'Profile of an Alpha(bet) Predator,' introduces the notion of informational entropy. Human language has moved further and further away from signals that carry dense information. Many animals are still relying on single calls having single meanings (such as 'eagle!,' 'snake!,' 'food!'), which of course invites other animals to mimic those calls for deception (e.g. pretending that there is an 'eagle!' so the animal runs away from its 'food!'). To protect themselves from such deceitful mimicry, some animals have taken to using calls that are by themselves not very informative but create specific meaning through their combination. Outsiders have a harder time fooling them now. Humans have ramped up the encryption by several levels, by *combining combinations*: vowels and consonants > morphemes > words > phrases > clauses > sentences > narratives, each level with its own set of combinatorial rules, and all levels interacting simultaneously. The complex cortical connectivity needed for such massively parallel, hierarchical processing seems to set human brains fundamentally apart.

The cognitive requirements for the competence to put such a multi-layered system to use are extraordinary. Since the informational content of the individual signals is so much lower than in other naturally occurring communication systems, humans compensate by inferring what they think the speaker *means* to say, using context, past history, knowledge of the speaker's preferences, etc. Other animals have a Theory of Mind, too (predicting what other individuals can and should know and what they will do—see Chapter 2). Humans, however, *must* use Theory of Mind to understand each other's words, and they must continually negotiate each other's assumptions. This kind of mental cooperation works very well. Humans are hyper-social and can cooperate to the point of sacrificing their own needs for the sake of others. Humans are also top predators; in fact, human evolution is characterized by humans eliminating *other* top predators—including each other. Our linguistic cooperation cuts both ways: altruistically subordinating our own interests to others', or forming alliances to destroy a third party.

concept
The idea of *what*
something is.
Perceiving *that*
something is,
in the moment,
without labeling
and classifying
it is a meditation
exercise—difficult,
but strangely
peaceful.

Chapter 2, 'Thinking Animals,' explains the most important ways
that language use exercises and, thereby, enhances—individually
and evolutionarily—the very capacities that make language possible. Language use indeed requires a suite of mental capacities. For
example, we couldn't use 'The cat is sleeping on the mat' to describe
a particular cat as sleeping on a particular mat if we didn't have the
mental capacity to form concepts of objects and events. But when
we use language, we exercise and thereby exponentially enhance—
individually and as a species—those very mental capacities.

Like some other animals, we have the mental capacities to form
basic concepts of objects, events, and relations; to perform basic
thinking tasks, such as remembering, analyzing, comparing, synthesizing, and imagining; to perform more complex thinking tasks,
such as doubting, wondering, and planning; to perform basic social
thinking tasks, such as paying attention to what others are paying
attention to; and to perform more complex social thinking tasks,
such as attributing mental states to others. But by using language,
human beings have exercised these capacities and taken them to
places that no other species—and no individuals among those
species—can come close to taking them. Human beings can now
conceive 'objects' and 'events' as complex and abstract as *universe*,
existence, and *Big Bang* and can collectively intend to send a person
to Mars within 25 years.

Chapter 3, 'The Narrating Brain,' explores what our brains and
minds do to compensate for the fact that we do not have 'total
recall': We create stories. Language, involving most of the brain
to begin with, has become its information management system. We
forget the majority of what we experience in a given day (some say
90 percent or more), and if we really need to reproduce a particular
piece of information after all, then we create a likely story to produce
that information. It may even be right.

**memory
implantation**
The creation of
a false memory.
One setup involves
showing someone
a (Photoshopped)
picture from a
fictitious childhood
event. If the
depicted event is
not too implausible,
the subject
will sometimes
'remember' it and
volunteer details.
Skillful orators
and advertisers
have comparable
techniques for
creating false
certainties that
amount to memory
implants.

Just as likely, however, our memory will differ from what 'really'
happened. First of all, our very perceptions are already conceptual in
the sense already explained, that we typically see or hear something
as something. Second, we recall to accommodate a purpose, and that
purpose can guide the story we create to produce that memory. Third,
someone may have asked us for past information and framed that
question in a way that biases us because we want to cooperate. How
fast would you say was the defendant's car going when it {*tapped /
slammed into*} the plaintiff's car? Frames provide a selective focus
on a narrative, and that focus is its own message; we pick up on that
message subliminally. In fact, given the degree to which we read
and affect one another's minds, it is actually possible to plant a *false
memory* in someone else. There are trained professionals who know
how to create false certainties by using frames and by triggering
plausible predictions. However, those dangers cannot take away
from the rewards of linking our brains in stories: reading to a child,
devouring a book by a favorite author, or listening to a storyteller as
part of an audience.

1 Profile of an Alpha(bet) Predator

POINT BY POINT

- Using single calls to warn each other, animals can react instantly, but they can also be co-opted by imitators.
- Languages instead spread information over combinations of combinations of signals (=high entropy).
- High entropy invites variation and change and allows creativity.
- Variation acts as encryption, offering obscurity to outsiders and presuming trust and cooperation from insiders.
- As a hyper-social species, humans can cooperate altruistically, but they can also cooperate to deprive and destroy.
- A cognitive arms race has made humans capable of learning multiple languages, hence capable of making alliances with outsiders (e.g. to raid a third party). Language is a power tool.
- Language is processed through intricate pathways connecting brain areas that did not evolve for it.

Entropy and Cooperation

> Cooperation augments the information contained in speech / writing.

To understand the nature of human language, we must be willing to embrace paradoxes. One of the great paradoxes underlying this book is this: Human language gets more information across by detaching meaning from individual speech signals. From the wealth of intended information active in the speaker's mind and creatively reconstrued in the listener's, words convey only a fraction. The speech sounds themselves (consonants like /t/ and vowels like /æ/) and letters (<t>, <a>) are downright meaningless. A complex system is required to create the sparse information in speech: Consonants and vowels combine and recombine in a hierarchy of levels (morphemes, words, clauses, sentences, discourse), each prone to variation and change. Visual communication—intonation, gestures, movements, facial expressions—and speech mutually enhance each other for added bandwidth (which is why we feel more connected talking face to face rather than over the phone). But why did our species put so much stock in speech, an informationally unpredictable and relatively inefficient encoding system?

Languages are high in informational entropy (entropy increases as information gets spread out over many signals). Informational entropy is low in a word like *huh?*, but high if we spread out the equivalent information over the sequence *Could you say that again, please?* Nonetheless, we don't rely on utterances like *oh?* and *ugh!* much and prefer more 'polite' expressions like *Is that so?* and *Bless your heart!* Monosyllabic bluntness is not safe. Indeed, raising signal entropy and, thereby, lowering informational predictability started as a survival strategy in nature—on two fronts. First, unless the animal already is a top predator and has little to fear from being imitated (like a chimpanzee), the creation of an encrypted communication system increases protection from being duped by tricksters and predators. Second, going beyond a system that relates signal and meaning in unambiguous one-to-one mappings affords improvisational room for creative flexibility.

Flexibility allows change. In human languages (but also among birds, whales, and prairie dogs), flexibility quickly results in the formation of dialects. New varieties of communication separate groups *within* the species that might be competing for the same resources. The rate of change can be fast enough to create regional distinctions within a generation, but not so fast as to preclude alliances between local groups in contact with each other (e.g. for raiding resources from a third party or, in the case of humans, for warfare or for building megastructures or coordinating controlled burns). As one would expect, a complex, flexible, high-entropy communication system requires cognitive resources: creativity, a theory of mind (being able to anticipate what others might not know and what they would or should understand), and a sufficient understanding of events to communicate about them instructively. The interaction between language and cognitive faculties shall be explored in Chapter 2.

Human languages have achieved a delicate and remarkable balance: High entropy provides much creative flexibility, drifting linguistic change, and secure enough encryption to exclude 'others'; and mental resources compensate for that lossiness. To communicate a complex three-dimensional mental model of associations that is 'in her head,' a speaker must compress it into a linear sequence of words that can only reflect the original complexity as abstract, arbitrary tokens; that is to say, a multidimensional, hierarchical neural representation has to interface with a flat serial string (such as underline). From that string, the listener/reader again constructs a complex mental model. How closely the mental model co-created by the recipient resembles the sender's is a matter of cooperation and of matching associations ('neural mirroring' between brains). Human communication thus relies in good measure on mind reading, on empathy, and on adducing information pragmatically (Wilson and Sperber 2004). Human communication works on the premise that a conversation partner intends to cooperate—a reliance that also

entropy
In thermodynamics, the degree of randomness or disorder within a system. In information theory, a measure of the unpredictability of information content (Shannon 1948). Low entropy means high predictability; high entropy means low predictability.

Theory of Mind
The ability of an individual to anticipate and track what other individuals believe, feel, or can be aware of.

lossiness
The reduction of information as content is transmitted or compressed. The term originally described the loss of electrical energy in transmission.

creates opportunities for *pretending to cooperate* but with harmful intent, i.e. using what we refer to in this book as 'contaminated language.' The power of languages cuts both ways: A language is nutrition for our brains and maintains the safety of an in-group, but it can also be contaminated and even weaponized.

DNA and Philosophy: Unambiguous Information?

> A completely unambiguous information system lacks flexibility.

To study an unambiguous information system design (a nearly one-to-one mapping between code and content, with lossless transmission), we could take a brief look at DNA, which has been described as life's anti-chance device (Campbell 1982:165). As such, DNA has a 'grammar' that orders nucleobases—adenine (A), cytosine (C), guanine (G), and thymine (T)—into information-carrying sequences (nucleotides). To ensure absolute faithfulness of transmission, there are several corrective mechanisms of repair and backup. The 'grammar' of sequencing A, C, G, and T is fairly well understood, and genetic engineers now can manipulate those codes. For example, a researcher might decide to alter the DNA of E. coli bacteria so they become hungry for copper and maybe out-compete cancer cells that are likewise hungry for copper. Genetic engineering relies on low entropy in the genetic code.

But truly entropy-free transmission would prevent DNA from ever changing. One potential for change comes from undetected errors in transmission—mutations and transmutations that the genetic design would normally prevent. Mutations can be harmful (cause cancer), harmless (change eye color), or useful (improve camouflage). If they are adaptive, they are so *diachronically* (over generations) via natural selection from large numbers (the Darwinian model of evolution). Adaptation within a single generation (e.g. to a change in the biotope) requires learning; however—and this is the other potential for genetic change—cutting-edge research is now looking into whether important learning during formative years can be passed on to the next generation in the epigenome (which influences how genes manifest). Epigenome research resurrects a notion by Jean Baptiste Lamarck that inheritable change can occur over short time periods.

A flexibly adaptive system should not be rigid. Communication systems can have that flexibility; they can make a social group collectively adjust its behavior. The advantages for the group accrue as flexibility increases, and the members can adapt even to new biotopes and conditions. The champion of flexibility appears to be human language. It has, in the cognitive domain, catapulted humankind from Darwinian to Lamarckian evolution. For example, the human epigenome appears to bootstrap human infants' language acquisition by biasing them towards expecting a certain amount of consonants in the language they are about to grow into (Pembrey 2018).

Attempts to create a low-entropy human language free of ambiguity have in fact been made. In 1668, for example, Bishop

Lamarckian evolution
Jean Baptiste Lamarck's theory of evolution precedes Darwin's. It is based on the idea that changes in the biotope cause physical adaptations. For example, if a giraffe needs to stretch its neck more to reach higher, nervous fluid in the neck will cause growth. The gains accumulated in the animal's lifetime pass on to the next generation (as ongoing divine creation).

John Wilkins published *An Essay towards a Real Character, and Philosophical Language*, in which sounds whose meanings can be looked up in a spreadsheet of concepts divided by genus, species, etc. combined into words such as *conceived* (1668:429):

> cᴚambab (ca) is the Genus of corporeal action; (b) is the first difference, and (a) the second species; the adding of the second Radical Consonant (b,) denotes this word to be adjoyned in the tables, by way of affinity, and consequently to signifie Conception, (ᴚ) signifying *Adjective*, and (m) *Passive*.

At about the same time, German philosopher and polymath Gottfried Wilhelm Leibniz began his quest for a universal reference system (*characteristica universalis*) of his own, a numerically calculated 'alphabet of human thought' (*dissertatio de arte combinatoria*, 1666).

Of course, Wilkins and Leibniz were envisioning an ideal, universal language free of entropic unpredictabilities, uniting all philosophers in clear, logical expression. That is not what natural languages have developed for.

Interpreting Single-Signal Communication Systems: Cooperation and Co-option

> A one-signal-one-meaning communication system is reliable but penetrable.

In split-second situations, a single signal can be the lifesaver for a social animal. A single specific call is fast and unambiguous. Assuming there is trust that all calls are made appropriately and reliably, it is not necessary for a robin to verify that a raptor is indeed approaching. Instantly, the bird heeds the call of another robin and scrambles to safety. However, single signals can be imitated ('vocal mimicry'). The Margay cat of the Amazon jungle, for instance, can imitate the distress call of a pied tamarin monkey pup in an attempt to lure the cat's intended prey, a concerned adult monkey (Calleia et al. 2009). The tiny brown thornbill bird, on the other hand, uses vocal mimicry to turn the table on its natural predator. When the nest is threatened by a currawong bird, the thornbill imitates an array of warning calls for 'hawk' from several other birds. That deception usually causes the currawong to retreat: While clever enough to doubt the warning call of a single bird, it errs on the side of caution when hearing multiple warning calls from (apparently) different birds (Igic et al. 2015).

The fork-tailed Drongo bird of the Kalahari Desert has a yet more elaborate strategy for the deceptive use of single signals: It takes the issue of trust into consideration. It invests time when its food sources are plentiful to *gain* the trust of other species by (correctly) warning them with its own 'hawk' call. In times when its food sources are scarce, however, the Drongo may choose to make that call deceptively. With a false alarm for 'hawk,' it can send an entire colony of meerkats rushing into their burrows—dropping whatever food they had just dug up. Meerkats are smart animals, however, and decide when the level of deception is no longer symbiotic. When the Drongo's own call for 'hawk' no longer does the trick because the meerkats no longer trust the bird, the Drongo can still mimic the *meerkat's* trusted call for 'hawk' (Morell 2014). Note that winning the trust of another species amounts to a strategic prediction of what the other animals will think and do.

Some researchers (Dworschak 2007, Heinrich and Bugnyar 2007) have come to believe that ravens and wolves are able to keep track of each other's signals and possibly anticipate the behavior of a *third* species. Ravens have been seen to attract wolves by circling over weak game and making calls, even flying back and forth between the predators and the prey to show the way. Ravens and wolves live in a mutually beneficial symbiosis (ravens relying on the sharp teeth of predators to open up a large-game carcass). The predatorial association between these two species is proverbial down to biblical antiquity (Judges 7:25), and to the observer it could certainly appear that they are 'fully aware of the other's capabilities' (Mech 1970:288), though the bird is possibly the smarter of the two species (Dworschak 2007).

Imitating and predicting other animals, for better or for worse, was a catalyst for change in communication. To become less vulnerable to co-option by making signals more obscure, some species stepped up their game and became less predictable by raising informational entropy: To their split-second single-signal systems they added combinatorial rules. And the adoption of combinatorial rules for signals ignited something of a cognitive arms race: The additional cognitive power required had a cascading effect in a competitive environment. Humans are the champions of that mental arms race.

Humans still are born with a low-flexibility, low-entropy communication system: Newborns have several distinctive cries that parents know to interpret, or can learn to. For the parentally curious, there are videos that will play some of those distinctive cries (e.g. Priscilla Dunstan's 'Baby Ears' app), and there has even been at least one attempt to develop an Android app that recognizes and 'translates' some neonate cries (Saha et al. 2013). Each of those cries apparently signals a specific internal state of the newborn, such as hunger, sleepiness, discomfort, gassiness, or the need to burp. In addition, however, infants also have 'functionally flexible' signals (squeals, vowel-like sounds, and growls) that apply less specifically in positive, neutral, and negative contexts, respectively (Oller et al. 2013).[1] From there, they soon embark upon a high-entropy system whose flexibility is not even clear to themselves at the time: babbling.

Babbling is initially unpredictable. It is systematic, though, in that it has a regular progression towards predictability that all babies follow ('babbling drift'), which indicates a genetic endowment.

babbling drift
The genetically determined, universal progression from first vocalizations to first words. The genetic origin was first hypothesized by Eric Lenneberg (1967).

---

1 Bonobos have less specific calls ('peeps') as well (Clay et al. 2015), but that is as far as functional flexibility goes for them.

After cooing and experimenting with closure (gurgles, raspberries), the infant begins to produce consistent 'resonant forms' that soon turn into babbles. With increasing control, babies produce repetitive babbles, echolalic babbles (where they superimpose the typical melodies of their native languages over their babbling), and jargon babbles (which contain recurring sound sequences that sound like possible words but are not yet tied to context) that lead to actual first words. It takes a year for a baby to discover how they can create meaning with speech sounds (that an adult can understand without an app).

So why would babies venture beyond communicating with just their cries in a way that is, after all, perfectly adequate to get caretakers to cater to their physical needs? What would entice them to move from the predictability of low entropy to the 'great blooming, buzzing confusion' of babbling? The answer is straightforward: They are born into a hyper-social species. They are able to extract meaning from adult speech before they are able to pronounce words. From expressing inner states with cries, they quickly (miraculously quickly) progress to referring specifically to external objects, states, and events. Labeling leads to classification, i.e. abstractness: foods, toys, body parts, things that can be manipulated by hand.

blooming, buzzing confusion
A phrase coined by William James in his 1890 book *Principles of Psychology* to describe babies' presumed initial state (1890:488). Current research is revealing a more complex initial state of cognitive endowments.

We will see in Chapter 2 that animals have concepts, too. When a robin, for example, makes a 'danger from the air' call, the danger may originate from various flying predators such as owls and hawks, but they are probably all in the general category of raptors (as opposed to the concept of earthbound predators such as raccoons and the deadly house cat). Combinatorial communication systems probably accelerate that existing ability to conceptualize.

The Cognitive Arms Race: Combinatorial Communication Systems

Combinatorial communication is less penetrable but requires more cognitive resources and cooperation.

To become less vulnerable to being co-opted by outsiders, some species combine signals. The chestnut-crowned babbler, a highly cooperative bird of Australia, has such as system. Call A followed by call B is a 'flight call' (produced in the context of short, low natural flights), but the sequence BAB is a 'prompt call' (produced for events of providing for nests). On their own, A and B are meaningless (Engesser et al. 2015). To lure a babbler towards its nest with a false prompt call, any would-be deceiver first has to figure out that there is a code in the first place, and then understand it.

Beyond the security added through encryption, combining signals also allows nuances: The animal can adopt qualifier signals. A sharp *hok* from a Campbell's monkey means 'crowned hawk-eagle' or 'eagle attack'—immediate danger from the air. If the monkey adds a "suffix" *-oo* to *hok*, the sequence *hok-oo* means 'disturbance in the canopy' (Ouattara et al. 2009). A Campbell's monkey's communications can be specific (attacking eagle or leopard, falling tree or branch) or general (nearby animals in the trees or on the ground). The *-oo* suffix means something like '-ish.' Prairie dogs have developed signal combining way beyond '-ish.' They modify their specific calls (for hawk, human, coyote, dog, red-tailed hawk, etc.) to add information about size, shape, and color. For example, a prairie dog can specifically communicate the approach of a tall, thin human with green attire (Slobodchikoff et al. 2009).

With a combinatorial system, babblers, Campbell's monkeys, and prairie dogs showcase two qualities of advanced communication: Besides being harder to imitate by outsiders, combining signals *creates* meaning that must then be interpreted (another creative act). Such systems surely put a premium on cooperation: Not only must group members select the correct calls, they must now also combine them appropriately and trust that the combination was made appropriately. An understatement by a Campbell's monkey ('disturbance on the ground' as a leopard approaches) could have deadly consequences.

One may speculate how that level of cooperation, creativity, and theory of mind affects overall cognition. Can animals reflect (think *about* things)? And if they can reflect about what they see, could they find some things funny? Might Campbell monkeys be smart enough to have a sense of humor, for instance? What if the monkeys are aware of a beautiful butterfly above them, and one of the gang pointedly looks at it and says *hok*? Would the other monkeys laugh at the joke? The question is not all that outrageous. The brain areas that trigger laughter are ancient in evolutionary terms (such as the limbic system), and recent research has identified what appears to be the equivalent of laughter in mammals.

We already know anecdotally about humor among social mammals, and even social birds such as ravens can be playful, act silly, and entertain/impress each other with crazy stunts such as riding a boar's back for an impromptu rodeo. Bird sculptor and parrot expert Sally Blanchard once owned an African Grey parrot, Bongo Marie, who harbored a particular dislike for an Amazon parrot she also owned, Paco, at whose expense Bongo Marie made the following joke:

> Bongo Marie's cage sits next to Sally's dining room table. One day Bongo Marie was watching as Sally cooked a Cornish game hen. Bongo Marie slid over to the side of her cage to get a better look when Sally pulled the bird out of the oven. As Sally took out a knife to cut up her dinner, Bongo Marie threw her head in the air and said with great enthusiasm, 'Oh, no! Paco!' Trying not to laugh, Sally said, 'That's not Paco,' and then showed Bongo Marie that Paco was alive and well around the corner, saying, 'See? He's right over there.' Bongo Marie's response was to say 'Oh no' in a very disappointed voice, and then launch into a maniacal laugh.

(Linden 1999:40–41)

Koko the gorilla was not only partial towards the late comedian Robin Williams, but was herself observed to play harmless pranks on people. She once tied her trainer's shoelaces together, signed 'chase,' and then laughed at her own joke and signed 'gorilla funny.' Koko also engaged in verbal goofing around (Scott 2001):

Koko: THAT ME. (Pointing to a photo of a bird)
Exp: Is that really you?
Koko: KOKO GOOD BIRD.
Exp: I thought you were a gorilla.
Koko: KOKO BIRD.

   ...

Exp: Can you fly?
Koko: GOOD. ('Good' can mean 'yes')
Exp: Show me.
Koko: FAKE BIRD, CLOWN. (Koko laughs)
Exp: You're teasing me. (Koko laughs.) What are you really?
Koko: (Laughs, and after a minute signs:) GORILLA KOKO.

Watching a gorilla in a fit of laughter, writes Jesse Bering, is 'something that would stir up cognitive dissonance in even the heartiest of creationists' (2012), so it is no wonder that a new field of study has formed, gelotology, to study laughter's physiology in man and beast. We already know that laughter is infectious and promotes social health and bonding. Recordings of dog laughter (first described by Konrad Lorenz 1950) can be used in kennels to reduce tension and incite playful behavior (Simonet et al. 2005). Incidentally, dog laughter also has a tension-reducing effect on humans (Frazier 2014), which is apt to give additional meaning to the term 'therapy dog.'

Bonding and cooperative trust are paramount for social animals, especially if they rely on cohesion for common purposes such as defending local resources. Their stakes are high. Territorial animals such as wolves and chimpanzees must be able to stand united against intruders competing for the same resources, including intruders of the same kind. Humor and playfulness contribute to social bonding, as does grooming. Language has been described as 'vocal grooming' (Dunbar 1996). What better instrument for bonding, then, could exist than humorous language?

modern homo sapiens
This term is used here to refer to the last (and spectacularly surviving) member of the homo sapiens tribe. Denisovans and Neandertals were extinct by 25–30+ thousand years ago, though their genetic traces survive in modern man. Red Deer Cave people became extinct even more recently (ca. 12,000 years ago).

Creative Cooperation and Violence: Human Language

Language allows humans both to survive and to wage war through cooperation.

The human brain has several cortical areas (prefrontal cortex, etc.). Selective pressure has driven the brain of modern homo sapiens to link cortical areas to create complex modular hierarchies that process language and communication. Some of the components are old, such as facial expressions and gaze coupling, pointing and gesturing, speech sound perception, and maybe even the typical intonation contours we use in speech for warning, threatening, calming, teasing, begging, etc. Brain areas involved in language and speech are actually millions of years old and most certainly did not evolve for processing language, though they take on that added responsibility now ('overlaid function'). If brain areas had evolved specifically for language, there would probably be fewer bottlenecks in language processing. One of them is our short-term working memory for speech: It can routinely track only somewhere between five and nine words at a time before it needs to be flushed (Miller 1956). But there are also anatomically recent brain components, such as new loops between brain areas. One such circuit, for example, unique to humans, connects premotor areas and the prefrontal cortex in such a way that it endows humans 'with a unique ability for representing linguistic and non-linguistic sequences in a unified manner' (Wang et al. 2015). Language is a mental quantum leap, but it emerged from a 'Kluge' (Marcus 2008)—the complex interaction of a somewhat chaotic-looking hodgepodge of ancient areas and modern connections between them, probably with some added tweaks. One genetic change made it possible to cram more and smaller neurons together. Others involved decreasing the size of the visual cortex (compared to Neandertals, at least) while increasing the size of the prefrontal lobe. Yet another change may have been the ability for a brain area to go into a 'chimera' state, processing its traditional core function at one frequency (e.g. sequencing fine motor movements) and joining a network at another frequency for an overlaid function (e.g. pre-planning speech sounds) (Bansal et al. 2019).

overlaid functions. An organ that has evolved for one function (e.g. ingesting food) can, in the course of evolution, assume additional functions (e.g. articulating sounds), often assisted by other organs. Similarly, a brain area such as Broca's Area, which handles complex motor sequences, can be put into the service of producing speech sounds when tied into a neural network that processes language.

Without a modern, flexible language, modern homo sapiens might well have gone extinct. Evidence indicates that some 200,000 years back, the species was in perilous decline due to a period of global cooling that lasted until about 125,000 years ago and turned Africa into something of a food desert for our ancestors. Rich food sources were still available, however, at the coast lines of that time in the form of shellfish beds, which can yield up to 4500 calories per hour of foraging (Marean 2015:36). Maritime food provides not only calories, but also the best-absorbed omega-3 fatty acids for the brain—it is the ultimate brain food, in other words, which makes sense considering that brains evolved in the sea to begin with (Michael A. Crawford quoted in Stetka 2016:31). That said, the opulent abundance of oysters in the New York City harbor, which had sustained the Lenape people for generations, did not seem to have boosted European brains sufficiently to prevent depleting them out of existence by 1906 (www.billionoysterproject.org). The peak harvesting times for shellfish come around when the tide is lowest; when the waters rise, it is advisable to forage and hunt elsewhere. Hence, early modern humans had to learn to connect the lunar calendar to the tidal cycle to know when to return to the coastline, which requires intelligence (Marean 2014:18). An atavistic reminder of coastline foraging may survive in human physiology today: Human hands may have adapted to picking up submerged objects. Wrinkled fingertips, an autonomous nervous response unique to humans, make better surface contact under water (Kareklas et al. 2013).

Possession of desirable local food sources, as the fate of the Lenape sadly illustrates, invites violence. Just as chimpanzees secure their borders and launch murderous sorties into neighboring territories to expand their own (Mitani et al. 2010), so apparently did/do humans survive by raids and warfare. An archeological site at Nataruk, west of Lake Turkana, Kenya, gives early evidence of the violent massacre some 10,000 years ago of at least 27 men, women (one pregnant), and children. Two skeletons were in a position that suggested their hands had been tied together. The injuries were savagely human: sharp-force trauma to the head and/or neck probably associated with arrow wounds, blunt-force trauma to the head, crushed knees, hands, and ribs. The presentation, combined with findings nearby, is consistent with a scenario that this was a murderous raid to conquer a rich source of food on a fertile lakeshore (Mirazón Lahr et al. 2016).

Merely encountering a different dialect (cf. Crockford et al. 2004 for chimpanzee dialects) or language can already trigger aggression. To this day, human languages can be associated with genetic markers (Longobardi et al. 2015). This is not to imply that any such thing as human "races" exist—our variations affect a mere 1‰, i.e. one tenth of one percent, of the human genome (ASHG 2018:636)—but rather to indicate that an ethnic group sharing a language tends to remain cohesive long enough to share and preserve a genetic variation. To form alliances for raids against third parties, humans had to develop 'Machiavellian intelligence' (Byrne 1996), which surely includes multilingualism. Indeed, Vivian Cook has pointed out that 'knowing a second language is a normal part of human existence; it may well be unusual to know only one language' (2001:159). It makes sense to assume that the combination of (a) brain food and (b) Machiavellian language skills favored a genetic mutation all modern humans share in addition to pruned fingertips: brains disproportionately large in relation to body size. There is a gene for this; it is unique to humans, and the timing is right. ARHGAP11A is present in all homo sapiens fossils including Neandertals and Denisovans (Florio et al. 2015:1469).[2]

When the animals returned to the African grasslands, humans developed creative ways of improving their projectile weapons. The motor control needed to make and use them may also have some implications for language. William H. Calvin (1998) speculates that ballistic movement of the kind needed to hit a running animal with a throwing spear or arrow, where the entire sequence must be planned in advance and cannot be corrected once in progress, has a lot in common with speech and syntax. Humans have long-established

Machiavelli
Niccolò di Bernardo dei Machiavelli (1469–1527) was a Florentine polymath and diplomat whose name became eponymic for ruthless, ends-justify-the-means politics, as modeled in his book *The Prince*.

---

2 Neandertals and Denisovans are among the closest and most recently extinct members of our modern human tribe. Their genomes have been fully reconstructed, using fossils and referencing portions of their genetic material that survive in modern living humans.

neural pathways putting Broca's Area to good use for pre-planning complex sequences of movements. One gains a full appreciation of these ancient skills when one attempts to duplicate the knapping of ancient stone tools (Stout 2016). Certainly there is some genetic connection between processing goal-oriented motoric sequences and speech (Linden 1999:132). It is significant that an aphasia that disrupts fluency of speech (Broca's aphasia) also impairs dexterity for other motoric sequences (a condition known as dyspraxia).

aphasia
Literally, the absence of speech, though the term has come to be used for any speech or language impairment. To indicate specifically an *impairment* rather than a total loss, the term **dysphasia** can be used.

When another glacial period began between 74,000 and 60,000 years ago, modern humans were not endangered. If anything, they expanded. Their language and intelligence had made these comparatively wimpy humans (in comparison to a chimp) the 'alpha predators' (Marean 2015:39). Their 'ability to master any environment was the key that finally opened the door out of Africa and into the rest of the world' (ibid., cf. Tarlach 2019). Their violent ways stayed with them: Even nomadic hunters and gatherers that followed their prey instead of defending a little stretch of coastline engaged in warfare (cf. Blainey 2015). In the New World, Marean speculates, modern homo sapiens wiped out not only most megafauna but also the Neandertal and Denisovan populations, 'slaughtering men and children and taking the women' (Marean 2015:39). That said, we did coexist with Neandertals elsewhere for some 400,000 years (and if Aida Gómez-Robles 2019 interpreted dental records correctly, both may have split off from a common ancestor as much as 800,000 years ago).

Our modern language appears to have enabled large-scale violence through superior cooperation. Another paradox.

In a Class by Itself: A Hierarchical Combinatorial System

Language is a hierarchy of combinatorial brain systems powered by creativity.

Humans use languages for more than just bonding and cooperating. Languages are used to analyze, bicker, categorize, define, elaborate, fudge, generalize, hunt, insinuate, joke, kvell, lie, mourn, nag, pray, query, read, swear, tweet, understand, vow, write, xtemporate, yak, and surprise. We can talk about things that are not even there: memories, expectations, stories, and a Zizzer-Zazzer-Zuss, whose unlikely claim to existence is that, unlike the word *surprise*, it does begin with a Z (*Dr. Seuss' ABC*). The ancient Anglo-Saxons referred to their bard (essentially a poet, chronicler, PR specialist, journalist, political advisor, and walking literary anthology in one person—an early *homo Google*) as a *scop*, 'creator.' Language creates, and language explains.

The level of complexity with which humans create meaning is in a different ball park from the animal kingdom because the human brain puts its complex interconnectivity to use and operates across the entire hierarchy of linguistic levels. Each of those levels is itself combinatorial, and each distinct enough to have its own branch of linguistics devoted to it (linguists work in many more subdisciplines than these, of course):

- **phonetics**: The study of the speech sounds—how they are formed in the speech tract, how they are perceived by the ear, and their physical properties (made visible in spectrograms).
  ✎ <u>example</u>: [ˈbɛɾiʰæzˈtʲɾʌbl̩#wǝðǝˈwɪʔnǝsɪzˈtʰɛstǝmoni]

- **phonology**: The study of how speech sounds affect one another—how they take on features from each other (assimilation), how they create artifacts by coarticulation (e.g. when we pronounce an extra /p/ as the lips separate in the word *warmth* and it comes out as *warmpth*), how they have different realizations (allophones—note, for instance, the different /l/ sounds in *lip* and *elk*).
  ✎ /bɛti hæz trʌbǝl wɪð ðǝ wɪtnǝsǝz tɛstɪmoni/

coarticulation
Involuntary sound effect created as the articulators in the vocal tract transition from one sound to the next.

- **phonotactics**: The study of how phonemes combine. For example, a Spanish word may not begin with the consonants *st-* (as in the English word *study*—it must be *estudiar* in Spanish), and an English word may not begin with the sound sequence /kn/ anymore (that used to be okay centuries ago, as in the word *knee*, which is still pronounced /kni/ in German but /ni/ in modern English). Some languages allow only CV syllables (a single consonant followed by a vowel), others, like English, can have consonant clusters before and after the vowel 'nucleus' of a syllable (as in *strengths* [str·ɛ·ŋᵏθs] = CCCVCCᶜC, the /ᵏ/ again resulting from coarticulation). Since these layers of processing cooperate in real time, phonotactic knowledge is used at the levels of both phonology and morphology to establish boundaries between words.

- **morphology**: The study of how meaningful parts combine in forming words. The word *writers*, for example, consists of the verb *write* (a free morpheme), a suffix *-er* that turns a verb into a noun (derivational morpheme), and a suffix *-s* that indicates plural number (inflectional morpheme).
  ✎ *Betty*$_N$ · *have*$_V$ · *-s*$_{AGR}$ · *trouble*$_N$ · *with*$_P$ · *the*$_D$ · *witness*$_N$ · *'s*$_D$ · *testimony*$_N$

derivation
Changing the part of speech or altering meaning by adding a morpheme (e.g. turning the noun *nation* into the adjective *national* or changing the meaning of *social* into *antisocial*).

inflection
Adding a suffix to the end of a word to add features such as number or tense (e.g. adding *-ed* to a verb to mark it for past tense).

- **lexicon**: All the morphemes, words, idioms, expressions, and templates stored in the brain. A word is any unit that heads a phrase (a noun *writers* can head a noun phrase *my favorite writers*); sometimes English breaks them apart in spelling (e.g. *my favorite* [*chocolate chip cookies*]$_N$ —German tends to compound them: *meine* [*Lieblings-Schokoladenstreuselkekse*]$_N$). Idioms and expressions are stored and used unchanged (e.g. *she kicked the bucket*, but not *?the bucket was kicked by her*), and templates are stored sentence patterns (e.g. determining where the *by*-phrase goes in a passive construction: *He was stung <u>by a bee</u>*, not, as would be the correct template for German, *Er wurde <u>von einer Biene</u> gestochen* 'he was by a bee stung').

- **semantics**: The study of what words and sentences mean, how they get their meanings, and the nature of meaning. At this level, binary relations of words are stacked into complex sets. ✎ *have trouble, trouble with, witness testimony, Betty* ✎ { { {*have,trouble*},*Betty*},{*with*{ {*the,witness*},{*'s,testimony*} } } }

- **syntax**: The study of word order in sentences—how words relate to other words to form phrases, how phrases relate to each other to form clauses with subject and predicate, and how clauses relate to each other (main, subordinate, …) to form sentences. Also the study of how phrases move (e.g. in a question: 'What color is your new shirt?' from 'Your new shirt is what color?') and how they affect one another (e.g. how do we know that *John* is the subject of *read this book* in 'She wants John to read this book,' and not the object of *want*?).

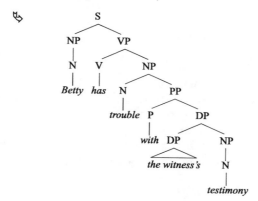

D (determiner)
Articles (*the, an*) are the best-known parts of speech with that function, but the possessive marker -'s occupies the exact same functional slot. Syntactically, -'s functions as determiner to *testimony* (note that it is impossible to say **the witness's the testimony*). Phonetically, however, it attaches to the noun phrase *the witness*. It is often confused with an inflection, but the behavior outlined above makes possessive -'s a 'determiner clitic.'

AGR (agreement)
(in this case, the only surviving English agreement suffix for third person singular (*he / she / it*).

- **pragmatics**: The study of how we know what a speaker intends to communicate within a given context (e.g. when a speaker can use 'Do you know Spanish?' as a request for assistance with translation), how sentences connect from one to the next (cohesion), how an entire passage hangs together (coherence), how a story is typically narrated, what counts as polite or impolite verbal behavior, what information the recipient adds to a message, and other interactions between speech, context, beliefs, and attitudes. ✎ DIRECTIVE (request for assistance) conveyed by means of an ASSERTIVE (information): 'Betty needs help with the witness's testimony' (implied information: 'The addressee needs to know this and may be in a position to help Betty').

Directive, assertive
These are terms from Speech Act Theory, which will be introduced in Chapter 4.

A speaker manipulates combinations across several levels simultaneously, with enough cognitive control to be able to tweak each layer's rules. For example, a speaker may elect to pronounce the word *find* like 'fahnd' (i.e. pronounce the two-vowel 'diphthong' /aɪ/ like a single vowel) to align with other speakers: The phonological level supports the much higher discourse level. Not only that: Linguistic creativity is also a source of delight for humans. New word creations tend to catch on quickly (*staycation* for a 'stay-at-home vacation,' or, alternatively, *glamping*, 'glamor-camping'). We enjoy when poets, rap artists, PR writers turn a witty phrase or word creation, such as Bounty's morphology-offending *quicker picker-upper*, which presumably inspired Theodor Geisel's *quicker quacker-backer* (*Oh Say Can You Say*, Dr. Seuss). Dr. Seuss, in turn, invented the *thnead* (in *The Lorax*), with a sound combination that is illegal at the onset of any English syllable. Mo Willems expressly wants his *Knuffel Bunny* pronounced with the initial /kn/, as in the Dutch word *knuffelen* 'to cuddle' (Willems 2015). Lewis Carroll made up new words that generations have quoted just for the sheer fun of saying them: ''Twas brillig, and the slithy toves / Did gyre and gimble in the wabe.' Gertrude Stein's poem 'Susie Asado' contains lines like 'A lean on the shoe this means slips slips hers. / When the ancient light grey is clean it is yellow, it is a silver seller.' Ildrenchay ayplay anguagelay amesgay.

Playful violations notwithstanding, each level of language obeys universal principles that are shared by all humans and adds inventories and rules specific to individual languages. Together, those layers of language can be played like an instrument. For some, like the poet T. S. Eliot, that instrument imposes a veritable obligation to be creative, to 'dislocate' his writing into meaning ('The Metaphysical Poets'). In language, universal principles interact with idiosyncratic thoughts.

One way to explain the apparent ease, speed, and sure-footedness with which children appear to acquire their first languages would be to assume that they do not need to discover the universal principles of human language (because those follow from the brain's neural architecture). They need only discover what is special about the language(s) they were born into, and soon they start creating forms and constructions that they *expect* to be grammatical. Occasionally, children apply the rules to the inventories of their language in a way that an adult would not: 'I am brooming the kitchen' or 'I holded the bunny.' Children are decidedly *not* learning from imitating what they are taught. In fact, they seem downright immune to linguistic correction, so caregivers typically do not even try to correct their grammar. Children do not "learn" their native languages the way college students learn foreign languages. They receive no instructions and no explanations. Adults simply trust that the children will eventually 'get it' by themselves. If it were otherwise, imagine explaining to a three-year-old why we can omit *do* in

'I do so like green eggs and ham' /
'I __ so like green eggs and ham'

but cannot omit *do* in

'I do not like green eggs and ham'
*'I __ not like green eggs and ham'

* An asterisk marks a form as ungrammatical (not possible to produce by a grammar). A grammar may, however, produce grammatical forms that are not acceptable to all speakers, such as double negatives. But since such forms *were* produced by a grammar and accepted by a speech community, this book distinguishes grammaticality from usage.

(though 'I like not green eggs and ham' sounds antiquatedly possible). That kind of detail is for children to fill in for themselves; their brains are designed to do so as their neural areas and pathways mature. Please note that children are the most miraculous creatures of the universe.

The Neural Architecture of Universal Grammar

Languages have the same neural architecture, processing in parallel vertically and horizontally.

The popularly best-known areas associated with speech processing are Broca's Area (which pre-plans motoric sequences, including for speech) and Wernicke's Area (which integrates structure, sound, and meaning). Other areas are hubs for finding the right words, associating written and spoken word, associating one abstract idea with another, etc. This specialization has given us the paradigm of the brain as a modular arrangement of faculties, linked to cooperate like task forces in a society of mental organs. However, such an arrangement is quite unlike an assembly of subroutines in a computer program.

If the brain is in any metaphorical sense a 'computer,' it sure has an eccentric design. Not just language, but all information (vision, sound, …) is processed in hierarchies of increasing abstractness. Not only do processes cooperate or inhibit each other, but there are feedback/feedforward loops between higher and lower levels. For a machine, this is a largely uncharted operating system. For a mature human processing speech in real-life situations, it is self-optimizing. Our brains *anticipate* what we *should* hear next to optimize current processing towards likely results. That means that our expectations of what we are going to hear can very well override what was actually said. Such 'slips of the ear' happen especially with insufficient or unfamiliar context. If a child learns the 'Hail Mary' prayer and recites 'blessed art thou, a monk swimming,' note how the actual phonemes (of 'amongst women') were (mis-)perceived to accommodate the construed result of the perception. On-the-fly adjustments have two neurobiological reasons:

- during the first year of life, there is a period during which the brain locks in on the phonemes and variations (allophones) of the native language(s), in order to become a predictive speech processor, and
- our short-term memory is minimal and our brains have learned to commit, depth-first, to interpretations as fast as possible (even proactively) so that tiny workspaces can be flushed to accept new data.

To compensate for the short-term memory bottleneck, the brain abstracts away from the actual sounds and focuses on the predicted 'gist' of its perception. The immediate jump to abstraction to make sense of the data (how else would one '*make* sense'?) is not unlike the process that improvises visual information so as to avoid seeing a black hole where the optic nerves enter the retina (the 'blind spot'). No rods and cones there, but we still see the visual information that we probably ought to be seeing at that location.

How quickly we jump ahead to a processing outcome can be illustrated experimentally, with so-called 'garden path' sentences, where the listening brain commits to a structure even as the speaker has not quite finished speaking yet (and indeed may have quite another structure in mind). For example, listening in real time to the sentence 'We painted the wall with …' sets up the expectation of hearing some kind of 'paint' next. But then the word turns out to be 'cracks'—'We painted the wall with cracks.' The premature activation of 'paint' sets up so much bias that the brain wants to reject the actual word, because it also requires a different sentence structure (where 'with cracks' describes WHAT KIND OF WALL inside the noun phrase rather than, as predicted, HOW it was 'painted,' modifying the verb instead). In a very short sentence like this one, our short-term working memory is sufficient for the brain to make the repair and trace its way back the garden path, so to speak. But the point is that we have to. A computer can easily afford to have all theoretically possible readings open side by side even with larger sentences ('active-chart' parsing) and evaluate/commit in hindsight, because a computer has a lot of what humans have ridiculously little of: RAM—working memory. Our small workspace-memory leaves the brain no choice but to go 'depth first' and commit prematurely (deterministic parsing), which entails perceiving according to our predictions of what we are going to hear. In fact, one could describe early language acquisition as maturation from pattern recognition ("baby taking statistics") to rule-based predictive perception (Thiede 2019).

parser
A set of procedures and strategies for interpreting speech or writing in real time. The term is used specifically for perception ('decoding'), not production ('encoding').

Not only do our brains negotiate via feedforward and feedback loops, operating on the data and their anticipated interpretation hierarchically. Our brains also may have *competing* avenues of computing available and must privilege one vs. the other. In other words, of two possible processes leading to different (or even the same) results, one may try to inhibit the other. English forces especially younger speakers into such decisions, because the language contains so many irregular forms. For example, the superlative form of *good* is weirdly enough not **goodest* but *best*. The past tense of *read* is not *readed*, but *read* (pronounced like *red*, not like *reed*). Those forms are not rule-produced but irregular, so they are stored as anomalies and must be recalled as such the very instant they are needed. That can only happen when the rule-produced regular form is inhibited in time so that the stored form 'wins.'

The reverse happens as well: Sometimes, we block a stored form and deliberately apply the rule instead. For instance, in the song 'Diamonds are a Girl's Best Friend,' there is a line that complains: 'because that's when those louses / go back to their spouses.' The usual plural of *louse* is *lice*, of course, but now the produced form must inhibit the stored form to prevent a literal reading of *louse* as a 'wingless pesky insect.'

The brain has ancient pathways dedicated to extracting and storing patterns, and more recent pathways (in evolutionary terms) for rule-based processes. How-to constructive processes happen mainly in *dorsal* pathways of the brain (upper and posterior cortex), and stored-knowledge items and patterns are the specialty of *ventral* pathways below (lower and frontal). As the child grows older, there is an increasingly better-defined separation between the two, and we observe fewer failures to block rule-produced forms like *holded*. The interesting part about this competition between the two processes is that the child seems consciously aware of its different outcomes. In the following conversation between linguist Dan Slobin and his daughter Heida, then four years and seven months old, Dan notices that Heida uses both the listed past-tense form *read* (pronounced like *red*) and the rule-produced form *readed*. Dan Slobin mirrors her by saying *readed* himself, but after a couple of times of doing so, he draws a retort (1978:53):

> *Dan:*   Oh, that's right; yeah, I readed the beginning of it.
> *Heida:*   *Readed?!* [annoyed surprise] *Read!* [insisting on the obvious].
> *Dan:*   Oh, yeah—read.
> *Heida:*   Will you stop that, papa?

Heida's annoyance with her dad for mirroring her left Dan Slobin with no doubt that she knew which was the accepted form (the listed one) and which had to be 'stopped' (the rule-generated one, which she herself had produced just a few heartbeats earlier).

With the arrival of fast-and-precise imaging, neurolinguists have learned to appreciate just how much of the brain's cortex is devoted to Language, even in the absence of speech. It is well possible that the demands of an ever-changing, combinatorial system that relies on creative interpretation and that imposes a burden on the majority of humankind to know more than one language and understand many dialects came with considerable neural costs. The human brain grew in a 'within-species arms race' (Bailey and Geary 2009:77) and became highly complex—and developed a voracious appetite for energy in the process, consuming easily a quarter of the body's energy even at rest (up to a third when grading term papers).

The human brain actually became *too* big at one point in our evolutionary past. To slim it down, the brain probably not only packed more neurons into each square inch of cortex, but it created more pathways to allow areas to multitask. Areas can have multiple functions depending on which circuit they are part of at any given time. Broca's Area, as pointed out above, can chunk sequences of fine-motor actions (like signing a document) when it interfaces with one network, and structure speech when it interfaces with another network, or even analyze music (cf. Friederici 2011:1386). Such multitasking streamlined our processing and reduced the amount of calories needed for the comparatively huge brains of Cro-Magnon or Neandertal. Those not-so-distant members of our tribe (99 percent of the genes turned out to be identical) needed, by some estimates, up to 5000 calories per day for normal functioning, whereas modern humans other than Olympic swimmer Michael Phelps can do as much with about 2000. The trend towards smaller brains continued as population density increased (Bailey and Geary 2009), and cranial studies show that modern humans have jettisoned additional brain substance about the size of a tennis ball over the last 10,000 years. Part of this trend may be a domestication effect—for example, we do not need the large visual cortex of Neandertals to hunt by night. But the other part is surely due to smart-tuning the brain with more interconnections and denser neurons.

Language between Brains

Language is a power tool.

The linguistic output of one brain can lastingly affect another brain ('I hereby pronounce you ...'). A change in the definition of a single word can cause a communal change, e.g. through a new legal definition of 'marriage.' The US Supreme Court's decision on June 26, 2015 to admit same-sex unions into the legal definition of marriage is an example of how a *linguistically* created reality forces or licenses a *mental* paradigm shift. In everyday life, we tend to consult not the Supreme Court, but a dictionary, to 'look up' the meanings of words. Dictionaries chronicle contemporary and historical usage, so looking up words aligns the individual speaker's usage with that of the larger speech community (the Great Cycle of words mentioned in the introduction). The fundamental question is how meanings are negotiated between people. Not surprisingly, given what we know about the nature of language and humans, the most important factor in such negotiations is: power.

Part II of this book will take a close look at the role of power in language. The same person who says 'I hereby confer upon you the degree of ...' will usually preface that by saying 'by virtue of the power invested in me.' A soap opera graduation ceremony on TV presupposes no such power, hence confers no actual degrees even while using the same words. Power determines who gets to interrupt another speaker, who gets to say *ain't*, who takes longer turns speaking, who can tell someone 'you're fired' or 'shut up.' It is also reflected in who has to adjust to whose speech. Power allows an insurance company to define what an 'act of God' is (!) and what is not (see the definition of the term at the International Risk Management Institute at www.irmi.com/term/insurance-definitions/act-of-god). Power enabled missionary schools to discipline children for speaking Cherokee, governments to make languages "official" or illegal. It allows a math teacher to react to a first-grader's 'I don't got no dice' by saying 'You know, Joshua, we speak English in this class' (Charity Hudley 2014).

In the following two chapters, we will explore the mental capacities that have to interface for the use and understanding of human language.

(Im)pertinent Questions

- What stands in the way of humankind having a *lingua franca*, a universal language spoken across the globe?
- Why did 'ambiguity-free' languages like the ones developed by Wilkins and Leibniz (or modern ones like Loglan and Lojban) never really catch on?
- Why are humans attracted to well-spoken individuals just as much as to individuals who look attractive and/or wealthy?
- Does your dog have a sense of humor, and if so, why not?
- If only elites have preferred access to uncontaminated language (as to clean drinking water and air or organic food or pristine lakeshore properties), what are public schools for? And who contaminates language?
- Is the concept of 'human races' completely bogus or could we maybe apply it to Neandertals and Denisovans? And if so, is portraying them as dumb brutes racist?

References

ASHG (American Society for Human Genetics). 2018. ASHG denounces attempts to link genetics and racial supremacy. *The American Journal of Human Genetics* 103 (November 1).636. DOI: 10.1016/j.ajhg.2018.10.011.

Bailey, Drew H., and David C. Geary. 2009. Hominid brain evolution: Testing climatic, ecological, and social competition models. *Human Nature* 20.67–79. DOI: 10.1007/x12110-008-9054-0.

Bansal, Kanika; Javier O. Garcia; Steven H. Tompson; Timory Verstynen; Jean M. Vettel; and Sarah F. Muldoon. 2019. Cognitive chimera states in human brain networks. *Science Advances* 5(4).1–14. DOI: 10.1126/sciadv.aau8535.

Bering, Jesse. 2012. Rats laugh, but not like humans. *Scientific American* (July 1). Online: www.scientificamerican.com/article/rats-laugh-but-not-like-human/.

Blainey, Geoffrey. 2015. *The story of Australia's people*, vol. 1: *The rise and fall of Ancient Australia*. Melbourne: Penguin Australia.

Byrne, Richard W. 1996. Machiavellian intelligence. *Evolutionary Anthology* 5(5).172–80.

Calleia, Fabiano de Oliveira; Fabio Rohe; and Marcelo Gordo. 2009. Hunting strategy of the Margay (*leopardus wiedii*) to attract the Wild Pied Tamarin (*saguinus bicolor*). *Neotropical Primates* 16(1).32–34.

Calvin, William H. 1998. The emergence of intelligence. *Scientific American Presents* 9(4).44–51. Online: www.williamcalvin.com/1990s/1998SciAmer.htm.

Campbell, Jeremy. 1982. *Grammatical man: Information, entropy, language, and life*. New York: Simon and Schuster.

Charity Hudley, Anne H. 2014. Which English you speak has nothing to do with how smart you are. *Slate* (October 14). Online: https://slate.com/human-interest/2014/10/english-variation-not-related-to-intelligence-code-switching-and-other-ways-to-fight-linguistic-insecurity.html.

Clay, Zanna; Jahmaira Archbold; and Klaus Zuberbühler. 2015. Functional flexibility in wild bonobo vocal behaviour. *PeerJ—The Journal of Life and Environmental Sciences* 3 (August 4).e1124. DOI: 10.7717/peerj.1124.

Cook, Vivian James. 2001. *Second language learning and language teaching*. 3rd. ed. New York: Oxford University Press, Arnold.

Crockford, Catherine; Ilka Herbinger; Linda Vigilant; and Christophe Boesch. 2004. Wild chimpanzees produce group-specific calls: A case for vocal learning? *Ethology* 110(3).221–43. DOI: 10.1111/j.1439-0310.2004.00968.x.

Dunbar, Robin. 1996. *Grooming, gossip and the evolution of language*. London: Faber & Faber.

Dworschak, Manfred. 2007. Clever ravens: Masters of deceit. *Spiegel Online International* (April 10). Online: www.spiegel.de/international/spiegel/clever-ravens-masters-of-deceit-a-476266.html.

Engesser, Sabrina; Jodie M. S. Crane; James L. Savage; Andrew F. Russell; and Simon W. Townsend. 2015. Experimental evidence for phonemic contrasts in a nonhuman vocal system. *PLoS Biol* 13(6).e1002171. DOI: 10.1371/journal.pbio.1002171.

Florio, Marta; Mareike Albert; Elena Taverna; Takashi Namba; Holger Brandl; Eric Lewitus; Christiane Haffner; Alex Sykes; Fong Kuan Wong; Jula Peters; Elaine Guhr; Sylvia Klemroth; Kay Prüfer; Janet Kelso; Ronald Naumann; Ina Nüsslein; Andreas Dahl; Robert Lachmann; Svante Pääbo; and Wieland B. Huttner. 2015. Human-specific gene *ARHGAP11B* promotes basal progenitor amplification and neocortex expansion. *Science* 347(6339).1465–70.

Frazier, Ian. 2014. How dogs laugh with you, not at you: What man's best friend can teach us about being content. *Outside Magazine* (March). Online: www.outsideonline.com/1930446/how-dogs-laugh-you-not-you.

Friederici, Angela D. 2011. The brain basis of language processing: From structure of function. *Physiological Review* 91.1357–92.

Gómez-Robles, Aida. 2019. Dental evolutionary rates and its implications for the Neanderthal–modern human divergence. *Science Advances* 5(5) (May 15).1–9. DOI: 10.1126/sciadv.aaw1268.

Heinrich, Bernd, and Thomas Bugnyar. 2007. Just how smart are ravens? *Scientific American* 296(4).64–71.

Igic, Branislav; Jessica McLachlan; Inkeri Lehtinen; and Robert D. Magrath. 2015. Crying wolf to a predator: Deceptive vocal mimicry by a bird protecting young. *Proceedings of the Royal Society—Series B* 282(1809). DOI: 10.1098/rspb.2015.0798.

James, William. 1890. *Principles of psychology*, vol. 1. New York: Holt. Online: www.gutenberg.org/files/57628/57628-h/57628-h.htm.

Kareklas, Kyriacos; Daniel Nettle; and Tom V. Smulders. 2013. Water-induced finger wrinkles improve handling of wet objects. *Biology Letters* 9.20120999. DOI: 10.1098/rsbl.2012.0999.

Leibniz, Gottfried Wilhelm. 1666. *Dissertatio de arte combinatoria*. University of Leipzig dissertation. Online: https://archive.org/details/ita-bnc-mag-00000844-001.

Lenneberg, Eric. 1967. *Biological foundations of language*. New York: Wiley.

Linden, Eugene. 1999. *The parrot's lament: And other true tales of animal intrigue, intelligence, and ingenuity*. New York, London: Plume, Penguin.

Longobardi, Giuseppe; Silvia Ghirotto; Cristina Guardiano; Francesca Tassi; Andrea Benazzo; Andrea Ceolin; and Guido Barbujani. 2015. Across language families: Genome diversity mirrors linguistic variation within Europe. *American Journal of Physical Anthropology* (June). DOI: 10.1002/ajpa.22758.

Lorenz, Konrad. 1950. *So kam der Mensch auf den Hund*. dtv-Band 329. Munich: Deutscher Taschenbuch-Verlag.

Marcus, Gary F. 2008. *Kluge: The haphazard construction of the human mind*. Boston: Houghton Mifflin.

Marean, Curtis W. 2014. The origins and significance of coastal resource use in Africa and Western Eurasia. *Journal of Human Evolution* 77.17–40.

Marean, Curtis W. 2015. The most invasive species of all. *Scientific American* (August).32–39.

Mech, L. David. 1970. *The wolf: The ecology and behavior of an endangered species*. Garden City, NY: American Museum of Natural History, Natural History Press.

Miller, George A. 1956. The magical number seven, plus or minus two: Some limits on our capacity for processing information. *The Psychological Review* 63.81–97.

Mirazón Lahr, M.; F. Rivera; R. K. Power; A. Mounier; B. Copsey; F. Crivellaro; J. E. Edung; J. M. Maillo Fernandez; C. Kiarie; J. Lawrence; A. Leakey; E. Mbua; H. Miller; A. Muigai; D. M. Mukhongo; A. Van Baelen; R. Wood; J.-L. Schwenninger; R. Grün; H. Achyuthan; A. Wilshaw; and R. A. Foley. 2016. Inter-group violence among early Holocene hunter-gatherers of West Turkana, Kenya. *Nature* 529(7586).394–98.

Mitani, John C.; David P. Watts; and Sylvia J. Amsler. 2010. Lethal intergroup aggression leads to territorial expansion in wild chimpanzees. *Current Biology* 20(12).R507–08.

Morell, Virginia. 2014. African bird shouts false alarms to deceive and steal, study shows. *National Geographic*. Online:

news.nationalgeographic.com/news/2014/5/140501-drongo-kalahari-desert-meerkat-mimicry-science.

Oller, D. Kimbrough; Eugene H. Buder; Heather L. Ramsdell; Anne S. Warlaumont; Lesya Chorna; and Roger Bakeman. 2013. Functional flexibility of infant vocalization and the emergence of language. *PNAS* 110(16) (April 16).6318–23. DOI: 10.1073/pnas.1300337110.

Ouattara, Karim; Alban Lemasson; and Klaus Zuberbühler. 2009. Campbell's monkeys use affixation to alter call meaning. *PLoS ONE* 4(11).e7808. DOI: 10.1371/journal.pone.0007808.

Pembrey, Marcus E. 2018. Does cross-generational epigenetic inheritance contribute to cultural continuity? *Environmental Epigenetics* 4(2).1–8. DOI: 10.1093/eep/dvy004.

Saha, Biswanath; Parimal Kumar Purkait; Jayanta Mukherjee; Arun Kumar Majumdar; Bandana Majumdar; and Arun Kumar Singh. 2013. An embedded system for automatic classification of neonatal cry. *2013 IEEE Point-of-Care Healthcare Technologies (PHT)* (Bangalore, India, January 16–18).248–51.

Scott, Sam. 2001. Chimpanzee theory of mind: A proposal from the armchair. *Carleton University Cognitive Science Technical Report.* Online: https://carleton.ca/ics/wp-content/uploads/2001-06.pdf.

Shannon, Claude E. 1948. A mathematical theory of communication. *Bell System Technical Journal* 27(3) (July–October).379–423. DOI: 10.1002/j.1538–7305.1948.tb01338.x.

Simonet, Patricia; Donna Versteeg; and Dan Storie. 2005. Dog-laughter: Recorded playback reduces stress related behavior in shelter dogs. *Proceedings of the 7th International Conference on Environmental Enrichment* (July 31–August 5). Online: www.laughing-dog.petalk.org/LaughingDog.pdf.

Slobin, Dan. 1978. A case study of early language awareness. *The child's conception of language*, ed. by Anne Sinclair, Robert J. Jarvella, and Willem J. M. Levelt, 45–54. New York: Springer.

Slobodchikoff, Constantine N.; Bianca S. Perla; and Jennifer L. Verdolin. 2009. *Prairie dogs: Communication and community in an animal society.* Cambridge, MA: Harvard University Press.

Stetka, Bret. 2016. In search of the optimal brain diet. *Scientific American Mind* 27(2).26–33.

Stout, Dietrich. 2016. Tales of a stone age neuroscientist. *Scientific American* 314(4).28–35.

Tarlach, Gemma. 2019. Return to Aquaterra. *Discover* 40(5) (June).54–62.

Thiede, Ralf. 2019. *Children's books, brain development, and language acquisition.* London, New York: Routledge.

Wang L., L. Uhrig; B. Jarraya; and S. Dehaene. 2015. Representation of numerical and sequential patterns in Macaque and human brains. *Current Biology* (July 22).

Wilkins, John. 1668. An *essay* towards a *real character*, and *philosophical language.* London: Royal Society. Online: https://archive.org/details/AnEssayTowardsARealCharacterAndAPhilosophicalLanguage.

Willems, Mo. 2015. I want my books to be played. Transcript of 'Ask me Another.' NPR (February 12). Online: www.npr.org/2015/02/ 12/ 385546965/mo-willems-i-want-my-books-to-be-played.

Wilson, Deirdre, and Dan Sperber. 2004. Relevance theory. *The handbook of pragmatics*, ed. by Laurence R. Horn and Gregory Ward, 607–32. Malden, MA: Blackwell. Online: www.phon.ucl. ac.uk/publications/WPL/02papers/wilson_sperber.pdf.

2   Thinking Animals

POINT BY POINT

- To use languages, human beings must have a suite of mental capacities.
- Some of the more fundamental are the capacities to form concepts of objects and events and to remember, analyze, compare, and synthesize.
- Some of the more complex are the capacities to believe, desire, doubt, wonder, fear, hope, imagine, and plan.
- Some of the more social are the capacities to imitate, conventionalize, pay attention to what others are paying attention to (joint attention), attribute mental states to others (theory of mind), and do things 'as one' (collective intentionality).
- Language is powerful because it forces us to exercise, and thereby to thoroughly develop—individually and evolutionarily—those very mental capacities that make language possible in the first place.
- The results for individuals and our species are the extraordinary capacities to conceive of highly abstract 'objects,' such as truth, justice, liberty—even existence—and of events extremely distant in place and time, such as the Big Bang; to compare Juliet to the sun; to imagine what life could be like; to plan for a 35-year retirement or a 100-year community.

> Language is powerful because it forces us to exercise, and thereby thoroughly develop— individually and as a species— the very mental capacities that make language possible.

Chapter 1 highlighted a range of actions that human beings perform using languages. Here are several more: jest, joke, jump down one's throat, kibitz, kvetch, label, learn, lie, limit, lift up, marry, mention, motivate, move hearts and minds, …. The range of linguistic actions is extraordinary. To perform them, we need an equally extraordinary set of mental capacities. This chapter aims to answer two questions: What types of mental capacities must we have to use and understand language to this extraordinary extent? How does our use of language exercise and exponentially enhance, individually and evolutionarily, what those capacities allow us to do?

To think—to doubt, wonder, believe, fear, hope—is to do something mentally, which requires that we have something to think *with*. What we think with are *concepts*, and our human conceptual system is extraordinarily rich. This chapter begins by describing this rich conceptual system. Since thinking also requires that we mentally do something with those concepts, this chapter next explains several types of thinking that are fundamental, in the sense that these types of thinking (remembering, analyzing, comparing, synthesizing, imagining) make possible more complex types of thinking (doubting, wondering, fearing, hoping, planning). Next, the chapter identifies mental capacities that develop as we begin to recognize others, including those required to imitate, conventionalize, jointly attend to things in the world, and attribute mental states to others. The chapter concludes by highlighting the mental capacity that allows us to be hyper-cooperative and, therefore, radically social—the capacity to intentionally do things 'as one.'

The strategy throughout the chapter is to identify, for each of the capacities explained, some of the few non-human species that also exhibit that capacity and, then, to compare the extent to which non-humans and humans exemplify that capacity. That strategy should pay off twofold. First, that strategy will help us appreciate our capacities for language and thought more naturalistically as endowments of our evolutionary heritage. Second, that strategy will bring into sharp relief just how fully human beings enjoy these mental capacities and how much of that enjoyment results from linguistic exercise.

Two points before diving in. The first is a caution arising from the point just made. Most, if not all, of the mental capacities highlighted in this chapter are exemplified in some animal species or other, but not in very many and not nearly to the extent human beings enjoy them. However, this does not imply that our linguistic-cognitive capacities place human beings at the top of some hierarchy of animal importance any more than does a bat's extraordinary capacity for navigating in the dark place it at the top of such a hierarchy. It simply means that our linguistic-cognitive capacities constitute a fascinating, powerful part of what it is to be a human being. The second, and more important, point is that the mental capacities highlighted in this chapter will re-emerge in later chapters, when we highlight language's important social, political, and moral consequences.

Rich Concepts

Human beings have an extraordinarily rich conceptual system.

To think is to do something mentally: to doubt, desire, deliberate, decide, and so on. But doing these requires that we doubt, desire, deliberate, and decide with something or about something. Thinking requires having 'something in mind.' What we have in mind—the constituents with which we think—are *concepts*. For example, if we doubt *that Smith will catch the ball*, we have something in mind; our doubting has *content*. In this case, we are thinking with the concepts SMITH, BALL, CATCH, FUTURE.[1] These concepts already exhibit complexity, abstraction, and relationship. For example, to grasp the complex concept CATCH requires that we grasp its component concepts, which might be analyzed as PREVENTING-DROPPING-OBJECT-FROM-CONTACTING-GROUND. In turn, grasping just one of these component concepts, DROPPING, requires that we grasp the abstract concept MOTION and the relational concepts ABOVE and BELOW. It doesn't take many examples like these to demonstrate that the human conceptual system is extraordinarily rich. We can appreciate just how rich if we focus nearer to the beginning of the evolutionary story, on brain states and reflexes.

concepts
Common constituents of thought. What thinkers think *with*. What thinkers "have in mind" when thinking.

Brain States and Reflexes

Concepts are more than merely brain states that help thinkers partition experience.

A frog sits peacefully and, like a whip, lashes its tongue to feed on an approaching fly. How does this happen? We need not go into precise detail to understand this much: When an object of a certain size, mass, and constitution approaches within a certain distance and at a certain angle of a frog's eyes, that event causes the frog's brain to enter a certain state that nearly instantaneously causes the frog to open-its-mouth-and-lash-its-tongue-toward-that-object, retract-tongue, and close-its-mouth. Thus, there is some particular brain state of the frog that enables it to partition its experience in ways helpful to it, perhaps into [FLY$_f$] and [NON-FLY$_f$], [FOOD$_f$] and [NON-FOOD$_f$],[2] or some such helpful partition, and to consistently react accordingly.

If allowed to speak loosely, we can say that by entering this brain state, the frog accesses the mental representation of (let's say) [FLY$_f$]; some might want to say that this particular brain state of the frog *is* a mental representation of a fly. But in so doing, there is usually no suggestion that frogs understand the concept FLY$_f$ (and especially no suggestion that such a concept would be anything like a human's concept FLY). That is because there is usually no suggestion that frogs think about flies. There is usually no suggestion that frogs wonder whether flies will appear, expect flies to appear, hope that flies appear, dream about flies, plan to catch flies, or remember this morning's fly. Rather, the frog's brain state serves only as a direct,

---

1 In this chapter, we use SMALLCAPS to signify concepts, [SMALLCAPS] (in brackets) to signify brain states, and *italics* to signify either properties or contents of thoughts. The context should disambiguate whether the italics are signifying properties or thought-contents.

2 The subscript 'f' simply clarifies that this brain state is of a frog so as not to suggest that the frog's brain state upon perceiving a frog is like a human being's brain state. Likewise is the subscript used to clarify the concepts and mental representations of various species, e.g. 'SNAKE$_v$' will indicate a vervet's concept of a snake.

real-time link between its perceptual system and its motor system—it causes an immediate reflex comparable to the sucking reflex in newborn mammals.

Like frogs, all animals and insects are able to partition their experiences in ways helpful to them. This is unsurprising, since if they could not, then they, like frogs, would not have evolved as they have. But also, as with frogs, there is no suggestion that all animals and all insects grasp concepts, for there is no suggestion that all animals and all insects wonder, expect, hope, dream, plan, or remember. (Although as we'll see shortly, many animals, though likely not many insects, surely do.) Still, our brain's capacity to partition experience is necessary, if insufficient, for grasping concepts and, therefore, is necessary but insufficient for thinking and for using and understanding language. That is, it is necessary but ultimately insufficient for thinking about, referring to, and talking about things, such as flies.

Concepts of Objects and Events

> The human capacity to conceive of objects and events is astonishing and astonishingly complex.

Many wonder how a concept and, more generally, consciousness can emerge from a particular brain state or series of brain states. They wonder for good reason. For how concepts and consciousness emerge from brain states—how a particular brain state gives rise to *what it is like* to see a fly or *what it is like* to feel a fly on your skin—remains one of humanity's mysteries. That mystery even has a name, 'The Problem of Consciousness,' which is the most pressing instance of the more general mystery called 'The Mind–Body Problem,' that of explaining how, exactly, mental phenomena are related to physical phenomena. But if the question is not how, but what it would be for a concept to emerge from a particular brain state or series of brain states, we can gain traction by having a closer look at vervet monkeys.

Vervet monkeys produce and respond to various types of alarm calls, including one for each of three dangerous predators. When a vervet perceives a snake, it produces a distinct snake alarm call that causes other vervets to stand tall and scan around. When a vervet perceives an eagle, it produces a distinct eagle alarm call that causes other vervets to move swiftly into covered brush. When a vervet perceives a leopard, it produces a distinct leopard alarm call that causes other vervets to climb to the end of a branch too weak to support a leopard's weight. Given our previous discussion of frogs, it is easy to wonder: Are vervet alarm calls and responses to them simply reflexes? Or do vervets actually think about snakes, eagles, and leopards? In other words, do vervets have the mental capacity to form the concepts $SNAKE_v$, $EAGLE_v$, and $LEOPARD_v$?

There is evidence that they, or at least their close relatives, Diana monkeys, do form such concepts. Consider one interesting experiment in which Klaus Zuberbühler (2000) recorded four sounds: two

Diana alarm calls, one for their predator eagle and another for their predator leopard; and two predator noises, an eagle's screech and a leopard's growl. In one experimental condition, Zuberbühler first played an alarm call followed five minutes later by the noise of its corresponding predator. For example, he first played the recorded eagle alarm call, then five minutes later the recorded eagle screech. In a second experimental condition, Zuberbühler played an alarm call followed five minutes later by the noise of the other predator. For example, he first played the recorded eagle alarm call, then five minutes later the recorded leopard growl. The Diana monkeys showed significantly less alarm in the first experimental condition than in the second, which suggests that the Diana monkeys were *expecting* the predator corresponding to the alarm call. Expecting something is a type of thinking *about* something, which requires that Diana monkeys grasp the appropriate concepts. Again, one should not take these results too far by inferring that the Diana monkeys' concepts $EAGLE_d$ and $LEOPARD_d$ are just like our human concepts of such animals. Still, Diana monkeys must have some concepts $EAGLE_d$ and $LEOPARD_d$ if they are in fact expecting an eagle or a leopard—as must we when we are alarmed by someone screaming, 'Leopard, run!' Diana monkeys appear to have the capacity to form concepts of objects.

Many other animals must also have the capacity to form concepts of objects. For many other animals form concepts of events, and forming a concept of an event requires forming concepts of objects. For example, rats appear to dream. In a series of experiments, Kenway Louie and Matthew Wilson (2001) recorded the brain-'firing' patterns of rats as they ran a maze and, afterward, during the rats' REM stages of sleep, the period of sleep in which humans dream. Louie and Wilson found patterns of the rats' neural activity during sleep, patterns which lasted sometimes for minutes, that so overlapped the patterns of the rats' neural activity while running the maze that the researchers could actually pinpoint where the rats "were" in the maze while asleep. Louie and Wilson reasonably concluded that a good explanation for these results is that the rats were dreaming about—mentally reliving—running the maze, which requires forming some such concept as $BARRIER_r$ or $WALL_r$. If so, this means that the rats were thinking about and, therefore, conceiving of a past event and of the objects constituting that event.

Shortly, we'll encounter more telling examples of the capacity of some non-human animals to form concepts of objects and events. But even from this very start, it is important to appreciate how the exercise of human language has exponentially enhanced the human capacity to conceive of and to talk about objects and, especially, of events. The human conceptual system is astonishingly complex. Many people remember fondly and reminisce with others about their first kiss. Those who do, grasp, among other object-concepts, the concepts SELF, OTHER, TOUCH, and LIP, which, somehow, are bound together by the event-concept KISS. ('Somehow,' because how an event-concept binds together object-concepts also remains a cognitive mystery.) And those who reminisce use language to mentally transport others to a distant time and place. To take an astoundingly more complex, if more emotionally difficult, example, this chapter was drafted on the verge of another anniversary of 9/11. Most people living in the United States at the time would find it astonishing to reflect upon and appreciate just how many different events and just how many different objects of which they are conceiving—NEW YORK CITY, PENTAGON, SHANKSVILLE PA, SKY-SCRAPER, AIRPLANE, FIRE, SMOKE, COLLAPSE, TERRORIST, ATTACK—that compose an event-concept as complex as their concept 9/11 and to reflect upon and appreciate just how complex, subtle, and fine-grained human language must be to effectively communicate about that tragic day.

More Complex Capacities

The human capacities to remember and analyze underwrite our capacities to compare, synthesize, imagine, and plan, and they require more developed capacities to grasp abstract and relational concepts.

Human beings perform many types of linguistic acts. We can perform these linguistic acts, in part, because we have the mental capacities to form concepts of objects and concepts of events. In this section, we'll highlight more complex types of mental capacities, including the capacities to remember, analyze, compare, synthesize, imagine, and plan. These types of mental capacities are complex in the sense that exercising them requires that we exercise still other mental capacities, including the capacities to form some extremely abstract and relational concepts. These types of mental capacities are fundamental in the sense that performing them is required for more complex types of thinking, including doubting, desiring, believing, wondering, fearing, and hoping.

Remembering and Analyzing

Discerning an object's or event's more fine-grained properties and relations requires the corresponding mental capacity to analyze.

episodic memory Capacity to remember specific events.

The previous section presented three examples of the mental capacity to remember events. Rats dream about—mentally relive—running a maze. Many people fondly remember their first kiss. And many people soberly remember 9/11. The capacity to remember past events is called *episodic memory*.

Scrub jays also have episodic memory, or at least something very close to it. For scrub jays hide food, distinguish it as perishable or non-perishable, and remember where and roughly when they hid it (Clayton and Dickinson 1998). For example, when a scrub jay hides a maggot, which is perishable, and is kept away from the hiding place long enough for the maggot to decay, then, when released, it will not go to that hiding place. However, when a scrub jay hides a nut, which is not as immediately perishable, and is kept away from the hiding place for the same amount of time it was kept away from the maggot, then, when released, the scrub jay will go straight to the hiding place. Although one cannot conclude from these observations that scrub jays remember the *event* of their hiding the maggot or the *event* of their hiding the nut, it is reasonable to conclude that scrub jays remember what they hid, where they hid it, and roughly when they hid it. Thus, scrub jays remember at least objects and locations and have a sense of duration.

By classifying something as significant or nonsignificant, as perishable or nonperishable, as at location X or at location Y, etc., scrub jays also demonstrate the capacity to discern of a specific object its bundle of properties and relations and to form their corresponding concepts. Thus, a scrub jay might discern of its particular maggot the bundle of properties *soft, perishable, located there$_{xs}$, N amount of time ago* and, consequently, its concept of that particular maggot might be analyzed accordingly into the bundle of simpler concepts SOFT$_s$-PERISHABLE$_s$-LOCATED THERE$_{xs}$-N AMOUNT OF TIME AGO$_s$. Likewise, a scrub jay might discern of its particular nut the bundle of properties *hard, nonperishable, located there$_y$, M amount of time ago* and, consequently, its concept of that particular nut might be analyzed accordingly into the bundle of simpler concepts HARD$_s$-NONPERISHABLE$_s$-LOCATED THERE$_{ys}$-M AMOUNT OF TIME AGO$_s$.

Some animals, especially those who live socially, such as primates, have the capacity to remember events that occurred years earlier (Martin-Ordas et al. 2013) and to discern of certain objects an extremely fine-grained set of properties and relations and to conceive of them accordingly. Using such fine-grained analyses, these animals can remember particular objects, especially particular individuals of the same species from whom they've been separated for years. Baboons and gorillas, for example, can remember years later another individual baboon by its face, size, friendliness, level of aggression, and other fine-grained properties (Usher 2012).

By using language, human beings have exercised and developed those capacities to extraordinary levels. Human beings can remember and use language to talk about a specific person, object, or event decades later, even if we neither see that person or object again nor repeat a similar event. Indeed, if the accompanying emotion is strong enough, we can do so even if we've encountered only for a few minutes that person (our first love), object (The Grand Canyon), or event (the birth of our child). By using language, we can even talk and think about people and objects that existed and events that occurred thousands—even billions—of years ago! We can talk about and conceive of Aristotle in terms of his bundle of complex properties (*ancient Greek philosopher, student of Plato, teacher of Alexander the Great, founder of the Lyceum*). Likewise we can talk about the Buddhist Horyu-ji Temple (*oldest wooden structures still standing, Ikaruga, Nara Prefecture, Japan*), Caesar crossing the Rubicon, and the Big Bang. We can even talk and think about people, objects, and events that *have never and will never exist*, such as King Arthur, Excalibur, and setting up a royal palace at Camelot.

Comparing and Synthesizing

> Memory and analysis permit comparison and synthesis.

Classifying objects and events according to their bundle of finely grained properties and relations; conceptualizing those objects, events, properties, and relations accordingly; remembering them: These provide the foundation for comparing. To compare requires that one identify and pay attention to multiple items, classify each according to its respective properties and relations, remember those items accordingly, and discern similarities and differences among them.

To appreciate just how complex is this mental capacity, consider the case of Alex the African Grey parrot, trained by researcher Irene Pepperberg and her assistants (2002). African Grey parrots can mimic human language. Over 30 years with Pepperberg, Alex developed the capacity to apply words to various colors, such as 'red,' 'black,' 'blue,' and 'green'; to various shapes, such as 'round,' 'square,' and 'flat'; and to various materials, such as 'wool,' 'rock,' and 'wood.' When shown a flat, wooden, green object and asked, 'What color?,' Alex could correctly respond, 'Green'; when shown a round, woolen, blue object and asked, 'What shape?,' Alex could correctly respond, 'Round'; and Alex could correctly respond to such questions at rates greater than chance. Alex could do things even more remarkable. For example, if shown a tray of three objects with one property in common—for example, if all were black—and asked, 'What same?,' Alex could correctly respond, 'Color.' If shown three objects with all but one property in common—for example, if they differed only in that one was square, another round, and another flat—and asked, 'What different?,' Alex could correctly respond, 'Shape.' In fact, if the three objects had no property in common and Alex was asked, 'What same?,' Alex could correctly respond, 'None.' And, again, Alex could correctly respond to such questions at rates greater than chance.

high-order property Property of a property or relation. *Being red* is a first-order property and *_is the same as_* is a relation that some objects or set of objects exemplifies. *Being a color* and *being symmetrical* are higher-order properties than *redness* and *_is the same as_* respectively exemplify.

The seeming simplicity of Alex's tasks belies their complexity. For such tasks require the additional mental capacities to discern that properties have properties—i.e. higher-order properties—and to grasp quite abstract concepts. Consider the first case, in which Alex is shown a tray of three objects having only their black color in common and asked, 'What same?' To successfully complete this task, Alex must:

*   discern and maintain attention to three objects;
*   discern of each of the three objects at least three properties;
*   discern and remember that the first object is (say) wool, the second wood, the third rock;
*   discern and remember that the second object is (say) round, the second cubed, the third flat;

- discern and remember that the first object is (say) black, the second object is black, and the third object is black;
- compare the 'sameness' of the three objects in terms of the same property types (so that Alex is comparing *blue* and *green* and *black*, not *blue* and *round* and *wool*, etc.);
- grasp that wool, wood, and rock are different materials; that is, Alex must grasp that the properties *wool*, *wood*, and *rock* have the further property *being materialled* and, consequently, Alex must grasp the higher-order concept MATERIAL$_a$ and the relation _DIFFERENT FROM$_a$;
- grasp that round, cubed, and flat are different shapes and, consequently, must grasp the higher-order concept SHAPE$_a$;
- grasp that the *black* of all three objects is the same color and, consequently, must grasp the higher-order concept COLOR and the relation _SAME AS$_a$;
- recognize that what is being asked for is not the particular color that the three objects share (*black*), but the particular higher-order property that is the same (*color, shape,* or *material*);
- recognize that what is being asked for is not the relation *different from* but the relation *same as*;
- be moved to answer correctly; and
- select the right words.

The complexity required for even this "simple" task of successfully answering what type of property three objects have in common and, therefore, the complexity of Alex's mental capacities are remarkable. Still, the exercise of human language has made such mental feats almost trivial for human beings. We accomplish such feats easily, thousands of times per day, discerning properties of an even higher order, grasping concepts correspondingly even more abstract, talk with others about them—and think nothing of it. Consider just the abstract and higher-order concepts humans must grasp that are expressed by the following highlighted words from the US Declaration of Independence:

abstract concept
Concept of higher-order properties. The concepts COLOR and SYMMETRY are more abstract than the concepts RED or SAME. Some of the more important human concepts are extremely abstract, such as TRUTH, BEAUTY, JUSTICE, and FAIRNESS.

> **We hold** [believe] these **truths** to be **self-evident**, that **all** men are **created equal**, that they are **endowed** by their **Creator** with certain **unalienable Rights**, that among these are **Life, Liberty** and the **pursuit** of **Happiness**. — That to **secure** these rights, **Governments** are **instituted** among Men, **deriving** their **just powers** from the **consent** of the **governed**, — That **whenever** any **Form** of Government **becomes destructive** of these **ends**, it is the Right of the People to **alter** or to **abolish** it, and to institute new Government, laying its **foundation** on such **principles** and **organizing** its powers in such form, as to them shall seem **most likely** to **effect** their **Safety** and Happiness.

Our extraordinary capacities to analyze, compare, and grasp abstract and higher-order concepts and to use languages to talk about and understand such properties and comparisons provide the foundation by which we communicate using aphorism, analogy, simile, symbol, and metaphor. And our language in turn enhances what these capacities allow us to do. Were these devices ever in better hands than in Shakespeare's?

But, soft! what light through yonder window breaks?
It is the east, and Juliet is the sun.
…
The brightness of her cheek would shame those stars,
As daylight doth a lamp; her eyes in heaven stream: shine.
Would through the airy region stream so bright
That birds would sing and think it were not night.

(*Romeo and Juliet*)

… a rose by any other word would smell as sweet.

(*Romeo and Juliet*)

Shall I compare thee to a summer's day?
Thou art more lovely and more temperate
…
But thy eternal summer shall not fade,
Nor lose possession of that fair thou ow'st;
Nor shall Death brag thou wander'st in his shade,
When in eternal lines to time thou grow'st:
So long as men can breathe, or eyes can see,
So long lives this, and this gives life to thee.

(Sonnet 18)

Life is a tale told by an idiot—full of sound and fury, signifying nothing.

(*Macbeth*)

Alex the African Grey parrot's capacity to compare is remarkable, and it is no slight to his cognitive achievements that he would not have been able to compare life to a box of chocolates (*Forrest Gump*).

conceptual synthesis
Capacity to mentally combine simpler concepts to construct more complex concepts.

If an animal can discern of an object or event its more finely grained properties and relations and form concepts of those more finely grained properties and relations, then it is mentally breaking the object or event down into smaller components. If so, then it has smaller mental components with which it might be able to perform other kinds of metal activities. For example, we've seen that some animals, including Alex, can find similarities and differences between the properties of multiple items. With their stock of corresponding concepts, some animals can then begin shuffling—can begin synthesizing—these more finely grained concepts in novel ways. The capacity to synthesize provides the foundation for more complex mental and linguistic capacities, including the capacities to imagine and plan.

Imagining and Planning

Comparison and synthesis permit imagining and planning.

imagination
Capacity to think about something not present or never before perceived.

For the basic idea, consider a stock example. Most of us have seen horses or, at least, pictures of horses and, consequently, most of us grasp the concept HORSE. We've also discerned that horses usually stand upright on four legs, have a peculiarly shaped head, and so on, so we grasp the concepts LEG, HEAD, etc. In fact, most of us probably have the more finely grained concepts HORSE-LEG, HUMAN-LEG, HORSE-HEAD, and HUMAN-HEAD. We have also likely seen various birds and flying insects, discerned that they have wings, and so we grasp the concept WING. Because we now have the more finely grained concepts HORSE-HEAD, HORSE-LEG, and WING, we can now mentally shuffle these and other concepts, such as WHITE, together in novel ways, for example, to imagine a fully white horse with wings. If so, we are beginning to imagine the mythical Greek creature Pegasus, an object. If we also imagine this object flying around in the sky, we are imagining an event. And in case we didn't know anything about Pegasus, someone could simply use language to enhance our capacity to do so: 'Pegasus is a mythical Greek white horse that has wings and, sometimes, flies around.' Our capacity to use and to understand this sentence requires our capacity to synthesize 'smaller' mental components—it requires our capacity to imagine.

In this stock example, we are imagining a nonexistent object and a fictitious event. Since this fictitious event involves an unlikely-to-exist object, our imagining in this case is an act of fantasy. We can, of course, imagine existing objects and actual events, which we do when we remember an object or event, visualize an existing object that is described to us, or envision ourselves moving about in a country we are about to visit for the first time. But imagining is not simply, nor does it necessarily require, visualizing. For example, it would be using our capacity to imagine to sincerely answer when we're asked how it would feel to be the best in the world at something important to us or how it would taste if we mixed some well-aged white balsamic vinegar, the juice of one-eighth of a lemon, a slight pinch of white pepper, and just the right hint of fresh thyme.

Since remembering an event is an act of imagining, then any animal with episodic memory, such as rats, can imagine. But some animals, especially primates, seem to have a gift for imagining. Many can imagine objects, use an object as if it were another object, play, pretend, and even feign emotions (Do animals? 2013). Recall Koko, the prank-playing, joking, American Sign Language-using gorilla, who tied her trainer's shoelaces together, signed 'Chase,' and laughed at her own joke. Koko clearly seemed able to imagine what would happen if her trainer were to chase Koko. Recall that Koko also joked with her trainers that she was a bird, signing at the end that, of course, she was actually a gorilla. Koko clearly seemed able to distinguish fantasy from reality, which means that Koko could actually *pretend* to be a bird.

Once we begin reflecting on our linguistically exercised power to imagine, we realize at once how much it empowers us. With it, we can remember and pretend, wonder and hypothesize, relive and anticipate, construct and create, review and set new goals, honor and storytell, fear and hope, envy and love. (If you don't yet believe these mental and linguistic capacities are powerful, please turn directly to Chapter 3!) And we can enhance each of these capacities exponentially by using language. We can read diaries and write memoirs to learn about and pass on family and personal history; write and read fairy tales about once upon a time; wonder and fantasize about galaxies far, far away; hypothesize and summarize research about deoxyribonucleic acid (DNA), as did Watson and Crick (1953); write and read novels that stir our emotions.

We can also use language to exponentially enhance our capacity to plan.

planning
Preparing a sequence of actions to accomplish a goal. Requires one to imagine, to understand cause and effect, and to control impulses.

And how: life-planning workshops, mission statements, vision statements, five-year plans, retirement plans, goal-setting workshops, strategy sessions, project-management timelines, contracts, calendars, brainstorming activities, to-do lists, grocery lists, dissertation outlines are but a few ways in which we use language to help us plan.

Planning is preparing a script, a sequence of actions to accomplish a particular goal. That means that planning requires imagining a series of future events, understanding cause and effect, intending to make these future events happen, and controlling impulses. Planning imposes a heavy cognitive load.

So heavy it used to be thought that only human beings could plan. True, birds make nests, beavers construct dams, and squirrels bury nuts, which are all future-directed activities. Most likely, though, these animals are caused to perform these behaviors. It's unlikely that these animals are imagining these *particular* future events, or intending these future events to happen, or controlling impulses to do so.

We say these 'particular' events, because it now seems clear that some birds can plan. We've already mentioned scrub jays, which store food, such as maggots and nuts, for later consumption. Are scrub jays planning dinner? There is some evidence that they are in fact planning for dinner—or at least breakfast (Raby et al. 2007). Researchers housed scrub jays in a three-room cage. In the evenings, the researchers fed scrub jays powdered pine nuts in the middle room (since the nuts are powdered, the jays cannot easily store them) and, in the mornings, placed the scrub jays in one of the end rooms. For three consecutive mornings, the scrub jays would first go in one of these end rooms where they had breakfast, the next three mornings in the other end room where there was no breakfast. After three days, researchers gave the scrub jays whole pine nuts for dinner, some of which they promptly stored in the other rooms. The long-term results showed that the scrub jays stored three times as many pine nuts in the non-breakfast room, suggesting that they were planning things so that in whichever room they would be placed the next morning, they would not go hungry.

In later experiments intended to rule out the competing hypothesis that the scrub jays were simply associating the non-breakfast room with hunger (Correia et al. 2007), researchers fed the scrub jays peanuts for breakfast in one room and dog kibble for breakfast in the other room. When the scrub jays were again given whole pine nuts for dinner, they tended to store some of the nuts in both rooms equally so that each room would have food it lacked, suggesting they were not only planning to be well-fed in whichever room they would be placed the next morning, but that their breakfast would also be varied.

Perhaps there remain other hypotheses that need to be ruled out before concluding that the scrub jays are planning. But now consider some feats by a variety of primates that should leave little doubt that some other animals can plan, sometimes ingeniously. In one experiment, for example, researchers Mathias and Helena Osvath (2008) showed two chimpanzees and an orangutan a hose and how to use it to extract a soup of their favorite fruit. A soup of a fruit is tastier and can be enjoyed with less work than eating a piece of the same fruit. Later, researchers placed in front of them a hose and a piece of their favorite fruit. The idea was to test the primates' ability to suppress their desire for immediate gratification by eating the fruit that was in front of them in favor of greater gratification by using the hose later to extract some fruit soup. The primates selected the hose more frequently than the piece of fruit, suggesting that they were not only imagining the future goal and understanding how they could use a hose as a tool to achieve it, but doing so while controlling their impulses. In another experiment (Osvath and Osvath 2008), researchers gave the primates a choice of three objects, one that worked like a hose and two other distractor objects (e.g. a blue toy car, a wristwatch, etc.). They chose the hose more frequently and, later, used it appropriately, suggesting that they were selecting the tool because it could help them accomplish down the line something that to them was worthwhile.

There have now been published numerous field studies observing primates and other animals using, even fashioning, a tool to acquire food, to groom, and other future-directed goals: using leaves to sponge or pour water (Tonooka 2001); using grass stalks to lure termites (termite fishing); stripping twigs of their leaves so they could use the remaining stem to spike ants or bees (Boesch and Boesch 1990); sharpening sticks to spear bush meat (Pruetz and Bertolani 2007); searching for rocks to hammer open nuts (Boesch and Boesch 1982). In fact, adult chimps have even been observed hammering open nuts using multiple complementary tools: a rock to hammer, a slightly curved stone on which to hammer—an anvil—and other material to stabilize the anvil (Visalberghi et al. 2015). Fu Manchu, an orangutan at the Omaha Zoo known as a particularly shrewd escape artist, was eventually observed hiding a wire from sight in his cheek; when the opportunity arose, he used it to trip the latch of a door that led to the furnace room and from there to stairs and to a door to freedom. His clandestine lock picking earned him an honorary membership in the American Association of Locksmiths (Linden 2000:6, 147–48).

These planning feats are complex, awe-inspiring, cognitive achievements. We do not diminish them even when we remember that human beings use language to conceive, strategize, chart, manage, and revise 35-year retirement plans, 30-year wars, and a 25-year mission to Mars.

Social Cognition

> Acquiring a human language requires the capacity to recognize behaviors and mental states of others.

Human babies and infants acquire a first language as they develop mental capacities that, in various ways, require them to recognize the behaviors and mental states of others. These include the capacities to conventionalize, imitate, refer to objects and events, attend to the same object or event as others, read others' minds, and collectively engage with others. Language, in turn, enhances those mental capacities.

Conventionalizing and Imitating

> Human language is a set of linguistic conventions acquired in party by imitation.

When something can recognize patterns, grasp the relational concepts CAUSE and EFFECT, imagine the future, and plan, it has some of the most important mental capacities required to develop conventions. It's actually tricky to say precisely what constitutes a convention, but several examples should suffice to get the idea.

convention
Acquired or learned purposeful behavior produced in part because of its past success.

One type of convention often develops between adults and infants. Adults typically lift babies and infants by reaching under their arms, causing the child's arms to raise. After some time, infants grasp a connection between arm-raising and being lifted. After a bit more time, infants begin raising their arms when they want to be picked up. Adults and their infants develop an arm-raising convention: Infants raise their arms to signal that they would like to be picked up. Several important points. First, arm-raising is a type of behavior. Second, this behavior is not instinctual, it is acquired or learned; there is nothing in a child's biology or neurology or chemistry that causes the child to raise her arms when she desires to be picked up. Third, the behavior is goal-directed; the child wants to be picked up. Fourth, the arm-raising-and-lifting pattern tends to take on a life of its own, being reproduced because its past reproductions have been successful. Thus, a convention is at least an acquired or learned purposeful behavior that continues to be reproduced in part because of its past success (Millikan 1998). These features capture the sense in which driving on a particular side of the road and buttoning one's shirt top-down are conventionalized. However, unlike these latter conventions infant arm-raising also carries information—it is a signal. So some conventionalized behaviors have a fifth feature, that they carry information. This additional feature helps to capture the sense in which a turning green light informs drivers that they may proceed, so that drivers conventionalize the behavior of proceeding at a green light. Those are communicative conventions.

communicative convention
Convention that carries information.

Some animals, especially primates, can generate communicative conventions. Robbins Burling (2005:105–11) describes several types of communicative conventions generated by chimpanzees. For example, consider chimpanzee infant–mother nursing pokes. Chimpanzee mothers nurse their babies. Over time, babies learn that they can nurse more easily after having shoved their mother's arm to the side. In short order, the mother recognizes from the first feel of her baby's poke that her infant wants to nurse and, consequently, moves her arm more easily. In turn, the baby chimp begins to recognize that it may poke more gently, and so on until the mother and her infant symbiotically arrive at their personal poking convention: When the infant chimp pokes in a particular place and in a particular way, the mother gives the infant easier access. Mother and infant don't engage in this symbiotic behavior because they are causally determined to do so by their biology or neurology or chemistry. They learn this purposeful, communicative behavior and reproduce it because it has proven successful.

Adult human beings rarely raise their arms to signal that they want to be picked up, least of all by their babies, and adult chimps obviously do not poke their mothers or their infants when they want to nurse. So neither infant human beings nor infant chimps develop these conventions because they have seen adults do it—these infants, in these cases, are not mimicking adults. But many conventions, including communicative conventions, are acquired or learned by mimicking members of their linguistic community. That is why children from different linguistic communities acquire different languages. At the beginning, infants simply mimic—they do not recognize that certain types of linguistic behavior carry information or that these types of linguistic behaviors achieve goals. Once infants mimic with the intention of achieving a particular goal, they pass into the realm of imitation.

imitation
Goal-directed mimicry.

Imitation is goal-directed mimicry, and the capacity to imitate communicative conventions seemingly creates magic. For once individuals can imitate communicative conventions, those conventions can spread among multiple individuals, thereby generating communicative conventions that are shared community-wide. As a community refines its conventions, so thereby it refines its culture—where 'culture' is understood broadly enough to include the evolution and accumulation of a community's conventions.

culture in the narrow sense
Evolution and accumulation of a *human* community's conventions.

Some non-human species have generated respective cultures by developing community-wide conventions that are non-communicative. For example, neighboring chimpanzee populations in Uganda use different practices to extract honey trapped within a fallen log (Gruber et al. 2009). Kibale Forest chimpanzees extract the honey using sticks, while Budongo Forest

culture in the broad sense
Evolution and accumulation of a community's conventions.

chimpanzees extract the honey using wet-leaf sponges. Neither of these practices is necessary, since both communities could use either, or some other, practice to extract the honey. Each community, by way of shared imitation, simply passes to its members, including to its next generation, its own conventional practice—i.e. its own cultural tradition.

Have any non-human animal species generated their own cultures by developing community-wide conventions that are communicative? Have any established their own communicative traditions? Alex the African Grey parrot, who imitated the communicative conventions of (a subset of) English, and Koko the Gorilla, who imitated the communicative conventions of (a subset of) American Sign Language, constitute evidence that some non-human species have the capacity to generate some community-wide communicative conventions. Do any in fact do so?

Some species of songbirds, dolphins, and whales certainly do. For example, as male songbirds develop, they imitate the songs of their fathers and other nearby males, so that community-wide songs emerge so finely that researchers can easily tell the precise region from which a songbird hails. Likewise, some dolphins and whales imitate songs of others in their regions. In one case, the song of a whale community off Australia's east coast changed completely within two years to match that of a whale community off Australia's west coast, apparently as a consequence of several west-coast whales being introduced to the east coast (Noad et al. 2000). Songbirds and whales sing these songs for non-communicative purposes, such as to more effectively navigate (e.g. through echolocation) or, in the case of some whales, to move sea animals (e.g. sea lions) via vibration to a particular location for easier feeding. But songbirds and whales also use these songs to mark territory or attract mates, which is a form of communication. Neither songbirds nor whales need to sing the particular songs they do, since, as their fellow songbirds and whales attest, other songs suffice to mark territory or attract mates. Each community, by way of shared imitation, refines and passes to its members, including to its next generation, its own communicative convention—i.e. its own communicative traditions.

It is difficult to tell whether songbirds or whales use their songs to communicate more specific information, as opposed to simply marking territory or attracting mates, so some might wish to remain cautious that these animals imitate communicative conventions. But that caution seems too restraining, grounded, it seems, by conflating communication with language and, consequently, by conflating communicative conventions with linguistic—more specifically, with semantic—conventions. For even if songbird and whale songs are more music than lyric, these animals still use their music in part to communicate.

This caution, however, does compel us to ask whether other species imitate semantic conventions, that is, whether they have their own semantic cultural traditions. Alex and Koko, recall, could imitate semantic conventions, but neither African Grey parrots nor gorillas generate such semantic conventions among their respective species or groups. Vervets and prairie dogs, recall, can communicate discrete information, but there is no compelling evidence at this time that they do so by convention (they may be biologically and environmentally caused to communicate discrete information).

Human beings seem to be, for all we know at this point, the only species that imitates conventions among themselves that communicate such discrete information. Indeed, human beings can imitate communicative conventions so discrete, and of such complexity, that we even have communicative conventions to convey information about conventions! That is, human beings have communicative conventions that can tell us what our conventions actually mean—as when we use language to explain what a word or phrase means—and even what they are to mean. For example, we could use the linguistic conventions of English to set up in seconds the convention that the consecutive symbols '&' and '^' are to be understood as *Keep calm*. If we then posted '&^' on Facebook and it went viral, millions of people would have a new convention in a matter of one day, LOL. The exercise of human language has helped make human beings the masters of linguistic culture. As we'll see in Chapter 4, we even use semantic conventions to construct out of thin air new features of reality, such as money, nations, universities, corporations, chess matches, and football games.

Joint Attention and Theory of Mind

Paying attention to what something else is paying attention to requires a theory of mind, the capacity to attribute mental states to others.

Joint attention, as that notion will be used in this chapter, is the capacity to adjust one's own attention to that which something else is paying attention to. Joint attention thus differs from collective attention, which will be discussed in the next section.

The key term is 'adjust,' for joint attention requires, first, noticing that something else is paying attention to something and, second, iteratively inferring from clues based on their behavior and the environment whether one is paying attention to the same thing. Chimpanzees and other apes are superb followers of another's gaze. Chimps, for example, will look at a ceiling when a person enters the same room and looks up and, should the chimp find on the ceiling nothing of interest, will look back at the person's face to determine if the person is still looking in that direction (Call et al. 1998). When strategizing how to procure food, chimps will take into account whether other chimps can see the same food and, sometimes, conceal from other chimps their attempt to procure the food, lest they draw another chimp's attention to that food (Tomasello 2008:47–48). Michael Tomasello cites ample evidence that other apes have the capacity for joint attention. For example: When a person looks behind a wall, an ape will move to get a better look at what is behind it; when a person looks in the

joint attention
Capacity to adjust one's attention to that which something else is paying attention to.

direction of a wall that has behind it a more distant object that the ape can see, the ape will look only at the wall; when an ape requests food, it takes into account whether the person from whom they are requesting it can see their gestures (Tomasello 2008:47).

Like other apes, human beings can of course adjust their own attention in light of what others are paying attention to, but uniquely, we can also intentionally and skillfully guide others' attention. We can do so, for example, by looking in a certain direction when we know others are watching, by holding up something for others to see, by smiling while closing our eyes and breathing in deeply to direct others' attention to a pleasant smell, or by pointing with a finger or chin. It is worth quoting Burling in full as he describes the difference between the chimp and human capacity to (or, perhaps, motivation to) direct others' attention:

> Here is a place where young human beings are utterly different from young chimpanzees. Well before they start to talk, children delight in sharing attention with others. They look with interest at what others show them, and they eagerly hold up objects for others to see. They enjoy sharing their interests, and it soon becomes easy to attract a child's attention to something, simply by pointing to it. Children even recognize adult signs of satisfaction and dissatisfaction. When an adult experimenter tells a child that he is looking for a *blurg*, and then looks dissatisfied when inspecting one object, but pleased when inspecting another, the child will understand the second object to be the *blurg*. Young chimpanzees don't play these games. With noises or gestures they can call attention to themselves easily enough, but they do not hold objects up for others to inspect, and they do not have a human child's easy understanding of pointing. Even when searching eagerly for hidden food, a chimpanzee does not respond to explicit pointing that would be utterly obvious even to a very young human child ... Wild chimpanzees do not point and, except when they call attention to themselves, they appear never to make any deliberate attempt to direct the attention of another ape.
>
> (Burling 2005:73)

How does the capacity for joint attention, including the capacity to direct others' attention, make language use possible? And how does language use enhance this capacity? In no fewer than six important ways. First, only by paying attention to what another person is doing and paying attention to while speaking can babies and infants acquire knowledge of what certain sounds or symbols mean—or that they mean anything at all. Second, intentionally directing one's attention to something is an especially efficient way to create what has lately been called 'common ground,' the common objects or events that multiple individuals can think about, which is required for any type of communication. Third, since joint attention often establishes common ground, and since common ground is required for the important capacity that will shortly be identified as collective intentionality, joint attention prepares the way for collective intentionality. Fourth, once we acquire a language, we can enhance our capacities for joint attention by guiding another's attention quite easily, for example by referring to an object and describing its properties ('That car is fast'), asking a question ('What's that smell?'), or directing someone's attention ('Look at that'). Fifth, using language, we can jointly attend to something that is not even in the vicinity, either because it does not exist (pointing to an empty glass to direct a bartender's attention to Scotch) or because it is far away in time and place ('Refugees have been crossing the Mediterranean Sea'), and even to things that are not physical, such as ideas, thoughts, or highly abstract concepts, such as TRUTH, FAIRNESS, and JUSTICE.

Again, it is worth quoting Burling in full:

> Words are highly efficient tools for achieving joint attention. When I use a word, I show you what I am thinking about and you can then turn your attention to the same thing. The referent of the word, the thing to which it refers, does not need to be present. When I use a word, I am really drawing attention to a concept, not necessarily to an object, and since I can have concepts for parts of objects, for collections of objects, and for the characteristics and actions of objects, I can as easily draw your attention to one of these as to a whole object. I can just as easily draw your attention to phenomena that have not even existed except in the worlds of our imagination.
>
> (Burling 2005:74)

As we'll see in later chapters, the human capacity for joint attention, especially the capacity to use language to draw others' attention to something, makes coordination and cooperation—for better or for worse—quite easy.

The capacity for joint attention, more specifically, its sub-capacity to attribute to another the mental state of attention, is but one instance of the broader capacity to attribute to other things a variety of mental states, including beliefs, goals, and intentions. One who has such a capacity is said to have a 'Theory of Mind.'

Theory of Mind
Capacity to attribute mental states to other things.

Primates have such a Theory of Mind. If a person passes food to a chimpanzee, then fails to do so shortly thereafter because the person appears, say, to drop the food by accident, the chimp will wait patiently for the person to try again. However, if the person fails to pass the food successfully because, say, he or she is not trying to do so, the chimp becomes frustrated (Call 2004). If a person shows a human-raised chimp an action that is, in fact, a failed attempt to change the state of an object—say, the person's hand 'slips' while attempting to move a ball—the chimp will actually move the ball rather than demonstrate a slip of the hand; if a person demonstrates to a human-raised chimp two actions, one successful and the other unsuccessful, the chimp typically performs only the successful action (Tomasello et al. 2005). These are but a few examples that strongly suggest that chimpanzees can attribute to others goals and intentions.

Human beings, of course, can also attribute beliefs, goals, and intentions to others even as early as two years old. In one study (O'Neill 1996), two-year-old's observed an attractive toy being put on a high shelf while their parent was either present or absent. Children whose parents were absent were significantly more likely than those whose parents were present to name or gesture to the toy. This result suggests that even two-year-old's attribute beliefs (or lack thereof) to others and modify their behavior accordingly. Other studies strongly suggest that even children younger than two years old can attribute to others pretense (Leslie 1987), goals (Csibra et al. 1999, Gergely et al. 1995, Woodward 1998), intentions (Carpenter et al. 1998, Meltzoff 1995), and attention, especially when the other is using a new word (Baldwin 1991).

In short order, aided by the exercise of human language, humans' theory of mind becomes exceptionally developed. We can also attribute to others knowledge, desire, doubt, pain, agony, fear, hope, wonder, surprise, joy, guilt, shame, anger, resentment, resignation, sorrow, and more. Indeed, as we acquire our first language, our capacities to attribute mental states to each other are exponentially enhanced, because we can simply *tell* each other what we are thinking and feeling. How much easier it is to coordinate our mental and social lives when we can simply tell people what we believe, doubt, know, want, intend, fear, hope, wonder, and resent and about or toward what we are happy, joyful, sad, angry, and look forward. No wonder human beings are hyper-cooperative.

Collective Intentionality

> The capacity to collectively engage with others ignites human hyper-cooperation.

When a troop of chimpanzees hunts a troop of colobus monkeys, the chimps cooperate at least in the sense that their individual behaviors typically lead to the successful killing of several monkeys. To do so, one chimp, the driver, will attack the colobus monkeys, which causes some of the monkeys to scatter between other awaiting chimps, the blockers, which in turn causes a few of the monkeys to funnel straight toward another awaiting chimp, the ambusher. The ambusher and the blockers are usually sufficient to narrowly surround and kill two to seven colobus monkeys during a single hunt. A fine dinner, at least for the chimps. But are the chimps cooperating in the stronger sense that they are hunting together?

Consider: That two people are out for a walk in the park does not imply that they are walking together. That thousands of people are cheering for a particular team at the same time does not imply that they are cheering *together* (as they would be when doing 'the wave'). That two people are attending to the same object does not imply that they are attending to it jointly. That multiple people are talking at the same time does not imply that they are talking together. For to do something together requires that minds be collectively directed, that they exhibit the mental capacity called 'collective intentionality.'

There is no direct evidence that chimpanzees, or members of any other species, have the capacity for collective intentionality. (For different sides of the debate, see Krause 2009). But by the exercise of human language, human beings can collectively intend to raise a child, promote a candidate, win a game, and rebuild a city. We can collectively attend to a work of art, to others walking nearby (people watching), and precisely to how that chocolatier makes the perfect cup of hot cocoa so we can make some together on Valentine's Day. We can collectively feel school spirit, national shame, collective guilt, cultural pride, and common values. We can collectively accept a constitution, a resignation, and a new leader. Collective intentionality means that *we* are in it together. *We* makes human cooperation 'hyper.'

Collective intentionality is the cornerstone of human languages. For that a critical mass of language users collectively accepts that particular arbitrary strings of discrete shapes, sounds, and finger movements mean what they do and collectively intends to continue using those signals with those meanings *makes* those arbitrary strings mean what they do. Likewise, that a critical mass of language users collectively decides to begin using a particular string of shapes, sounds, and finger movements in a new way is the mechanism that causes the evolution of a human language. Without collective acceptance and collective intention, nothing would exist akin to human languages.

In turn, we use language to enhance our capacity for collective intentionality. We use language to unite in group protest, express group grievances and their redresses, declare independence, affirm allegiances, use our party's talking points to maintain party harmony on political talk shows, and take each other as husband, wife, and partner.

This chapter has taken us on a tour of some of the most important mental capacities that make possible the fascinating extent to and precision with which human beings use and understand languages and, in turn, the extent to and by which our use and understanding of languages exercises and enhances, individually and evolutionarily, those mental capacities. Our capacities to have both fine-grained and abstract concepts of objects, events, properties, relations; our cognitive capacities to remember and analyze, compare and synthesize, imagine and plan; our more social cognitive capacities to conventionalize and imitate, jointly attend, attribute mental states to others, and collectively engage others: These are the suite of mental capacities that make possible the rich, deep, extensive, precise, discrete contours of human language—precisely the contours that make human beings the most hyper-cooperative creatures in the natural world.

collective intentionality
Capacity of minds to be jointly directed at objects, states of affairs, goals, or values. Often accompanied by a sense that *we* are doing something together.

Again, human hyper-cooperation can be used for good or ill, for better or worse. Demonstrating how we can use language to hyper-cooperate for either is the purpose of Part II. Before turning to Part II, however, we'll explore our mind's capacity to tell stories.

(Im)pertinent Questions

- Lev Vygotsky (1962/2013) theorized that social interaction precedes cognitive development. We don't "naturally" develop more complex cognitive capacities and then learn, as Piaget (1936) theorized; rather, we learn by interacting with others and then develop more complex cognitive capacities. What percentage of social interaction do you estimate involves the use of language? Assuming Vygotsky is right, does your estimate support or detract from the plausibility of the view that immersion in the uses of language is a moral imperative?
- Vygotsky also hypothesized that more complex types of thinking, such as believing, doubting, fearing, imagining, wondering, hypothesizing, and planning is just talking to oneself using a natural language (albeit, in abbreviated form). To what extent do you agree with this hypothesis? Does your answer have any further implication about the plausibility of the more general notion of linguistic moral imperatives?
- Has the advent of written languages changed the course of human cognitive development? How so?
- Consider the shared conversations, sometimes occurring over decades or even millennia of a community of scientists, a community of scholars, a community of teachers, a community of legal experts, a community of religious leaders, a community of local leaders. Do such communities believe, fear, hope, dream, imagine, plan, and know things? Or is that just a fancy way of saying that the individuals in such communities believe, fear, hope, etc.?
- By listening, reading, and talking to others over the last 20 years, many people's highly abstract concept of marriage has been refined in various ways. What are some of your highly abstract social, moral, and political concepts—perhaps truth, morality, justice, civility, privacy—that have been refined by listening, reading, and talking to others?
- What do you think would be the long-term cognitive and behavioral effects of comparing a group of people to roaches, rats, or filth? What would be the long-term cognitive and behavioral effects of finding the various ways others are very much like you?
- What do you dream of and want for yourself and those you care about 20 years from now? What is your (revisable) plan?

References

Baldwin, Dare A. 1991. Infants' contribution to the achievement of joint reference. *Child Development* 62(5).874–90.

Boesch, Christophe, and Hedwige Boesch. 1982. Optimisation of nut-cracking with natural hammers by wild chimpanzees. *Behaviour* 83(3–4).265–86.

Boesch, Christophe, and Hedwige Boesch. 1990. Tool use and tool making in wild chimpanzees. *Folia Primatologica* 54.86–99. DOI: 10.1159/000156428.

Burling, Robbins. 2005. *The talking ape: How language evolved.* Oxford: Oxford University Press.

Call, Joseph. 2004. Inferences about the location of food in the great apes (*Pan paniscus, Pan troglodytes, Gorilla gorilla,* and *Pongo pygmaeus*). *Journal of Comparative Psychology* 118(2).232–41.

Call, Joseph; Brian A. Hare; and Michael Tomasello. 1998. Chimpanzee gaze following in an object-choice task. *Animal Cognition* 1(2).89–99.

Carpenter, Malinda; Nameera Akhtar; and Michael Tomasello. 1998. Fourteen- through 18-month-old infants differentially imitate intentional and accidental actions. *Infant Behavior and Development* 21(2).315–30.

Clayton, Nicola S., and Anthony Dickinson. 1998. Episodic-like memory during cache recovery by scrub jays. *Nature* 395.272–74. DOI: 10.1038/26216.

Correia, Sérgio P. C.; Anthony Dickinson; and Nicola S. Clayton. 2007. Western scrub-jays anticipate future needs independently of their current motivational state. *Current Biology* 17(10).856–61.

Csibra, Gergely; György Gergely; Szilvia Bíró; Orsolya Koós; and Margaret Brockbank. 1999. Goal attribution without agency cues: The perception of 'pure reason' in infancy. *Cognition* 72(3).237–67.

Do animals have imagination? 2013. BBC Future. Online: www. bbc.com/future/story/20130207-can-animals-imagine.

Gergely, György; Zoltán Nádasdy; Gergely Csibra; and Szilvia Bíró. 1995. Taking the intentional stance at 12 months of age. *Cognition* 56(2).165–93.

Gruber, Thibaud; Martin N. Muller; Pontus Strimling; Richard Wrangham; and Klaus Zuberbühler. 2009. Wild chimpanzees rely on cultural knowledge to solve an experimental honey acquisition task. *Current Biology* 19(21).1806–10. DOI: 10.1016/j.cub.2009.08.060.

Krause, Kenneth W. 2009. Doubting altruism: New research casts a skeptical eye on the evolution of genuine altruism. *eSkeptic* (January 28). Online: www.skeptic.com/eskeptic/09-01-28/.

Leslie, Alan M. 1987. Pretense and representation: The origins of 'theory of mind.' *Psychological Review* 94(4).412–26. DOI: 10.1037/0033-295X.94.4.412.

Linden, Eugene. 2000. *The parrot's lament and other true tales of animal intrigue, intelligence, and ingenuity.* New York: Plume, Penguin Putnam.

Louie, Kenway, and Matthew Wilson. 2001. Temporally structured replay of awake hippocampal ensemble activity during rapid eye movement sleep. *Neuron* 29(1).145–56.

Martin-Ordas, G.; Dorthe Berntsen; and Josep Call. 2013. Memory for distant past events in chimpanzees and orangutans. *Current Biology* 23(15).1438–41.

Meltzoff, Andrew N. 1995. Understanding the intentions of others: Re-enactment of intended acts by 18-month-old children. *Developmental Psychology* 31(5).838–50.

Millikan, Ruth Garrett. 1998. Language conventions made simple. *Journal of Philosophy* 95(4).161–80.

Noad, Michael; Douglas H. Cato; M. M. Bryden; Micheline-N. Jenner; and K. Curt S. Jenner. 2000. Cultural revolution in whale song. *Nature* 408.537. DOI: 10.1038/35046199.

O'Neill, Daniella K. 1996. Two-year-old children's sensitivity to a parent's knowledge state when making requests. *Child Development* 67(2).659–77.

Osvath, Mathias, and Helena Osvath. 2008. Chimpanzee (*Pan troglodytes*) and orangutan (*Pongo abelii*) forethought: Self-control and pre-experience in the face of future tool use. *Animal Cognition* 11(4).661–74.

Pepperberg, Irene Maxine. 2002/1999. Can a parrot learn the concept of same/different? *The Alex studies: Cognitive and communicative abilities of Grey Parrots*, ed. by Irene M. Pepperberg, chapter 5. Cambridge, MA: Harvard University Press.

Piaget, J. 1936. *Origins of intelligence in the child.* London: Routledge & Kegan Paul.

Pruetz, Jill, and Paco Bertolani. 2007. Savanna chimpanzees, *Pan troglodytes verus*, hunt with tools. *Current Biology* 17(5).412–17.

Raby, Caroline; D. M. Alexis; Anthony Dickinson; and N. S. Clayton. 2007. Planning for the future by Western scrub jays. *Nature* 445.919–21. DOI: 10.1038/nature05575.

Termite fishing. The Jane Goodall Institute. Online: youtu.be/inFkERO30oM.

Tomasello, Michael. 2008. *Origins of human communication.* Cambridge, MA: MIT Press.

Tomasello, Michael; Malinda Carpenter; and R. Peter Hobson. 2005. The emergence of social cognition in three young chimpanzees. *Monographs of the Society for Research in Child Development* 70(1).

Tonooka, Rikako. 2001. Leaf-folding behavior for drinking water by wild chimpanzees (*Pan troglodytes verus*) at Bossou, Guinea. *Animal Cognition* 4(3–4).325–34. DOI: 10.1007/s100710100110.

Usher, Michael. 2012. The reunion. *60 Minutes.* Australia (June 3).

Visalberghi Elisabetta; Giulia Sirianni; Dorothy Fragaszy; and Christophe Boesch. 2015. Percussive tool use by Taï Western chimpanzees and Fazenda Boa Vista bearded capuchin monkeys: A comparison. *Philosophical Transactions of the*

Royal Society B 370(1682) (November 19).1–15. DOI: 10.1098/rstb.2014.0351.

Vygotsky, Lev. 1962/2013. *Thought and language*. Revised ed. Cambridge, MA: MIT Press.

Watson James D., and Francis H. C. Crick. 1953. A structure for deoxyribose nucleic acid. *Nature* 171.737–38.

Woodward, Amanda L. 1998. Infants selectively encode the goal object of an actor's reach. *Cognition* 69(1).1–34.

Zuberbühler, Klaus. 2000. Causal knowledge of predators' behaviour in wild Diana monkeys. *Animal Behaviour* 59(1).209–20.

3   The Narrating Brain

POINT BY POINT

- Language (with a capital L—the inner language faculty) is an integrative information management device that creates stories and narrates them.
- Perception is therefore telic: Language imposes itself upon perception guided by schemata and scripts (=apperception).
- Apperception is thus itself predictive, which adds even more cognitive power.
- Humans also predict and co-create each others' stories through shared language.
- Sharing stories is cooperative (co-creative), hence based on trust. A skilled abuser of such trust can use contaminated language (harmful frames offered as altruism) to great effect as the target audience experiences bonding over jointly merging to such frames.

Cognitive Control through Language

> Language is powerful because it frames and tells stories.

The human mind has a hard time coming to terms with its brain. Generations of minds have puzzled over where they come from, each guided and satisfied by notions of technology and science of the time, by 'the habits of thought and the metalanguage of the day' (Bouton 1991:26). One accepted notion in ancient Greece was that the brain dissipates surplus heat from the blood. That theory had sufficient plausibility to resist questioning, given the knowledge of the time that cold-blooded animals have 'no brain' and given that brains do generate heat because they are the largest consumer of energy in the body. By resisting questioning, however, a theory becomes stagnant and protected against change—a dogma.

Of course, any frame of thought is a 'closed system' (ibid.:155). Progress therefore comes from the willingness to sidestep frames, to question and unlearn and step back from what is accepted to see what else there might be outside the frame. We most remember the questioners and un-learners—such as Socrates speculating about, essentially, embodied cognition (Plato, *Phaedo* 96:a8–b8):

> I was always unsettling myself with questions such as these ... Is it the blood, or air, or fire by which we think? Or is it none of these, and does the brain furnish the sensations of hearing and sight and smell, and do memory and opinion arise from these, and does knowledge come from memory and opinion in a state of rest?

Thankfully, there have always been thinkers willing to unsettle themselves, venturing into dissenting theories about what brains do. As early as 4500 years ago, the Egyptian healer and polymath Imhotep had already associated head injuries (such as battle axe blows to the skulls of soldiers) and certain speech- and language disorders, which are now called *dysphasias*. This was perhaps the earliest documented systematic association of the brain with language, and of course the brain's function as a language organ is confirmed by modern science.

The inquiry into how the mind/brain processes and communicates thoughts has created a history of successive frames. The workings of the brain have been narrated in terms of pneumatics, hydraulics, mechanics, and electricity. The brain has been likened to an automaton, a spider web, a telephone switchboard, an engine, a computer, a city, a large corporation. We take a different approach. Instead of finding a metaphor for what the brain *is*, we concentrate on a metaphor for what the brain *does*. Why not narrate the brain as a narrating device?

Language-imposed Telic Apperception: Schemata and Scripts

Apperception
= sensation +
sense.

Chapter 2 reviewed the mental capacities of thinking animals. There are indications that animals indeed think, drawing upon cognitive faculties (to a higher or lesser degree, depending on the species and the complexity of its social structures). Those facilities include not just reflexes, but the abilities to

- form rich concepts of objects and events,
- analyze and sort and recall,
- synthesize and compare,
- imagine/anticipate and plan,
- and, for social animals to
  - imitate and thus conventionalize,
  - to have a theory of mind,
  - to use that theory of mind for joint attention and collective intentionality.

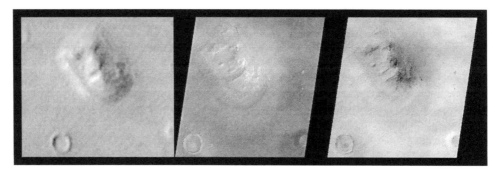

Figure 3.1 The 'Face' on Mars

Source: http://photojournal.jpl.nasa.gov/tiff/PIA01442.tif. NASA/JPL public domain.

We can find these mental faculties in animals such as birds, primates, monkeys, cetaceans (whales, dolphins, and porpoises), prairie dogs, among others. This chapter explores what powers are unlocked when Language assumes cognitive control over these faculties.

A popular example illustrates how Language, when put in control of mental faculties, guides our very perception. In 1976, a spacecraft by the name of Viking 1 sent home pictures of an expanse on Mars known as the Cydonia region. One of the geographical features, a mesa about 1.2 miles long, became known as the 'Face' on Mars (Figure 3.1). Since Mars missions to this day are in part designed to answer the question whether the planet once might have supported life (which indeed seems increasingly so), we are not just looking *at*, but also looking *for*. The perception of that formation as a face was licensed by an instant narrative of why it could indeed be a face. Richard C. Hoagland, host of the discontinued show 'Other Side of Midnight' on the Dark Matter Digital Network, promoted his views that the face was indeed a monument, part of a city built on Mars by an ancient civilization, a story that helped earn him the 1997 Ig Nobel Prize for Improbable Research in Astronomy. Subsequent pictures of the same feature have revealed that the perception of a face was an optical illusion. The point here is that we perceive by 'making sense.' Note that NASA calls the elevation a *mesa*, which is Spanish for 'table,' which is an interpretive association as much as is calling it a 'face' (except that it is even less likely that an ancient civilization would have made a monument depicting a giant table). Attentive perception interprets; the interpretation in turn biases the very perception. Mind/brains think that way. The technical term for such willful, biased perception is 'apperception.'

As we have seen in our discussion of warning calls among animals, the ability to extract features and interpret them flexibly and instantly can be a lifesaver. Scientists are aware that subjectivity introduces biases, and they try to control those biases by controlling the controller, Language, with scientific language (defined terms and academic editing). When one of us (Thiede) took physiology classes in Medical School at the University of Missouri–Columbia, the instructions for writing lab reports included what amounted to an explicit injunction against apperception: 'The first- and second-person pronouns do not exist.' Even as a budding linguist, "I" knew that that wasn't true, but I also understood the subtext: The very omission of *I, we,* and *you* would imply that no 'I,' 'we,' or 'you' was vested in the experimental setup, in the execution of the experiment, or in the recording of the results. Lab reports recast the experimenter from intentional doer and interpreter to disinterested observer. In truth, a set of conditions creates a situation, and a sequence occurs because of that situation—as intended (or else the experiment "failed"). We will refer to the set of conditions as a *schema*, and to the ordered sequence that is triggered as a *script*.

Ironically, it took Artificial Intelligence research to make cognitive scientists appreciate schemata and scripts, because psychology had set out on a path that attempted to reduce human learning to a system of 'lawful responses' to stimuli ('lawful' suggesting much more certain responses than 'biased'). 'Behaviorism' harkens back to the days of Ivan Petrovich Pavlov's nineteenth-century experiments on the digestive system of dogs. The editorial effort to select a *frame* for narrating those experiments makes all the difference, however. Note what happens when the same setup is described in the language of lab reports and the language of intentionality:

schema
The set of conditions that add up to a 'situation.'

script
A planned/expected sequence of events appropriate for a situation (as measured by favorable outcomes).

frame
The choice of a schema and script to represent an event or constrain a narrative. The frame can be a metaphor (e.g. describing a war in financial terms of costs, investments, benefits, dividends, collateral losses, etc.), often to delimit the addressee's understanding and acceptance (see p. 72).

a. Following the presentation of food, the animals would produce measurable amounts of saliva, though just a sound that would regularly precede the feeding (such as a buzzer) could already trigger this physiological response.
b. A lab assistant would give (or just show) the dog food to elicit the production of saliva. The assistant also observed that the dog would produce saliva just on hearing a sound that would be associated with the feeding, such as a buzzer.

Only presentation b. reveals that there was a human responsible for the dogs (i.e. that they were not machine fed), and with that, we are free to allow that dogs and caretakers tend to bond over time. Was there any such bonding with Pavlov's labs? Did the dogs trust the humans? Was that trust itself a factor in how the dogs reacted to a familiar sound announcing food? One lab assistant (*praktikant* in Russian), Ivan Lobasov, wrote a doctoral dissertation with a scope that went considerably beyond the 'conditioning' frame by admitting such variables in the dogs' responses:

Dogs exhibit a great variety of characters, which it is well to observe in their relation to food and manner of eating. There are passionate dogs, especially young ones, who are easily excited by the sight of food and are easily subject to teasing; others, to the contrary, have great self-possession and respond with great restraint to teasing with food. Finally, with certain dogs it is as if they understand the deceit being perpetrated upon them and turn their back on the proffered food, apparently from a sense of insult. These dogs only react to food when it falls into their mouth … Certain dogs are distinguished by a very suspicious or fearful character and only gradually adapt to the laboratory setting and the procedures performed upon them; it stands to reason that the depressed state of these dogs does not facilitate the success of experiments. The age of dogs is also important in determining their character: the older the dog the more restrained and peaceful it is, and vice versa.

(Lobasov 1896, cited by Todes 1997:228)

Each dog brings her or his own set of 'variables' to the experiment, resulting in different behavior. Framing the experiments in terms of the dogs' attitudes towards the researchers allows us to see different schemata and scripts. Dogs are complex beings; they have biases and make choices. Having coexisted with humans for more than 10,000 years, they naturally aim to please humans, or they disdain or fear them. They are not gullible enough to fall for the same stimulus again once they have recognized it to be deceptive; neither, as Chapter 1 pointed out, can wild meerkats be 'conditioned' to respond 'lawfully' to the deceptive alarm call of the Drongo bird. Chapter 2 demonstrates that what we call 'thinking' has a characteristic that is diametrically opposed to conditioned lawful responses— flexibility: the ability to *assess* the conditions to find an *appropriate* response. And appropriateness depends on anticipated favorable outcomes. Humans use Language to narrate even ongoing events in light of their anticipated outcomes. Our apperceptions are telic.

telic
Guided towards an outcome.

phrase structure
In linguistics, a representation of the structure of a phrase, as in a tree diagram. For example, a prepositional phrase (PP) typically has the structure of preposition (P) plus a noun phrase (NP): PP → P NP.

Nowadays, the 'objective' experiment that students describe in lab reports is to modern science what writing Pascal programs is to computer science, or what drawing classical phrase structure trees is to modern linguistics: a training tool, not a discovery tool. The deceptive 'objectivity' of the cause-and-effect conditioning frame that led to Pavlov's simplifications and eventually to the reductionist approach of Behaviorism to human psychology has yielded to Bayesian inference modeling. Thomas Bayes' approach is essentially probability statistics. It formulates hypotheses based on best available evidence and updates them when additional evidence becomes available. That readmits the inevitable human dimension into scientific experimentation and modeling: A hypothesis is an ad-hoc inference that bridges given data and outcomes. This is self-adjusting, outcome-oriented 'telic' thinking.

An example from Artificial Intelligence will serve to illustrate just how ingrained telic thinking is in the human mind. Assume a 'box world'—a surface with objects that can be manipulated by a robotic assembly. Currently on the surface are five numbered blocks, and they can be stacked with a robotic arm linked to a computer with a camera (that setup can also just be a simulation on the screen, of course). The command is to build a tower with three blocks. The program first verifies the schematic position and availability of each block—including that they are not already arranged in a tower and that the robotic arm is not already holding a block. Then it runs a script 'tower' with a routine such as this one (Hardy 1982):

```
define tower();
    setup();
    grasp([b1]);
    ungraspto([b2]);
    grasp([b2]);
    ungraspto([b3]);
enddefine;
```

The order of grasping first block 1 to put on block 2, and then block 2 to put on block 3 may have a certain logic to it—but not for an outcome-aware human. Even a human baby would anticipate an unfavorable result here, because this script (as Hardy of course points out) puts block 1 onto block 2, then grasps block 2 to move it on top of block 3. But with block 1 now on block 2, a likely outcome is that block 1 will slide off and fall in the process. Or, as a baby would conceptualize it, 'uh-oh.' Moving block 3 on top of block 1 is more 'practical'—a human concept for a higher chance of a favorable outcome.

Children think in terms of outcomes at a very young age. Eleven-month-old babies snap into exploration mode when they see an object defy expectations, e.g. by *not* falling when it rolls over the edge of a block (Stahl and Feigenson 2015). An unsupported object can be expected to fall—that is why block 3 belongs on block 1. A human will bias any mental calculation towards its anticipated result. Computers can run through simulations as well, but they have to complete them before evaluating the results. Humans think ahead and adjust on the fly.

'Slips of the ear' (so-called Mondegreens) are excellent examples of such anticipatory adjustments. Listening to a Beatles' song in real time, one hears 'she's got a tic—,' at which point the brain may already decide that the word boundary has been reached and this is about someone's *tic*. As the line completes—'*she's got a tic* ket to ride'—the brain can decide to rescind the early commitment and revisit what is still in working memory or (which is easier) stick with it and perceive still incoming phonemes to make sense *toward* the predicted outcome: 'she's got a tic in her eye.' Apperception senses and makes sense simultaneously; it is a creative telic act utilizing rules and knowledge. Incoming data are perceived (altered, in effect) to confirm the predicted outcome. No ordinary computer does that. We would likely no longer call them 'computers' at that point—we designed them *not* to take the shortcuts we take.

Anticipation shows up in electroencephalograms (EEG's). A subject outfitted with all those electrodes on her or his scalp may be presented with a word sequence such as the following (this particular experiment was run on 15 healthy, young, gluten-tolerant German adults):

encephalogram
The measurement of electrical activity in the brain in response to events (event-related potentials, ERP). The ERP's are measured on the scalp at specific locations and fed to a computer, where they are analyzed for patterns (waves).

Die Pizza wurde   im   gegessen.
the   pizza   was PASSIVE in-the eaten
'The pizza was in the eaten.' (Friederici et al. 2003)

Omitted from the sentence is a noun between the last two words, *Restaurant*. For a native speaker of German, everything is going to plan until that omission is noticed. The auxiliary *wurde* clearly sets up expectations for a passive construction, like 'was eaten.' A possible next word could be *von* for the German equivalent of the English *by*-phrase (cf. p. 24 above). But we get *im* instead, so we no longer expect the agent at this point. The word *im* is a contraction of the preposition *in* and the definite article *dem*, inflected for dative of location, so a location is expected. Then the word *gegessen* is presented. The verbal base is *ess-*, 'eat,' but the participial form used for the passive verb is marked by a circumflex: a combination of prefix *ge-* and suffix *-en* wrapped around the verb. Hence, just hearing the prefix *ge-* (unambiguously identified by the de-emphasized vowel /ə/ typical for function morphemes) is enough for the brain to notice that there is an anomaly. And the measurable reaction to that surprise is blazingly fast: a mere 150ms or so into the onset of the word *gegessen*—before the word is even heard completely. With reactions that fast, it is not easy to see the exact location by real-time imaging, which is too slow, so electroencephalograms are commonly used. The reaction shows as a negative wave measured in the front of the left hemisphere, which was dubbed ELAN (early left anterior negativity). It appears to indicate the earliest syntactic response of the brain, 'fast template matching' (Friederici 2011:1378). In the example above, the brain was processing the schema for 'prepositional phrase' structure and found the incoming data (a verb instead of a noun phrase) incompatible.

> **dative**
> A case inflection reserved for indirect objects and locations in German; the case has effectively disappeared from English grammar.

The brain does *not* shut down processing right then and there if the subject trusts that some kind of sensible outcome was intended. Instead, it shifts from schema-based template matching to script-based rule operations. That involves forwarding the processing to another brain area, an effect called 'upstream delegation' (Friederici 2011:1373) that adds about half a second. Some 600ms after the onset of the word *gegessen*, a positive wave is detected over a more posterior area (P600). At that point, the brain attempts to reanalyze or repair the syntactic structure to see if it can be rescued somehow. If the sentence is syntactically well formed but has a semantic violation (e.g. *he spread his bread with socks*), the upstream delegation is to another brain area instead and a different brain wave is measured—the famous N400 first described in 1980 (Kutas and Hillyard 1980).

A computation suspending, adjusting, delegating itself, improvising towards a desired outcome—that is classic brain behavior. Telic apperception is in essence a local narrative, subjugating experience to sense making. It so constitutes our thinking that the experiencing self is regularly overruled by the narrating self.

A study by Redelmeier, Katz, and Kahneman (2003) shows this most graphically.

Kahneman and his colleagues picked an unlikely population to test his theory that brains think in narratives: patients undergoing a colonoscopy. In the early days of the procedure, patients without sedation would occasionally experience sharp pain. In the study, some procedures were terminated as soon as possible; the patient usually experienced the pain at the end (of the procedure). Other patients were allowed to rest up before the colonoscope was removed. The follow-up was with those two groups: Group A, who had the shorter procedure but experienced a sharp pain at its conclusion, and Group B, who had experienced the exact same pain but with the intense sensation of pain towards the middle of the procedure. Even though the patients in Group B experienced the same pain and actually suffered through more discomfort than Group A, it was Group B who *remembered* the procedure as less traumatic. Brains narrate towards outcomes, discarding most details of the actual experience along the way.

Understanding both perception and memory as creative narratives sheds light on some puzzling idiosyncrasies—and surprising strengths—of our brains. We construct our reality through Language, filtering it by imposing the schemata and scripts that are most likely to make sense of it. We see the patterns that make sense to us (like a face on Mars) and we weave them into events that make sense to us (a civilization that must have built it there). I narrate, therefore I am.

The Predictive Power of Narrative Computing

Storying is more powerful than storing.

Telic apperceptions are mini-stories turning sensation into sense. Memories are stories: The remembering self's Language writes the experiencing self's sensations into narratives, retaining only what is deemed inalienable for the story. Most significance is ascribed to outcomes. In telic apperception, lower-order processes optimize by interacting with their own anticipated outcomes at a higher level of abstraction. We could say that we already have a 'hunch' of what we process before we have finished the processing, and we retain the 'gist' of what happened—not what *actually* happened. For a high-performance brain, creativity is thus the workaround for a subpar memory: Limited workspace is populated only with what we anticipate to be relevant; if something appears to be missing, it can be retrojected from that anticipation. Magicians make their living knowing this.

The above example of encountering an unanticipated constituent in a sentence shows that predictive processing characterizes languages just as much as it characterizes Language. When a verb such as *bury* rises to syntax, it comes with a narrative template: An agent causes an affected object to have an underground location. If, again

Cogito, ergo sum 'I think, so therefore I exist.' René Descartes was very aware that what we call 'reality' is what the brain makes of it. He became doubtful that we can *know* anything as it really is and ended up with just this certainty: By doubting, we confirm that we are thinking, thus that we 'are.'

in real time, a human parser is presented with the sequence 'The ·
treasure · buried ...,' the brain commits to the sentence's remaining
structure, because a *treasure* is not an agent. Given no more than the
first three words of the clause, the parser can already anticipate a
reduced relative clause with a passive voice: 'The treasure [that was]
buried ....' Predictions, as discussed above, keep demands on short-
term memory low. The parser works without keeping an increasing
number of words in working memory to decide what the sentence
structure is (simple or complex, in this case). The commonly used
term for committing to linguistic structure before all the facts are in
is 'predictive' or 'deterministic parsing,' which is 'depth first.' As
mentioned in Chapter 1, predictive parsing is in complete contrast
to machine parsing in Natural Language Processing: Computers,
with their gigabytes of RAM, can handily afford to wait until all
the words are in place, keep multiple alternative parses open side by
side, and commit after a final evaluation. That is known as 'active-
chart parsing,' which is 'breadth first.'

> **predictive parsing**
> Deterministic
> strategies that
> commit early to
> what grammatical
> structure is
> currently being
> processed. Parsing
> is the 'perceptive'
> grammar, not the
> speaker's grammar.

Given the fantastic speed and memory capacities of computers,
it is intriguing to contemplate why computers are *not* better than
humans at understanding language. At stake is the definition of
'understanding,' of course. And yet. Consider the historic set of
chess matches between Garry Kasparov and IBM's 'Big Blue'
in 1996 and 1997. Deep Blue now resides in the Smithsonian
Museum, but in its time it was a formidable beast of a processor,
capable of computing 'up to 200 million possible chess positions
per second' (IBM n.d.). Nonetheless, even against the computer's
massive breadth and depth of evaluative processing, Kasparov
won the first set of games and lost the second set only after the
computer was upgraded further. Kasparov's creative, intuitive,
and experienced predictive parsing stood its ground quite well.
Feedforward and feedback loops operating in parallel across
layers of abstraction may have developed as a compensation for
memory limitations, but they have turned the human brain into an
intelligently adaptive processor. We just 'know' what chess moves
are 'worth' exploring, in the way that we 'intuitively' know if a
sentence is going to be active or passive in voice, simple or complex in structure.

And the nature of that kind of intelligence can be summed up with
the word 'storying.' Once the brain's way of narrative computing
is understood, it can be trained and enhanced. For example, there
are tournaments for something that should really be an oxymoron
when it comes to human beings: Memory championships. Memory
champions use their storying skills, creating coherence where there
was a list.

One time-honored coherence-generating mnemonic technique is
to mentally line up things in a sequence of virtual locations through
which we can mentally 'walk.' That technique likely takes advantage of an ancient strength of humans, who, lacking sensory abilities
such as keen smell or detecting magnetic fields, resorted to *naming*

and imaging their territories, thereby creating semantic mental maps and thus enabling 'members of a group to reidentify a range or a trail from the restated calls or names' (Jerison 1977:57). The Greek poet Simonides (556–468 BCE) had recommended exploiting that very ability for rhetoric. He recommended mapping an entire speech onto an imagined building in which each room contains items reminiscent of the next topic to address (Wittrock 1977:155). Caitlin Schiller offers a rhetorically more mundane example—how to remember a shopping list:

> Imagine standing in front of the place you've chosen, opening the front door, and navigating around. As you move through your personal palace, you'll place images of things you want to remember at specific points along your path or in the visualized room. For example, you could mentally place a loaf of bread and a bag of tomatoes from your shopping list next to your bedside table. Then, when you need to retrieve your shopping list or those facts for your history final, simply walk along the route and conjure up the images you placed there.
>
> (Caitlin Schiller n.d.)

A more ambitious version of the technique was dramatized in the television series 'Sherlock' (BBC). In the episode 'His Last Vow' (season 3, episode 3) both the famous detective and a powerful media mogul, Charles Augustus Magnussen, file vast amounts of knowledge in their respective 'mind palace.' Our brains' new connectivities (for Language) can compensate powerfully for the shortcomings of the old ones (for retention). It is surprising that narrative information management techniques are not taught in our schools.

Narrative computing explains not only how humans remember, but also how they make decisions. Some of our decisions may be based on stories with anticipated bad outcomes—fears. In her TED talk 'What Fear Can Teach Us,' novelist Karen Thompson Walker narrates the story of 20 sailors of the whaleship *Essex*, which was rammed and sunk by an apparently infuriated sperm whale (the original 'Moby Dick') on November 20, 1820. The crew launched their small whaleboats and collectively made a horribly wrong decision by *not* navigating towards the Marquesas Islands (which they assumed to be inhabited by cannibals) but by deciding on a dramatically longer route towards South America instead. That decision cost the lives of more than half of the crew (and made the survivors turn to cannibalism themselves). Walker makes the point that fears are stories with characters, plots, vivid imagery, suspense, and anticipated results. How we choose to 'read' the stories of our fears (emotionally or analytically) directly influences our decisions. Fixating on anticipated bad outcomes can make the narratives of our mind self-defeating: I was never any good at …, I am powerless against …, I will be laughed at ….

Setting the Parameters of Narrative Computing: Framing

Frames set the parameters within which a narrative is to be processed— and can be stealthy manipulators.

The 'lab-report' vs. 'intentional' language of Pavlov's dog experiments above illustrates how much our inner narratives respond to the choice of frames. Because it predetermines the outcome of the recipient's narrative, framing a story for others requires a Theory of Mind. It is an acquired skill. Children's earliest narratives lack any sense of strategic framing, relying on sequencing the mini-narratives contained in each verb and proceeding from one verbal episode to the next (usually with *and*):

> Once there was a table
> and he was taking a walk
> and he fell into a pond of water
> and an alligator bit him
> and then he came up out of the pond of water
> and he stepped into a trap that some hunters had set for him,
> and turned a somersault on his nose.
>
> (Mitchell 1921:24)

In contrast, this earliest preserved piece of writing by Charlotte Brontë (age 10) already has a frame—let's call it 'being a good girl' (Alexander 1987:3):

> There was once a little girl and her name was Anne. She was born at a little village named Thornton and by and by she grew a good girl. Her father and mother were both very rich. Mr and Mrs Wood were their names and she was their only child, but she was not too much indulged.
>
> Once little Anne and her mother went to see a fine castle near London, about ten miles from it. Anne was very much pleased with it.
>
> Once Anne and her papa and her Mama went to sea in a ship and they had very fine weather all the way, but Anne's Mama was very sick and Anne attended her with so much care. She gave her medicine.

Young Charlotte (who grew up in Thornton) had adopted values and constructed a social identity for herself and began to frame both.

When *someone else* to whom we are willing to extend consensus sets the frame, our inborn human hyper-cooperativeness allows stealthy manipulation. We accept that someone else has already gone through the trouble of eliminating and selecting processing outcomes to spare us that mental effort, presenting us with the schema that 'makes sense.' An experiment now known as the 'Asian disease problem' reveals our cooperative response to frames. Amos

Tversky and Daniel Kahneman (1981) framed a choice between two solutions to a problem in two different ways. The schematic situation they set up was identical both times: The US is preparing for the outbreak of an unusual Asian disease. It is expected to kill 600 people. Participants were asked to choose between two 'programs,' but the choices were framed differently in two presentations:

> **Presentation 1**: If Program A is adopted, 200 people will be saved. If Program B is adopted, there is a ⅓ probability that 600 people will be saved, and a ⅔ probability that no people will be saved.
>
> **Presentation 2**: If Program C is adopted, 400 people will die. If Program D is adopted, there is a ⅓ probability that nobody will die, and a ⅔ probability that 600 people will die.

To be sure, both presentations describe the same outcomes. Presentation 1 frames the outcome in terms of gains, prompting a risk-averse preference for 'Program A' (72 percent). Presentation 2 frames the outcome in terms of lives lost, prompting a risk-*taking* approach to prevent that loss: 78 percent opted for 'Program D' (decisively rejected when it was presented as 'Program B').

Public officials with expertise in framing (or with access to language consultants who can do it for them) can elicit inner narratives that create the kinds of majorities seen in Tversky and Kahneman's experiment above. On May 22, 2019, the town of Webbers Falls, Oklahoma, ordered an immediate evacuation after heavy rainfalls caused two barges to slam into a dam on the Arkansas River. Officials anticipated that the damn might break and unleash a massive deluge upon the town, but they also knew that evacuation orders are not always heeded by everyone, so they added this on the town's Facebook page: 'If you choose to stay we advise you write your name and personal information on your arm in permanent marker' (Wright and Wesner Childs 2019). A frame of preparing one's own corpse for identification surely overrode the frame of staying to protect one's home and possessions.

The power of framing to refocus others' certainty can be used to save lives, but it can equally be used to deprive (a.k.a. *disentitle*) if the frames only pretend to be offered in a cooperative spirit, i.e. when language that is trusted is in fact contaminated. Thus, it is possible to select frames that redirect voters' attention from their own interests. Appalachian Pike County, KY voted in 2015 to elect Matt Bevin as governor. Having hemorrhaged jobs and employees' health insurance with the closure of coal mines, that county in particular should have been wary of Bevin's platform. Bevin built his campaign on dismantling Kynect, the very health plan, established in Kentucky under the Affordable Care Act, on which many in that county relied (Goldstein 2015).[1] Bevin also 'opposes food stamps and supports cuts in Social Security, Medicare and Medicaid' (Karlin 2014). His

---

1 We owe this source to UNC Charlotte English Honors student Amy Crew.

campaign emphasized core Christian values and his outsider status as a businessman (Goldstein 2015). Governor Blevin reframed the debate about healthcare by claiming that his Democratic opponent profited, as partner in a law firm, from representing Purdue Pharma, the very manufacturer whose product, Oxycontin, triggered an opioid epidemic (Cross 2019). Out-of-work miners in Pike County then suffered the indignity of hearing their governor say that 'Every dollar we give to an able-bodied, working-age person with no disabilities and no dependents is a dollar we're not able to provide … for those truly in need in our state' (Cross 2019).

Framing can turn people into advocates against their own best interests. A bill introduced in 2009 (Senate Bill HR 3200) was intended to make sure that physicians are paid for their time when they *counsel* Medicare patients about living wills, advance directives, and end-of-life care options. Opponents of that bill chose to frame it as if the doctors used those sessions to *decide* whether to provide or to deny medical care:

> The America I know and love is not one in which my parents or my baby with Down Syndrome will have to stand in front of Obama's "death panel" so his bureaucrats can decide, based on a subjective judgment of their "level of productivity in society," whether they are worthy of health care. Such a system is downright evil.
>
> (Sarah Palin, Facebook entry, August 7, 2009)

The 'death panel' frame generated sufficient public outrage to prevent the inclusion of the provision to compensate doctors for beneficial work *they were already doing* (and continue to do pro bono) in the 2010 Patient Protection and Affordable Care Act.

Framing selects and deflects reality, a point developed at length by Kenneth Burke (1966; he uses the term *screen* instead of *frame*). The only defense against the diversional power of a language that seems altruistic but is contaminated with a deceptive frame is critical thinking. But in our 'cognitive arms race' (see Chapter 1), who would not want to blunt that weapon? 'No one in this world, so far as I know,' concluded H. L. Mencken (1926), 'has ever lost money by underestimating the intelligence of the great masses of the plain people. Nor has anyone ever lost public office thereby.' Maybe that is the reason why our schools do not provide students with an operating manual of their own brains' narrative information management strategies. 'The most dangerous man to any government is the man who is able to think things out for himself,' Mencken had concluded in 1922 (Mencken 1922). And don't our elected representatives know it—here is an actual quote from the 2012 platform of the Texas Republican Party:

> We oppose the teaching of Higher Order Thinking Skills (HOTS) (values clarification), critical thinking skills and similar programs that are simply a relabeling of Outcome-Based

Education (OBE) (mastery learning) which focus on behavior modification and have the purpose of challenging the student's fixed beliefs and undermining parental authority.

(2012:12)

Marketers and political agents avail themselves of research in cognitive science on how to match frames to identity and values and trigger the desired predictive processing (Lakoff in Karlin 2014). Charisma coaches now offer courses in 'frame control' for anything from dating to the art of the deal. Ever wondered why 'love,' of all things, should make a Subaru a Subaru?

If frames in slogans, sound bites, and tweets can be cognitive power tools, then the sustained attention and bonding of storytelling can be downright hypnotic.

Narrative Cooperative Computing: Story Time

> Stories promote social bonding. Teller and listeners experience similar neural processes and feel temporarily transported beyond themselves.

Sharing a language and a laugh are bonding devices in social grooming. So is storytelling—both on the side of the teller and on the side of the listener/reader. The predictive processing of *creating* narratives (anticipating outcomes) can be so intense that the writer/narrator can feel 'inspired'—a sensation that the words seem to come from outside. The author has the compelling feeling of being dictated to, which has led to the metaphor of a 'bicameral mind' in which an unconscious, creative brain takes control and dictates to a listening, analytical brain (cf. Crago 2014). On the audience's side, the listener/reader suspends disbelief so as to accept the frames, matches her or his own experiences and beliefs to the protagonists', merges to the story. A good story creates an experience of being absorbed, entranced (ibid.). In fact, Green and Brock (2000) have come up with a 'transportation scale' that measures the degree to which someone has become absorbed into a story.

The effect is enhanced in a social setting, as in storytelling with a live audience or at a political rally, when the listeners experience what has been described as 'neural entrainment' (cf. Stephens et al. 2010)—they feel on the same 'wave length,' laughing and expressing surprise and suspense (or anger) in unison. A skilled storyteller such as Garrison Keillor can turn an audience into a collective, experiencing not just shared intentionality (see Chapter 2) but distributed cognition. As Joshua Gowin (2011) described one gifted storyteller:

> When she really enlivens a story, the audience will nod their heads in unison and their eyes will grip onto her movements as she garnishes the plot. They inhale as a group, breathing in her story. She calls the experience 'story trance.'

As we saw earlier, storytelling is an acquired skill, but there are some qualities that appear cultural, if not universal. Humans usually structure their narratives for cooperation, and William Labov (2001) has described how stories are commonly structured cooperatively:

- **Abstract**: *An optional set-up for the story*—'I remember when my family went on vacation to the beach.'
- **Orientation**: *The who, when, where, and/or why of the story*—'My sister and I were walking along the shore and collecting shells.'
- **Complicating Action**: *The plot of the story*—'We saw a swimmer waving his hands in the air and calling out for help. A rip current was pulling him out to sea. We ran down the beach and alerted a lifeguard.'
- **Resolution**: *What happened, in which the problem posed by the complicating action comes to a conclusion*—'The lifeguard paddled out on his surfboard and rescued the swimmer.'
- **Evaluation**: *Optional comments, made at any point in the story, that explain why the story is being told or why the events are notable*—'It's a good thing we were there or who knows what might have happened!'
- **Coda**: *Returns the listener back to the present. This is the storyteller saying that the story is over*—'And we all lived happily ever after!'

With increasing skill, the storyteller can take more control over the audience's co-creative activity. Framing is of course one of these techniques, but so is the creation of suspense (delaying outcomes) and surprise (flouting predictions). Even the audience's speed of processing can be manipulated, as a quote from novelist Henry James will illustrate:

> Chad offered him, as always, a welcome in which the cordial and the formal—so far as the formal was the respectful—handsomely met; and after he had expressed a hope that he would let him put him up for the night, Strether was in full possession of the key, as it might have been called, to what had lately happened.
>
> (James 1922:307)

Zadie Smith (2009) suggests that Henry James deliberately overtaxed the reader's parser in order to slow down, 'to make you aware, to break the rhythm that excludes thinking'—a deliberate attempt to sabotage automatic predictive processing. We will explore those artistic techniques of manipulating cognitive load in detail in Chapter 7.

Our tribe of hominins is commonly referred to as *homo sapiens*, the 'knowing man.' It has also been dubbed *homo narrans*, 'narrating man' (e.g. Victorri 2002). Storying is the brain's information management system. It compensates for a short-term memory too constrained to hold all the details, overrides experiences in favor of remembered or anticipated outcomes, and operates predictively, i.e. simultaneously on lower and higher levels of processing. It has the power to be intensely cooperative and incredibly manipulative. We will see in the following chapters how this power can be put to use, for good and for evil intents.

(Im)pertinent Questions

- Find examples of jobs such as corporate storyteller or White House press secretary that seem dedicated to framing narratives so as to focus/divert attention and manage communal attitudes.
- What would be your definition of 'critical thinking'?
- Would you like your teachers to be subversive?
- Are liberal arts liberating, and if so, does that explain the current emphasis on STEM disciplines?
- Would you rather give children books that assist in their 'social construction' or avant-garde children's books that emphasize thinking outside the box?
- What is a meme? Implications?
- What is doxing? Implications?

References

Alexander, Christine. (ed.) 1987. *An edition of the early writings of Charlotte Brontë*, vol. 1. Oxford: Basil Blackwell.

Bouton, Charles P. 1991. *Neurolinguistics: Historical and theoretical perspectives*. New York: Plenum.

Burke, Kenneth Duva. 1966. *Language as symbolic action: Essays on life, literature, and method*. Berkeley: University of California Press.

Crago, Hugh. 2014. *Entranced by story: Brain, tale and teller from infancy to old age*. New York: Routledge.

Cross, Al. 2019. Is Bevin 'trying to rip health care away from our families'? Is it true Beshear 'sold out Kentucky' in an opioid lawsuit? Here are facts. *Kentucky Health News* (November 3). Online: http://kyhealthnews.blogspot.com/2019/11/is-bevin-trying-to-rip-health-care-away.html.

Friederici, Angela D. 2011. The brain basis of language processing: From structure to function. *Physiological Review* 91.1357–92.

Friederici, Angela D.; Shirley-Ann Rüschemeyer; Anja Hahne; and Christian J. Fiebach. 2003. The role of left inferior frontal and superior temporal cortex in sentence comprehension: Localizing syntactic and semantic processes. *Cerebral Cortex* 13(2) (February).170–77.

Goldstein, Amy. 2015. Kentucky's newly insured worry about their health under next governor. *The Washington Post* (November 9). Online: www.washingtonpost.com/national/health-science/next-kentucky-governors-aca-animus-raises-concerns-in-coal-country/2015/11/09/5143a0ea-8492-11e5-8ba6-cec48b74b2a7_story.html.

Gowin, Joshua. 2011. Why sharing stories brings people together. *Psychology Today* blog entry (June 6). Online: www.psychology today.com/us/blog/you-illuminated/201106/why-sharing-stories-brings-people-together.

Green, Melanie C., and Timothy C. Brock. 2000. The role of transportation in the persuasiveness of public narratives. *Journal of Personality and Social Psychology* 79(5) (November).701–21.

Hardy, Steven. 1982. Blocks. Online: www.cs.bham.ac.uk/research/projects/poplog/doc/popteach/blocks.

IBM. n.d. Deep Blue. Online: www.ibm.com/ibm/history/ibm100/us/en/icons/deepblue/.

James, Henry. 1922. *The ambassadors*. The Novels and Tales of Henry James, vol. 22. New York: Charles Scribner's Sons.

Jerison, Harry J. 1977. Evolution of the brain. *The human brain*, ed. by Merlin C. Wittrock, 39–62. Englewood Cliffs, NJ: Prentice-Hall.

Karlin, Mark. 2014. George Lakoff: In politics, progressives need to frame their values. (Interview, November 29). Online: http://georgelakoff.com/2014/11/29/george-lakoff-in-politics-progressives-need-to-frame-their-values.

Kutas, Marta, and Steven A. Hillyard. 1980. Reading senseless sentences: Brain potentials reflect semantic incongruity. *Science* (new series) 207(4427) (January 11).203–05.

Labov, William. 2001. Uncovering the event structure of narrative. *Linguistics, language, and the real world: Discourse and beyond*, ed. by Deborah Tannen and James E. Atlantis (Georgetown University Round Table on Language and Linguistics), 63–83. Washington, DC: Georgetown University Press.

Lobasov, Ivan O. 1896. Otdelitel'naia rabota zheludka sobaki [The secretory work of the dog stomach]. Doctoral dissertation. Military-Medical Academy Doctoral Dissertation Series. St. Petersburg.

Mencken, H. L. 1922. Le contrat social. *Prejudices* (third series).

Mencken, H. L. 1926. Notes on journalism. *Chicago Tribune* (September 19).

Mitchell, Lucy Sprague. 1921. *Here and now story book*. New York: Dutton.

Redelmeier, Donald A.; Joel Katz; and Daniel Kahneman. 2003. Memories of colonoscopy: A randomized trial. *Pain* 104.187–94.

Republican Party of Texas. 2012. Report of platform committee. Online: www.empowertexans.com/wp-content/uploads/2012/07/2012-GOP-Platform-Final.pdf.

Schiller, Caitlin. 2015. The science of memory: 4 award-winning tricks for remembering everything (10 April). Online: www.blinkist.com/magazine/posts/the-science-of-memory-4-user-tested-secrets-for-remembering-everything.

Smith, Zadie. 2009. Brief interviews with hideous men: The difficult gifts of David Foster Wallace. *Changing my mind: Occasional essays*, 255–97. New York: Penguin.

Stahl, Aimee E., and Lisa Feigenson. 2015. Observing the unexpected enhances infants' learning and exploration. *Science* 438(6230) (April).91–94.

Stephens, Greg J.; Lauren J. Silbert; and Uri Hasson. 2010. Speaker–listener neural coupling underlies successful communication. *Proceedings of the National Academy of Sciences of the United States of America—PNAS* 107(32).14425–30.

Todes, Daniel P. 1997. Pavlov's physiology factory. *Isis* 88(2).205–46.

Tversky, Amos, and Daniel Kahneman. 1981. The framing of decisions and the psychology of choice. *Science* (new series) 211(4481).453–58.

Victorri, Bernard. 2002. Homo narrans: Le rôle de la narration dans l'émergence du langage. *Langages* 36(146).112–25.

Wittrock, Merlin C. 1977. The generative processes of memory. *The human brain*, ed. by Merlin C. Wittrock, 153–84. Englewood Cliffs, NJ: Prentice-Hall.

Wright, Pam, and Jan Wesner Childs. 2019. Three killed in Missouri tornadoes; rising waters force entire Oklahoma town to evacuate. The Weather Channel (May 23). Online: https://weather.com/news/news/2019-05-22-flooding-storms-tornadoes-midwest-plains. Accessed May 23, 2019.

Part II Language and Power

Part I explored the connections between language and mind. Part II explores the relations between language and power.

Part I explored the powerful, fascinating triadic connections between language, brain, and mind. Chapter 1 examined the nature of language. Human language relies on entropy: Information is not carried by single signals, but is spread out over combinations of signals. From a finite number of meaningless sounds and a finite number of ways to combine them, human speech gives us the powers to express any thought we are capable of having and to grasp any thought anyone else can express—including thoughts we've never had, about things we've never experienced, about places we've never been, about any time in the past, present, or future. Because of language, we have extraordinary power to learn, believe, anticipate, fear, hope, wonder, and surprise. Language is a mental faculty, which is arranged in hierarchical layers that process simultaneously, and uses ventral brain circuits for information and dorsal circuits for how-to processes. Language so conceived can exist only for a species that is hyper-cooperative—with informational entropy so high, humans must do a lot of mind reading to 'understand' one another.

Chapter 2 identified important mental capacities we must have to use and understand human language and, in turn, how the exercise of human language exponentially enhances, individually and as a species, those very mental capacities. Thinking and expressing what we think requires that we have an extremely rich conceptual system of objects, events, properties, and relations; that we remember and analyze objects and concepts into more finely grained properties and concepts; that we compare and synthesize more finely grained concepts so that we can imagine and plan; that we pay attention to the same things as, attribute mental states to, and collectively engage with others. Language, in turn, empowers us to enhance what we can do with these very mental capacities that make language possible and, consequently, increases our social potential in ways that non-human animals cannot comprehend—for example, by working together to construct rich, intersecting cultures, to declare independence from other countries, to plan and carry out ten-year neighborhood reconstruction projects, and to understand the origins of the universe.

Chapter 3 supported the hypothesis that thinking is narrative. Our brains do not 'imprint' what we perceive, but, instead, our minds process, or interpret, incoming perceptions as something. Consequently, our brains do not 'store' representations or memories as raw data, but instead, our minds re-narrate them as needed. Consequently, our minds do not process computationally from a store of memories and rules, but instead, process by continually negotiating current data with anticipated outcomes. The way our minds frame experience profoundly affects what we ultimately think and how we ultimately behave.

How we ultimately behave: That is the focus of Part II, 'Language and Power,' to which we now turn.

Chapter 4, 'Doing Things with Words,' provides a general theory of the types of things we use languages to do and how we do them. In particular, it explains how we often say much more than what our words mean and how we can use words to construct social realities. The Hebrew Bible describes a deity that spoke us into existence in the likeness of that deity, a fitting creation story because humans, too, speak things into existence.

Of course, minds must cooperate to agree when such facts are indeed created so that 'I hereby pronounce you married' spoken by an actor on stage does not actually produce a married couple. We place the words into context, determine their sincerity and feasibility, even gauge whether the speaker fails to predict unintended consequences. In fact, at times we must determine whether the speech act is what it seems or has an ulterior agenda, or whether it was interpreted correctly but met with an evasive response. It takes a good amount of socialization to navigate this constant mind reading and second-guessing and delicate negotiating. Fortunately, we have the resources described in the first three chapters to balance our needs verbally.

Chapter 5, 'The Language of Cooperation,' analyzes how exactly humans cooperate when we use language. Given the nature of language, there are three levels of linguistic processing and cooperation. At the sentence level, the speaker presents structures that can readily be processed, arranges information strategically, adapts to others, etc. At the level of literal interpretation, there is negotiation over what the sentence says, with an eye on what the sentence means or implies at the third level (extended interpretation). Our languages allow us to pay proper respect to one another and not to make larger impositions than necessary (positive and negative 'face'). This is where politeness is ritualized in linguistic expression. Linguistic politeness is also an acquired skill, and experts can further develop face-saving skills to the point where they can perform mediation, conflict resolution, and hostage negotiations.

The reverse is also true: Language does not always seek harmony. It can get under one's skin in negative ways as well.

Chapter 6, 'The Language of Violence,' ties the most important material of the preceding chapters to an in-depth discussion of dispositions—general tendencies that strongly regulate, but do not determine, attitudes, beliefs, and behaviors—to explain how human beings can use, have used, and continue to use language to effect even extremely large-scale violence. Our ugly examples are genocide and widespread sexual assault, especially of women.

A genocide becomes possible when enough people are motivated to kill other people. But how could some from such a highly cooperative species kill entire groups of its own species? With a lot of linguistic preparation. By (i) producing a profuse amount of language with (ii) harmful content in (iii) contexts with certain features, individuals' dispositions for moral respect and restraint are weakened while their dispositions for aggressive, injurious behavior are strengthened. As they are, individuals' attitudes toward mass killing progress from revulsion, to approval, to moral permissibility, to moral obligation, to moral necessity, to moral valorization. Widespread sexual assault becomes possible in a community when certain social narratives and scripts, especially about male and female sexual roles, are accepted. Such acceptance shapes certain linguistic dispositions, including the troubling linguistic disposition to *cease* accepting what certain words are used in a community to do. The results are various types of silencing of the target group.

Chapter 7, 'Clarity from Managed Confusion,' returns on a more uplifting note to the language of cooperation. It presents a model of how concepts, ideas, and stories propagate across brains and minds via languages. To the linguistic inventory of Chapter 5, we add techniques of collaborative information management. To illustrate, we showcase the role of 'proforms' (words that refer to other words, such as pronouns) and how they interact with cognition. We also examine techniques of chaining 'given' and 'new' information, which likewise facilitate understanding. We conclude that clarity is not an absolute constant, but a successful alignment with audience needs. Since those needs will vary, there is mutual negotiation towards clarity, which we dub 'managed confusion.' We will illustrate that with a genre whose very definition is grounded on clarity: definitions.

Given how much interfacing exists between Language and other faculties of the mind, we conclude by asking whether highly accomplished authors of literary works owe their success to their superior skills in managing the audiences' cognitive demands. In particular, we analyze four representative passages (from Ernest Hemingway, Dylan Thomas, Theodor "Dr." Seuss Geisel, and Agatha Christie) to describe the demands placed on each of four kinds of processing: linguistic, logical, predictive, and event modeling. We assume that at such an advanced level of writing, the authors know exactly what they are doing. Reading good literature is, in the words of novelist Jonathan Evison, 'a sort of collaborative dance' in which the author leads.

The 'Conclusion' returns, full circle, to our call for linguistic equality.

4   Doing Things with Words

POINT BY POINT

- We use languages to do things.
- At the most general level, we utter meaningful sentences of a particular language ('How are you?') to achieve a specific linguistic purpose (ask a question) and which have specific effects (establish collegiality).
- There are a surprisingly small number of types of linguistic purposes. We describe things ('The cat is on the mat'), direct people to do things ('Go home'), express feelings and attitudes ('What a car!'), commit ourselves to future courses of action ('I vow to stick with it'), and construct certain institutional realities ('This court is adjourned').
- We can do these things very directly ('Close the window') or indirectly ('Aren't you cold?')
- We can do these things indirectly by performing what are called implicatures, that is, by exploiting in various ways certain conversational and social-political tendencies that grease the wheels of communication ('Say only what you believe to be true,' 'Be polite'). For example, to express frustration with a person's particular contribution to a conversation, we can flout the maxim 'Say only what you believe to be true' by saying something obviously false ('Oh, yeah, that's a good idea').
- Implicatures are morally, socially, and politically important. Among the most important reasons: With them, we can communicate much (much) more than what we say; their performance and uptake require extraordinary levels of cooperation and trust and, therefore, vulnerability; they are often used intentionally to provide the cover of plausible deniability ('That is not what I said ...'); they are often the means by which comedy, metaphor, protest, insult, and humor are pulled off.

> We use
> languages to
> do things.

Language is a power tool. In addition to those linguistic actions already mentioned throughout, here are 46 more: We ...

claim, affirm, assure, inform, predict, report, suggest, insist, hypothesize, admit, confess, blame;

request, ask, urge, demand, command, forbid, suggest, insist, recommend, implore;

apologize, thank, condole, congratulate, complain, compliment, praise, welcome;

promise, vow, pledge, swear, consent, refuse, assure;

fire, pronounce, appoint, confirm, endorse, renounce, denounce, excommunicate, name.

Impressed by such lists, philosopher Ludwig Wittgenstein claimed in the mid-twentieth century that we can use language to do 'countless' things (1958: §23). Indeed, so many things, and of so many kinds, that Wittgenstein despaired of systematizing all that we can use languages to do and how we can do it. Language use, he then believed, is too unruly.

If Wittgenstein were right that linguistic actions cannot be systematized, then it would be difficult to explain—to provide a theory of—linguistic actions and how we perform them. Fortunately, few shared Wittgenstein's despair. Since then, an entire subfield at the intersection of linguistics and philosophy of language has flourished whose aim has been to categorize what we use languages to do and to explain how we can, in fact, use languages to do them. Such theories form the subfield of pragmatics.

This chapter will explain some basic distinctions and components of pragmatics and, thereby, will lay groundwork for much that will be discussed in the remaining chapters. It begins by clarifying helpful distinctions made by early proponents of pragmatics, including John Austin, John Searle, and, especially Paul Grice, which help explain different types of linguistic actions. It then uses Grice's influential theory of implicature to help explain how we perform many of those types of linguistic actions. The chapter closes by highlighting more recent work in pragmatics.

pragmatics
The study of what we use languages to do and how we do it.

Speech Acts

To better understand the nature of linguistic actions, or 'speech acts,' it is helpful to grasp three important sets of distinctions.

Distinction 1: Types of Speech Acts

The first set of distinctions is best understood initially by analogy. Suppose Angelina arrives home in the dark and, of course, wants to see when she gets inside her home. She thus (1) flicks the light switch, (2) turns on the lights, (3) illuminates the room, and (4) causes the burglar to flee through the terrace door. What does Angelina do with

> Uttering 'I'm home' typically announces that one is home, often alerts one's family that one is home, and sometimes causes the dog to jump up and down.

the lighting apparatus? The most basic is to flick the switch. Of course, the switch is part of an apparatus whose point, which Angelina brings about, is to turn on lights. Angelina could be flicking the switch intending simply to exercise her finger, but in fact, her point in flicking the switch is to turn on the lights. By turning on the lights, she illuminates the room and, unexpectedly, also causes a burglar to flee.

Compare Angelina's 'lighting actions' to Bettina's linguistic actions. Suppose Bettina comes home and wants to let her family know that she has arrived. She thus (1) utters the meaningful English sentence 'I'm home,' (2) thus announces that she is home and (3) alerts her family that she is home, and (4) causes the dog to jump up and down. The most basic thing Bettina does with her words is to utter (with the intention of speaking English) the meaningful English sentence 'I'm home.' This is what John Austin called a *locutionary act* (1962: Lecture VIII).

Bettina could be uttering that sentence intending simply to exercise her vocal cords or to practice her pronunciation, but her linguistic point is to announce that she is home. This is what Austin called an *illocutionary act*. By announcing that she is home, Bettina alerts her family that she is home and causes the dog to jump up and down. Austin called these consequences, intended or otherwise, *perlocutionary acts*.

Austin's distinctions clarify the very general structure of what we use languages to do: We utter meaningful sentences (locutions) to accomplish specific linguistic purposes (illocutions) that effect intended and, sometimes, unintended consequences (perlocutions). We can use 'I'm home' (locution) to announce that we are home (illocution), alert our partner and children that we are home (perlocution), and cause our dog to jump up and down (perlocution). We can use 'Take two aspirins' (locution) to prescribe a certain course of action (illocution), lead the hearer to do as directed (perlocution) or to become angry that we are muddling in his business (perlocution). We can use 'Snake!' (locution) to warn others that a snake is nearby (illocution), cause them to flee (perlocution) and, perhaps, to scream (perlocution).

locution
Producing a meaningful sentence of a language while intending to speak that language.

illocution
Performing a locutionary act to achieve its linguistic point.

perlocution
Intended or unintended consequence of performing an illocutionary act.

Distinction 2: Types of Linguistic Purpose

Austin's distinctions between locution, illocution, and perlocution allow us to home in on the latter two types of speech act, which are more socially consequential. Thus, a second set of important distinctions is that between different types of illocution—different types of linguistic purpose for which we use meaningful sentences.

Searle identifies five types of linguistic purpose and distinguishes each according to some important properties that he calls *force, direction of fit*, and *sincerity condition* (1975 'Taxonomy'). Table 4.1 summarizes Searle's taxonomy.

Searle's taxonomy of illocutions
Assertives, directives, expressives, commissives, declaratives.

Table 4.1 Searle's Taxonomy of Illocutions

Illocutionary Act Type	Illocutionary Point	Illocutionary Force	Examples	Direction of Fit	Sincerity Condition
Assertives	To describe the way things are	Claim, affirm, assure, inform, predict, report, suggest, insist, hypothesize, admit, confess, blame	'The Red Sox will win tonight'	Word to world ↓	Belief that the world is how it is being described
Directives	To direct one's hearer to do something	Request, ask, urge, demand, command, forbid, suggest, insist, recommend, implore	'Please go home' 'Go home!'	World to word ↑	Desire that the hearer do what the speaker is directing
Expressives	To express (not describe) one's mental state	Apologize, thank, condole, congratulate, complain, compliment, praise, welcome	'Oops!' 'My condolences' 'Thank you!' 'Congratulations!'	None/ Presupposed	Possession of state expressed
Commissives	To commit oneself to a future course of action	Promise, vow, pledge, swear, consent, refuse, assure	'I promise to give you five dollars' 'I insist on giving you five dollars'	World to word ↑	Intention to do what one is committing to
Declaratives	To make something the case	Fire, pronounce, declare, appoint, confirm, endorse, renounce, denounce, name, repudiate	'This court is adjourned' 'You're out!' 'I do' 'You're fired'	Both ↕	Intention (or perhaps desire) to bring about what is intended

Assertives. Assertives are illocutions whose linguistic purpose is to describe. They are paradigmatically performed using a declarative sentence, such as 'I'm home,' 'The Patriots will win this year's Super Bowl,' 'Obama can no longer run for U.S. President.' There are various ways to describe: insist, suggest, hint, admit, blame, claim, state, predict, report, hypothesize. The various ways of describing are, as Searle puts it, the forces with which a speaker can assert. When speakers describe, they typically try to make their words match the way things are—or as Searle puts it, assertives have *word-to-world* direction of fit. If speakers are sincere in what they assert, then they believe that things are as they describe, or, as Searle puts it, an assertive's sincerity condition is *belief*.

Directives. Directives are illocutions whose linguistic purpose is to direct people to do things, and they are paradigmatically performed using imperative sentences, such as 'Go home,' 'Take two aspirins,' and 'Please turn off all mobile devices.' Sometimes, a particular kind of directive, that of directing someone to provide information, is performed by using an interrogative sentence, such as 'What time will you be home?,' 'Are you cold?,' or 'Where will you spend your vacation?' A speaker can direct others in a variety of ways, i.e. with a variety of forces: request, ask, urge, implore, command, demand, and forbid. When directing people to do things, speakers try to make the world match their words, or, as Searle puts it, directives have *world-to-word* direction of fit. If speakers are sincere in what they direct others to do, then they actually want others to follow their directives, so a directive's sincerity condition is *desire*.

Expressives. Expressives are illocutions whose linguistic point is to express, rather than describe oneself as being in, a certain psychological or phenomenological state. They are paradigmatically performed using exclamative sentences, such as 'Home, sweet home!,' 'Wow,!' 'Thank you,' 'Congratulations,' and 'Ouch.' Expressives are performed in a variety of ways. A speaker can: apologize (to express regret), thank (to express gratitude), condole (to express sorrow), complain (to express frustration), congratulate (to express respect or excitement), compliment (to express appreciation), or use 'ouch' to express pain. Searle claims that expressing a psychological or phenomenological state presupposes rather than intends a fit between the words used and the way things are, and thus claims that expressives have no direction of fit. If speakers sincerely express psychological or phenomenological states, they actually have the state they are expressing: regret, gratitude, sorrow, frustration, etc.

Commissives. A fourth type of illocution is commissives, whose linguistic point is to commit a speaker to a future course of action. Commissives are paradigmatically performed using first-person declarative sentences with performative verbs, such as 'I promise to make it up to you,' 'I vow never to let this happen again,' 'I swear to tell the truth, the whole truth, and nothing but the truth.' Thus, commissives have a variety of forces: promise, vow, swear, pledge, consent, refuse, assure, and the like. Commissives have world-to-word direction fit, and their sincerity condition is *intention*.

Declaratives. The fifth type of illocution, declaratives, contains especially interesting and powerful speech acts, for they literally create new social realities. Consider some paradigm cases of declaratives: A wedding officiant literally marries a couple by *pronouncing them married*; a manager can literally hire or fire someone by *saying* 'You're hired' or 'You're fired'; a judge literally adjourns her court *declaring* 'This court is adjourned.' Declaratives are paradigmatically performed by those on whom are conferred certain institutional powers (a wedding officiant, manager, judge), by using certain declarative sentences ('I now pronounce you ...,' 'You're fired,' 'This court is adjourned') under special conditions (wedding, hierarchical employment structure, court proceedings). Thus, declaratives are acts in which a speaker constructs a new social reality simply by representing it as being the case. Declaratives, therefore, have *both* world-to-word and word-to-world directions of fit, for speakers intend for the world to match what their words represent and for the words to represent the way things are. There are various forces of declarative: marrying, hiring, firing, adjourning, nominating, confirming. They are performed sincerely when the speaker intends to bring about what he declares, so their sincerity condition is also *intention*.

Declaratives, then, are an extraordinarily powerful type of illocution, for they construct and maintain social, or at least institutional, realities. Indeed, Searle (2010) has argued that declaratives are the foundation of all human civilization. This is an exaggeration—for example, civilizations have leaders, but a particular person rarely, if ever, becomes the leader of a group because someone performed a declarative speech act, such as an utterance of 'You're our leader'— but it is an exaggeration only slightly. Nations, governments, property, currency, laws, courts, judges, verdicts, prosecutors, defendants, witnesses, wills; universities, professors, students, grade-point averages; corporations, CEOs, employees, parental leave; marriages, husbands, wives; doctors, nurses, hospitals; baseball games, teams, coaches, umpires: All of these and much, much more come into existence and are maintained by mechanisms that represent them as existing—that is, by declaratives.

Of course, these come into existence and are maintained by more than their mere representation. Unless you are a judge, you cannot adjourn a court by representing it as adjourned. (Indeed, even a judge cannot adjourn just any court—it must be her court, and her court must actually be in session.) Unless you are a manager, you cannot hire your spouse at your place of employment simply by representing your spouse as being hired. Thus, many social realities are constructed and maintained only by means of formal arrangements and mechanisms. And still more is required.

For consider that you do not become an attorney in your area of the country simply by constructing your own formal mechanism to declare yourself an attorney in your area. A people and land do not become a sovereign nation simply because they construct a formal mechanism to declare themselves and their land sovereign. What is required, in addition to formal mechanisms and declarations, is collective acceptance, a form of collective intentionality (Chapter 2) in which 'we,' or at least a critical mass of 'us,' recognize, accept, and have the will to maintain what seems magically done by the mechanisms and its declarations.

It is difficult to identify an illocution that does not fall naturally into any of the five categories—assertives, directives, expressives, commissives, and declaratives—and even rival taxonomies that differ from Searle's on theoretical points largely overlap with his resulting categories. For example, Kent Bach and Robert Harnish (1999) disagree with Searle about why illocutionary acts fall into their respective categories, and, consequently, name their categories slightly differently. But their resulting categories still largely overlap Searle's.

That Searle's taxonomy appears sufficient may be surprising. For although Wittgenstein is right that we can utter meaningful words and sentences to do countless things, there actually turn out to be a rather limited number of *types* of linguistic purposes for doing so. We describe, direct, express, commit, and declare (bring about). Consider again the amendments at the beginning of this chapter to our list of linguistic actions, amendments that can now be seen to be various ways of describing, directing, expressing, committing, and declaring:

> *assertives*: claim, affirm, assure, inform, predict, report, suggest, insist, hypothesize, admit, confess, blame;
> *directives*: request, ask, urge, demand, command, forbid, suggest, insist, recommend, implore;
> *expressives*: apologize, thank, condole, congratulate, complain, compliment, praise, welcome;
> *commissives*: promise, vow, pledge, swear, consent, refuse, assure;
> *declaratives*: fire, pronounce, appoint, confirm, endorse, renounce, denounce, excommunicate, name.

Distinction 3: Performing Illocutions Directly or Indirectly

A third basic distinction is between illocutions (assertives, directives, expressives, commissives, and declaratives) that are performed directly or indirectly.

To take one of Searle's own famous examples (1975 'Indirect'), suppose a speaker asks a dinner companion, in front of whom lies a salt shaker for all to see, 'Can you reach the salt?' Rarely would the companion answer, 'Yes, I can reach it.' For although the speaker has

indirect illocution
Illocution performed by means of another illocution.

direct illocution
Illocution that is not indirect.

directly asked a yes–no question, its answer is so obvious that the companion would reasonably infer that the speaker was doing something indirectly in asking that question, namely, politely requesting that the companion pass the salt. That is, in *directly asking* (a type of directive) whether the companion can pass the salt, the speaker *indirectly requests* (another type of directive) that the companion pass the salt. Thus, an indirect illocution is one that is performed by means of performing another illocution. A direct illocution is one that is not indirect.

The Three Distinctions in Action

Locution, illocution, and perlocution; assertive, directive, expressive, commissive, and declarative; direct and indirect illocution: These three sets of distinctions, as we will see in the remaining chapters, can help explain language's powerful potential. For now, consider two examples.

The first is a slightly modified version of H. Paul Grice's famous, and humorous, example (1975:33), an example shortly to be explored more deeply. Suppose a college student, Mr. Smith, would like to attend graduate school and, accordingly, asks Professor Jones, from whom he's taken several courses, to write a letter of recommendation. Professor Jones writes the following letter of recommendation for graduate studies and sends it off:

> Dear Admissions Committee:
>
> Mr. Smith's handwriting is excellent and he attends class regularly.
>
> Sincerely,
> Professor Jones

A letter few graduate applicants would want sent on their behalf! For after reading the letter, the admissions committee, recognizing that Professor Jones is likely implying, suggesting, hinting, or otherwise intending to communicate that Mr. Smith lacks those qualities typically required to perform graduate-level academic work, sadly, places Mr. Smith's application in the 'No'-pile.

Professor Jones uses language to do several things. She writes (a special case of uttering) meaningful sentences of English (while intending to speak English)—several locutions. In writing those sentences, she asserts directly that Mr. Smith's handwriting is excellent and that he attends class regularly, two direct illocutions. That she does so in the context of providing no other relevant information about Mr. Smith's potential for graduate-level work is evidence that she also asserts indirectly that Mr. Smith lacks such potential, an indirect illocution. By doing so, the professor causes the admissions committee to infer that Mr. Smith in fact lacks such potential and to place Mr. Smith's application in the 'No' pile, two perlocutions.

For a more familiar example, consider the expression of minor domestic frustration:

| *Peter:* | 'How many times do I have to tell you that this dish goes on the top shelf?' |
| *Paul (nonplayfully):* | 'Five.' |

Here, Peter utters a meaningful English sentence, a locution. In uttering that sentence, he directly asks how many times he will have to inform Paul that the dish goes on the top shelf, a direct illocution. That he asks such an odd question in the context of (presumably) already having provided this information several times and given the common background knowledge that most people become frustrated when having repeatedly to provide the same information to the same person is evidence that Peter also indirectly expresses frustration at having to do so, an indirect illocution. Paul's nonplayful response ('Five') is evidence that Peter has, in turn, caused Paul also to become frustrated, a perlocution. Paul's nonplayful response is also a locution, a direct assertive (a shorthand statement *that Peter will have to tell Paul five times that the dish goes on the top shelf*), and an indirect expressive (expressing frustration). We can easily imagine that Paul's response causes Peter to become even more frustrated, perhaps even angry—another perlocution. Et cetera.

Conversational Implicature

A speaker performs an illocution indirectly by performing a distinct illocution directly. How is that possible? What linguistic mechanism makes it possible to perform a linguistic action indirectly? One of the earliest and still most influential theories of language use that can explain 'indirect illocution' belongs to Paul Grice, who articulated a theory of language use in terms of what he called *implicature*, especially of the kind he called *conversational implicature* (1975).

Sentence Meaning vs. Speaker Meaning

Grice's pragmatic theory is grounded in the distinction between sentence meaning and speaker meaning. *Sentence meaning*, is, surely enough, the meaning of a sentence.

Speaker meaning is what a speaker intends to communicate in using a sentence. Sentence meaning and speaker meaning often overlap, since speakers often intend to communicate what their sentences mean. If a person is going to be late, that person will often intend to communicate this to others by using the sentence 'I'm going to be late,' simply because that's precisely what the sentence means— *that the speaker is going to be late*. If that is all that the speaker intends to communicate, then in this case sentence meaning and speaker meaning perfectly overlap. But often, speakers intend to

Sentence meaning
What a sentence means.

Speaker meaning
What a speaker intends to communicate in using a sentence.

communicate more than what their sentences mean. In those cases, speaker meaning exceeds sentence meaning.

Returning to a previous example, Professor Jones' sentence means *that Mr. Smith has excellent handwriting and attends class regularly.* And Professor Jones intends to communicate at least that much. For that much is, in Grice's own terms, 'what the speaker says.' But Professor Jones means to communicate more than that. She also means to communicate that Mr. Smith does not have the qualities typically required to perform well in graduate school. Professor Jones means what her sentences mean, and more.

Conventional vs. Conversational Implicature

Implicature
What a speaker implies, suggests, or means over and above what her sentences mean.

The something more is what Grice called *implicature*, a technical term he introduced with another humorous example:

> Suppose that A and B are talking about a mutual friend C, who is now working in a bank. A asks B how C is getting along on his job, and B replies, *Oh, quite well I think; he likes his colleagues and he hasn't been to prison yet.* At this point, A might well inquire what B was implying, what he was suggesting, or even what he meant by saying that C had not yet been to prison ... I think it is clear that whatever B implied, suggested, meant, etc., in this example, is distinct from what B said, which was simply that C had not been to prison yet.

(1975:24)

conventional implicature
Implicature that is closely tied to the conventional meanings of the words. Using 'Even Granny is drunk' conventionally implicates that Granny's being drunk is surprising, though the speaker does not say so, and even though the sentence means no more than that Granny is drunk.

What B was implying, suggesting, or meaning is what Grice called *implicature*.

A speaker can implicate by using certain words that help implicate information in almost any linguistic context in which those words are used. In almost any context in which a speaker says of a certain person 'She is poor but honest' (1975:25–26), the speaker communicates without saying that being poor typically precludes being honest; in almost any context in which a speaker says 'Even Granny was drunk' (Barker 2000:269), the speaker communicates without saying that Granny's inebriation was unexpected. These are cases in which a speaker uses certain words ('but' and 'even') whose meanings convey in almost any linguistic context contrast and surprise respectively. Because such implicatures are generated by the conventional meanings of certain words, this type of implicature Grice called *conventional implicature*.

social-political implicature
Implicature generated by exploiting generally observed social, moral, or aesthetic principles.

By contrast, *nonconventional implicature* exploits certain generally observed principles that grease the wheels of cooperation. Some of these principles are aesthetic, moral, or social, such as 'Be polite.' For example, in the next chapter, we'll explore politeness theory, which can be understood as developing this type of social-political implicature. Another type of nonconventional implicature exploits principles that tend to govern the quantity, truth, relevance, or clarity of what one says during conversation. This type of implicature, on

conversational implicature
Implicature generated by exploiting generally observed conversational principles.

which the remainder of this chapter will focus, Grice called *conversational implicature*.

Grice noticed that conversation is a goal-oriented, cooperative activity:

> Our talk exchanges do not normally consist of a series of disconnected remarks, and would not be rational if they did. They are characteristically, to some degree at least, cooperative efforts; and each participant recognizes in them, to some extent, a common purpose or set of purposes, or at least a mutually accepted direction.
>
> (1975:26)

Thus, Grice claimed that conversation is governed by an overarching Cooperative Principle (1975:26):

> *Cooperative Principle*: Make your conversational contribution such as is required at the stage at which it occurs, by the accepted purpose or direction of the talk exchange in which you are engaged.

But how does one adhere to this super principle? Grice postulated that conversational partners exploit a set of subprinciples, which he calls maxims, governing a contribution's *quantity*, *quality*, and *relevance* and the *manner* in which it is contributed:

Quantity

- Make your contribution as informative as is required (for the current purposes of the exchange).
- Do not make your contribution more informative than is required.

Quality

- Try to make your contribution one that is true.
- Do not say what you believe to be false.
- Do not say that for which you lack adequate evidence.

Relation

- Make your contribution relevant.

Manner

- Make your contribution one that is easy to follow.
- Make your contribution perspicuous.
- Avoid obscurity of expression.
- Avoid ambiguity.
- Be brief.
- Be orderly.

As he presented them, Grice's maxims of Quantity and Quality concern the type of illocution whose sole linguistic purpose is to provide information, that is, to describe. Since assertives are the only type of illocution whose sole linguistic point is to describe, Grice appears to suggest that his maxims apply only to assertives. However, since Grice understood these maxims to apply to any type of cooperative activity—including fixing a car! (1975:29)—he likely would have welcomed their extension to other types of illocution. For example:

Quantity

Directives

- Direct others to do as much as is required (for the current purposes of the exchange).
- Do not direct others to do more than is required.

Expressives

- Express as many attitudes as is required (for the current purposes of the exchange).
- Do not express more attitudes than is required.

Quality

Directives

- Do not direct what you do not want done.
- Do not direct what you lack good reason to want done.

Expressives

- Do not express attitudes you do not have.
- Do not express attitudes that you lack good reason to have.

Likewise for *commissives* and *declaratives*. (As Grice presents them, the maxims of relevance and manner are suitable for all five types of illocutionary acts.)

Evidence that such conversational maxims are in play during conversation is the conversational phenomenon of hedging:

> 'I'm not sure what else to say other than ...' (hedging quantity).
> 'I might be mistaken, but ...' (hedging quality).
> 'I don't know if this is relevant, but ...' (hedging relevance).
> 'This is going to come out a bit jumbled, but I think ...' (hedging manner).

Such hedging would seem to make sense only in light of our (usually tacit) recognition that our talk exchanges are generally guided by the conversational maxims of quantity, quality, relevance, and manner.

Thus far, this section has explained what Grice's conversational maxims are and provided evidence that such maxims govern conversation. How can conversational partners exploit those maxims to generate conversational implicatures?

By exploiting the maxims in various ways. That is, by strategically adhering to or failing to adhere to them. Here are several examples:

By adhering to maxims.

> *A:* Are you ready to eat dinner?
> *B:* I'm not hungry.

In this case, B says only *that she is not hungry* but conversationally implicates *that she is not ready to eat dinner*. For without assuming additional contextual facts, there is little reason to think that B is failing to adhere to any of the conversational principles. But B's contribution can be relevant to the conversation only if there is some connection between one's lack of hunger and one's being ready to eat dinner. The obvious connection is that one usually eats only when one is hungry. Thus, A infers, in part because B intends A to infer, that B is not ready to eat dinner.

By *violating* a maxim because of a clash with another maxim.

> *A:* Where's the book?
> *B:* Somewhere in the office.

Here, B says (in shorthand) only *that the book is somewhere in the office*, but conversationally implicates *that B does not know the book's more precise location*. B's conversational implicature can be explained by a clash of maxims. B's contribution would typically violate the maxim of quantity, since it is not as informative as is required by the talk exchange. A reasons plausibly, however, that B violates the maxim of quantity because B cannot adhere to it while also adhering to a submaxim of quality, 'Do not say that for which you lack adequate evidence.' A thus reasons that B faces a clash of maxims and, consequently, that B's contribution is as informative as B can make it without violating the maxim of quality. A thus infers, in part because B intends A to infer, that B does not know the book's more precise location.

By *flouting* a maxim.

> Professor Jones' Letter of Recommendation to the Admissions Committee: 'Mr. Smith's handwriting is excellent and he attends class regularly.'

Professor Jones says only that Mr. Smith's handwriting is excellent and he attends class regularly, but conversationally implicates *that Mr. Jones does not have the qualities typically required to perform well in graduate school*. The conversational implicature is generated because Professor Jones not only violates, but actually flouts, the maxims of relevance and quantity. Clarity of handwriting and regular attendance are not qualities that are crucially relevant for determining

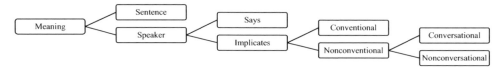

Figure 4.1 Important Distinctions in Grice's Theory of Implicature

one's potential for success in a graduate program and, even if they were, much more information about other requisite qualities—background knowledge, insight, initiative, ability to identify and solve problems, ability to work alone, ability to work with others—should be provided. Consequently, the admissions committee infers, in part because Professor Jones intends the committee to infer, that Mr. Jones does not have such qualities.

Figure 4.1 summarizes the most important distinctions of Grice's theory.

Although Grice never considered his theory of implicature, especially his theory of conversational implicature, as one that explains how a speaker can perform indirect illocutions, it is a natural extension of his theory. Indeed, in couching his own theory of indirect speech acts in terms of intentions and speaker meaning, inferable in part from 'rules that govern the utterance of the sentence' (1975 'Indirect'), Searle seems clearly to have taken Grice's theory of conversational implicature to be doing just that. For by explaining how language users converse in light of cooperative conversational principles, Grice's theory explains how speakers can perform at once both direct and indirect illocutions.

Contemporary Pragmatics

In the wake of Grice's theory of implicature, the field of pragmatics has flourished. A few scholars have objected on theoretical grounds to Grice's category of conventional implicature (Bach 1999) and even to the entire theory (Davis 1998). But most, intentionally or not, elaborate, refine, reduce, supplement, or otherwise attempt to improve upon Grice's theory.

For example, the next chapter will apply Grice's maxims of quantity, quality, manner, and relevance to the syntactic level of communication. Relevance theory as articulated by Sperber and Wilson (1986/1995) eliminates Grice's maxims of quantity, quality, and manner in favor of a more precise *communicative* principle of relevance and, indeed, argue that this principle can be explained, even predicted, by a deeper, more fundamental *cognitive* principle of relevance, which postulates that one's brain is hardwired to relate information coherently and, consequently, is one that no thinking creature could violate. Those attracted to relevance theory often sympathize as well with the theory of contextualism, which argues

that the pragmatic mechanisms Grice articulated, or at least something like them, are more powerful than even Grice realized. For,
according to contextualists, conversational partners bring so much
background information, contextual information, theory of mind,
collective intentionality, inferential ability, and outcome-oriented
processing to their conversations that speakers implicate and hearers
infer much (much!) more information during conversation than is
encoded by the semantics of the language they use. On that view,
informational entropy is *really* high.

Still other contemporary pragmatic theories can be understood
as enriching Grice's methodology and his rather barren notion of
social-political implicature, the type of implicature that he describes
as 'aesthetic, moral, or social in character' (1975:28). The theme
underlying the theory of conversational analysis is that the study
of language use should proceed not, as Grice appears to do, via
arm-chair reflection on a few artificial fragments of conversation,
but by data-driven hypotheses offered only after collecting and
interpreting a vast accumulation of data on actual conversations.
This bottom-up methodology reveals interesting social principles
that tend to govern conversation, such as 'Take turns' (turn-taking),
'Save face and help others to do so as well' (politeness theory),
'Accommodate to each other's speech patterns' (accommodation)
and powerful political principles, which critical discourse theories
aim to uncover, such as 'Speak only when your social standing
permits' and 'Select words and sentences that reflect the social
standing of each conversational partner' (see Chapters 5 and 6 for
further discussion of these social principles governing conversation). Other types of discourse theories argue that there are conversational principles, in addition to those governing fragments of
conversation, that apply to entire conversations (see Chapter 7) or
to other types of discourse, such as those that occur in journals or
in social media.

In one way or another, then, most contemporary pragmatic theories, intentionally or unintentionally, follow Grice in any of three
directions (Korta and Perry 2015: section 3): (a) distinguishing, on
the speaker-side, what a speaker says from what she implicates; and
accounting, on the hearer-side, for why a hearer arrives at one interpretation rather than another, (b) postulating a set of principles or
maxims, whether linguistic, cognitive, or social-political that tend
to govern conversation, and (c) recognizing the necessity, for human
language users, to anticipate and recognize each conversational
partner's communicative intentions.

The next several chapters will, in part, explain some of the ways
human language users can exploit such principles, either by adhering
to or violating them—as always, for good or ill.

(Im)pertinent Questions

- Consider speech acts that Bach and Harnish (1979) call acknowledgements, such as 'Hi.' Do these fall neatly into any of Searle's five categories of illocution?
- Consider again Searle's famous example, 'Can you pass the salt?' Do you think the speaker intends to ask a question? Or does the speaker intend only to request the hearer to pass the salt? If the speaker does not intend to ask the question, what, if anything, motivates the distinction between direct and indirect illocution?
- What is your most telling personal example of using implicature to communicate far more than what you said?
- Have you ever had the uneasy feeling that someone just insulted you, but just weren't quite sure? Can the notion of implicature help you understand how you might have been insulted?
- Suppose an imposing authority who is under legal investigation because of damning evidence says to a subordinate (who has the means to make the evidence disappear), 'It would be better for me if there were no such evidence.' What are all of the things the speaker might be doing with this sentence. Why does the speaker use this particular sentence?
- Suppose that in a particular culture children are raised to sometimes yell and shout back at adults as a means of helping the children develop a sense of independence. Would this mean that those in this linguistic community fail to abide by the social-political maxim, 'Be polite'?
- How might one perform an implicature by flouting the maxim 'Be polite'?

References

Austin, John L. 1962. *How to do things with words*. 2nd ed. Cambridge, MA: Harvard University Press.

Bach, Kent. 1999. The myth of conventional implicature. *Linguistics and Philosophy* 22.327–66.

Bach, Kent, and Robert Harnish. 1979. *Linguistic communication and speech acts*. Cambridge, MA: MIT Press.

Barker, Stephen. 2000. Is value content a component of conventional implicature? *Analysis* 60(267).268–79. DOI: 10.1111/1467-8284.00239.

Davis, Wayne. 1998. *Implicature: Intention, convention, and principle in the failure of Gricean theory*. Cambridge: Cambridge University Press.

Grice, Paul. 1975. Logic and conversation. Reprinted in *Studies in the way of words*, ed. by H. Paul Grice, 22–40. Cambridge, MA: Harvard University Press, 1989.

Korta, Kepa, and John Perry. 2015. Pragmatics. *The Stanford encyclopedia of philosophy* (Winter Edition), ed. by Edward N. Zalta. Section 3. Online: https://plato.stanford.edu/archives/win2015/entries/pragmatics/.

Searle, John. 1975. A taxonomy of illocutionary acts. Reprinted in *Expression and meaning: Studies in the theory of speech acts*, ed. by John Searle, 1–29. Cambridge: Cambridge University Press, 1979.

Searle, John. 1975. Indirect illocutionary acts. Reprinted in *Expression and meaning: Studies in the theory of speech acts*, ed. by John Searle, 30–57. Cambridge: Cambridge University Press, 1979.

Searle, John. 2010. *Making the social world: The structure of human civilization*. New York: Oxford University Press.

Sperber, Deirdre, and Dan Wilson. 1986/1995. *Relevance: Communication and cognition*. 2nd ed. Oxford: Blackwell.

Wittgenstein, Ludwig. 1958. *Philosophical investigations*. 3rd ed., trans. by G. E. M. Anscombe. Englewood Cliffs, NJ: Prentice Hall.

5   The Language of Cooperation

POINT BY POINT

- Languages work through cooperation (as required by their high entropy).
- Speakers/writers align with recipients' needs at all levels, from pronunciation, word choice, and sentence structure up to social conventions and preferences.
- Messages extend far beyond semantic content: Linguistic exchanges also negotiate identity.
- Factors affecting linguistic identity are politeness, 'face' (confirmation or imposition), and accommodation (or lack thereof). Much of this amounts to power relations.
- Since languages link minds, they can be used (and this can be learned) to bond and heal, to mediate between adversaries, or to resolve a hostage situation.

> The cooperation enforced by high informational entropy opens up additional levels of flexibility in social interaction.

The human language is a little bit like the game of chess: There is a finite set of game pieces and a limited set of combinatorial rules operating on them, but the results are infinite. Most importantly, playing chess rests on cooperation: It would be hard to think of anything more infuriating than a chess partner who just makes random moves; it would feel like a betrayal. Grice, recall, observed that our 'talk exchanges do not consist of a succession of disconnected remarks, and would not be rational if they did' (1975). In language, too, we expect that the conversation partner is trying to make linguistic sense, or else we tune out. Chapter 3 described the P600 brain wave measured in the left hemisphere when the brain is attempting to repair a syntactic structure that was flagged as an anomaly less than half a second earlier (by ELAN). That response kicks in *only* if the listener assumes that the speaker is cooperating by trying to make sense. When the majority of sentences presented to a subject contain a syntactic violation, the P600 stops showing up (Hahne and Friederici 1999). The brain gives up on any further attempts to co-create linguistic structure if the speaker appears to be making random errors.

Cooperation defines the nature of human languages, precisely due to their high entropy: Natural language processing has a hyper-social, collaborative prerequisite. Cooperation can of course have destructive aims, as was seen in Chapter 1 and will be seen again in the next chapter. The current chapter expands the insights of Philosophy of Language from the previous chapter to include insights from the field of Applied Linguistics. We will explore *language* (any language, such as English) as a tool to affect someone's internal *Language* (a mental faculty for linguistic processing) for purposes of cooperation.

We identify three levels of linguistic processing and cooperation: the level of syntactic structures and functions, the level of literal interpretation, and the level of extended interpretation. We then describe how experts can skillfully negotiate the three levels to help resolve conflict.

Three Levels of Linguistic Processing and Cooperation

Level 1: Negotiating Syntactic Structures and Functions

The linguistic faculty includes the principles of human Language. Whatever the specific settings of individual languages are, Universal Grammar (UG) implies them. The specific settings are domain specific. For example, whether a sentence is syntactically well formed is independent of social context; sentences can be syntactically correct even if they don't make sense. Noam Chomsky famously demonstrated this structural autonomy with the sentence 'Colorless green ideas sleep furiously,' which makes no sense in any readily imaginable context, but is nonetheless well formed at the syntactic level.

Syntactic rules are autonomous (must be described without reference to meaning, sound, etc.), but of course they are *put to use* in social context, in speech acts as the ones described in the previous chapter. And Chapter 4 also showed the subtleties and often deliberate ambiguities of speech acts, so the logic-like clarity of syntax does not directly carry over into the realm of interpretation. It just appeared that way in some of the older models of communication theory that one might still find in some textbooks, especially the 'encoding/decoding' model: A speaker encodes a message, which is sent to the recipient, who decodes it. As if decoding were the reverse of encoding! When it comes to natural languages, that is a fallacy: Our wording is not unambiguous enough to allow direct unraveling even of what H. Paul Grice called 'what is said,' the 'literal' meaning of an utterance (see p. 110 below). Rather, the 'recipients' engage in creating their own structures and interpretations in hopes that they match those of the 'senders.' How successful they are is

Internal Language
This concept is a modern concern in linguistics. Noam Chomsky (2000:70) refers to the abstract linguistic knowledge of generative procedures as 'i-language,' while Steven Pinker (1994:81) refers to the 'language of thought' more generally as 'mentalese.' Either way, the idea is to separate the faculty of Language (our competence) from 'external' speech (performance, or 'e-language' in Chomsky's terminology). A single Language faculty underlies all human languages, so *Language* is first and foremost a universal set of cognitive computing principles such as predication and embedding.

more a matter of cooperating (see the conclusion of Chapter 4) than 'decoding.'

Even just recognizing how signals (phonemes, words) combine is already a matter of apperception (recall the discussion of Mondegreens on p. 67). Syntactic structures, for all their structural clarity,[1] are no different. It could (and does) happen that a sequence of words may have been generated by one structural representation in the speaker's brain and prompt a different structural representation in the listener's. The words *cash in your couch* could have been meant as a trade-in offer ('go ahead and [*cash in* your couch]$_S$') but could also be parsed as a noun phrase instead ('there may be [*cash* in your couch]$_{NP}$'). Whether the parser opts for the clause reading (S) or for the noun-phrase reading (NP) depends on what the listener thinks ought to have been communicated. In 'disambiguation' tasks, context drives parsing: The parser selects (sometimes guesses—cf. p. 70) the syntactic structure that makes sense, as anticipated.

Making parsing decisions based on adduced real-life knowledge is fast, automatic, and effortless because Language can integrate a lot of information in real time. Without such massive and near-instant access to conceptual and experiential knowledge, the parser should come up with many more erroneous interpretations. This is *the* mattress-in-the-road challenge of Artificial Intelligence research. For an unbiased computer without human foresight, a "simple" sentence such as *Time flies like an arrow* has a variety of parses, all charted side by side as equally possible:

- You should time flies the same way an arrow times them;
- You should time flies with the same method used for timing an arrow;
- There are insects called 'time flies' that like an arrow;
- The newsmagazine *Time* flies (off the shelves?) as fast as an arrow can fly.

None of these possible parses are likely even tentatively pursued by a human being who already anticipates the speaker's intent. Following the conversation primes the parse that is most readily compatible with the current topic: 'The speed of the passing of time compares to the speed of a flying arrow.' Conversation partners cooperate (Grice's *Cooperative Principle*, p. 95) and interpret each other's contributions in terms of relevance (cf. Wilson and Sperber, pp. 14, 98)—something a 'chatbot' with limited contextual knowledge is not (yet) very good at.

---

1 We'll have to qualify that a bit. There are indeed some templates in English (such as *the more, the merrier* or *Just because you are smiling doesn't mean you are happy* or *I might could join you*) that elude a structural description that syntacticians agree upon.

In college rhetoric and composition teaching, there is a school of thought that emphasizes identifying the audience so as to make one's writing accessible. But what audience-specific adjustments are to occur when an audience has been identified? Even grammar books do not have much to say about how exactly writer and reader cooperate at the sentence level. That cooperation can be stated in Gricean maxims, here applied to grammar and usage:

Quantity (do not overload short-term memory):

- **Select the grammatical structure least likely to overtax the listener's short-term memory.** For example, *The software that some cars that Audi offers have is deceptive as well* is very near the limit of what a listener can parse in real time. Embed one more relative clause inside the other, and the sentence, while syntactically still well formed, becomes too hard to parse: *The software that some cars that Audi which Volkswagen owns offers have is deceptive as well.* The listener is forced to hold too much information in short-term memory: Parsing a relative clause cannot be completed because another relative clause is opened up, and completing that one is in turn suspended to process a third. The information of three clauses needs to be held in working memory before they can be resolved one by one, finally allowing the main clause to be completed (*The software ... is deceptive as well*). Human working memories typically cannot hold that much information. A selfish writer could just be content that the sentence is syntactically well formed and let it go at that. A *cooperating* writer, however, would want to allow for an individual constituent of the sentence to be parsed and flushed from the reader's memory workspace to make room for the next constituent: *Volkswagen owns Audi, which offers some cars with deceptive software as well.* The information is identical, but offered in chunks that the parser can finish piecemeal, without overburdening short-term memory.

- **Do not let too many words intervene between a pronoun and its antecedent.** There are two workspaces within which pronouns can be resolved: a push-down stack for processing syntactic information (about four items deep) and a push-down stack for which of these words are marked as topics (probably no more than two). Whatever drops out of *both* stacks is no longer available to the parser (though this two-stack model will be supplemented in Chapter 7). With too many words intervening, a listener may erroneously decide, for instance, that a change of topic has taken place: *Pete Rose amassed an unequaled record as a hitter, using his bat to do things no one else has ever done. Even after his betting scandal and even though he was banned from baseball, it still stands out today* (from Fowler and Aaron 2006:287). A reader, looking at the printed words, can re-scan the preceding sentence on the page all the way back to *unequaled record* for the antecedent of *it*, but a listener's short-term memory loses the connection because verbiage intervenes.

Quality (clearly mark constituents and their relations):

- **Use syntactic structure optimally to signal relations between syntactic components.** The downside to concentrating on bite-sized syntactic constituents that can be processed and flushed from working memory immediately is that a meandering stream-of-consciousness of sound bites may become incoherent as a text. That is, the listener can follow each utterance locally but feels adrift. A showpiece of incoherence, transcribed by *Slate Magazine*, is the following sentence from a 2016 South Carolina presidential primary-campaign speech ('Help Us Diagram' 2015): *Look, having nuclear—my uncle was a great professor and scientist and engineer, Dr. John Trump at MIT; good genes, very good genes, OK, very smart, the Wharton School of Finance, very good, very smart—you know, if you're a conservative Republican, if I were a liberal, if, like, OK, if I ran as a liberal Democrat, they would say I'm one of the smartest people anywhere in the world—it's true!—but when you're a conservative Republican they try—oh, do they do a number—that's why I always start off: Went to Wharton, was a good student, went there, went there, did this, built a fortune—you know I have to give my like credentials all the time, because we're a little disadvantaged—but you look at the nuclear deal, the thing that really bothers me—it would have been so easy, and it's not as important as these lives are (nuclear is powerful; my uncle explained that to me many, many years ago, the power and that was 35 years ago; he would explain the power of what's going to happen and he was right—who would have thought?), but when you look at what's going on with the four prisoners—now it used to be three, now it's four—but when it was three and even now, I would have said it's all in the messenger; fellas, and it is fellas because, you know, they don't, they haven't figured that the women are smarter right now than the men, so, you know, it's gonna take them about another 150 years—but the Persians are great negotiators, the Iranians are great negotiators, so, and they, they just killed, they just killed us.* If listeners construct any coherence, they find it in the delivery, i.e. they must construe it from the personality of the speaker rather than from the progression of thought.

- **Use function words to mark constituents.** There are really only five lexical categories in English (content words—nouns, verbs, adjectives, adverbs, prepositions); the rest are function words (articles, various types of proforms and conjunctions, complementizers, quantifiers, intensifiers, modals, auxiliaries, etc.). Function words greatly assist the parser in deciding how the content words relate to one another, or even how to interpret a single word. For example, an auxiliary helps identify a verb ending: The *-ed* ending on the verb *consulted* signals passive voice when the auxiliary is BE (*she was consulted*), perfective aspect when the auxiliary is HAVE (*she has consulted*), and past tense if there is no auxiliary (*she consulted*). Function words disambiguate (*cash [that is] in your couch*). The parser has fewer decisions to make. Taking in the words *Sherlock Holmes suspected the butler* ... in real time leaves open whether the clause stops here or whether there is more syntactic game afoot (*Sherlock Holmes suspected the butler did it*). Providing a complementizer reduces ambiguity: *Sherlock Holmes suspected that the butler did it*. Words that Miss Fidditch might have crossed out with a gloss of 'wordy' are not clutter at all, but increase reading speed.

Relation (mark how constituents relate to content):

- **Use definite and indefinite articles to signal whether the content of a noun phrase refers to something presumed known to the listener or to something newly introduced into the discourse.** The use of articles in Edited English helps negotiate topics. In the sentence *Chicago, at this time of year, should still be warm enough; {the/a} raincoat should be all you'll need*, the choice of articles signals to the listener that (a) a raincoat is immediately available or has been mentioned before, or else, (b) that it would be advisable to make up for the lack of a raincoat to prepare for the trip to Chicago. The article *the* refers the listener to previous discourse or to items that presumably populate the listener's mental model; the article *a* refers the listener to something new—here a suggested outcome (maybe the anticipated purchase of a raincoat).

- **Use less specific information to link back to more specific information.** In the sentence *I wanted Charlie to help me, but the bastard wouldn't do it*, the epithet *the bastard* refers back to Charlie; that relation is not so easily construed if the noun phrases are reversed: *I wanted the bastard to help me, but Charlie wouldn't do it* (Jackendoff 1969:57). To refer back to a specific reference, an epithet needs to refer to something less specific (e.g. by assigning *Charlie* figuratively to a popular category, *bastards*). This strategy allows the listener to relate current information back to past information and to decide whether a constituent relates to something already contained in the mental model.

- **Arrange information within a sentence according to how salient it is to the listener—proceed from presumed-known to presumed-new information.** This arrangement is known as the 'gradience of saliency' in sentences. If the default word order does not reflect that progression, English has a number of syntactic templates available to shuffle information around (see Table 5.1).

Miss Fidditch
Best described by Margaret B. Fleming (1983): 'the name given by Martin Joos in *The Five Clocks* to that terrible middle-aged spinster with sensible shoes and hair pulled back into a bun who corrected relentlessly every syllable we uttered in speech or writing, never satisfied with anything less than her own rigid standard of absolute perfection.'

epithet
A noun phrase referring to a preceding noun phrase.

Table 5.1 Linguistic Information Management Templates

Template	given > > >> > > new> >	
canonic	The snakes gave Melampus	the gift of talking to animals.
passive	The gift of talking to animals was given to	Melampus.
passive	Melampus was given the gift	of talking to animals.
'move dative'	The snakes gave the gift of talking to animals	to Melampus.
extraposition	The snakes gave the gift to Melampus	of talking to animals.
cleft	It was the gift of talking to animals that	the snakes gave Melampus.
pseudo-cleft	What the snakes gave to Melampus was	the gift of talking to animals.
topicalization	The gift of talking to animals, the snakes	gave Melampus.
there + cleft	There was a gift of talking to animals that	the snakes gave Melampus.

Manner (accommodate to parsing biases):

template
A learned sentence structure, stored as such in the lexicon, that allows for information to be distributed for salience.

register
Adjustment of speech to reflect the level of formality of the speech situation / status of the person(s) addressed.

- **Avoid syntactic templates that do not belong to the current register.** In an informal speech situation, a cleft sentence that would otherwise be ideal for presenting information by saliency might signal exclusion instead because the template is marked as too formal for the speech situation ('Vanilla or chocolate?' 'It is vanilla ice cream that I prefer.'). One or the other template from Table 5.1 may not even be familiar to some audiences. A 2010 study by James Street and Ewa Dąbrowska (2010), for example, studied a population of British high school students who never used the passive construction. A speaker thus needs to balance the need for presenting information according to its salience to the listener with the need to choose familiar and appropriate syntactic templates (so as not to signal exclusion).

- **Use stress to facilitate the recovery of presuppositions.** Consider the sentence *John called Mary a virgin, and then she insulted him* (taken from Lakoff 1971:63–64). It is not clear from the sentence structure itself whether Mary took John's remark as an insult. Stress can disambiguate that (see Table 5.2). Stress assignment by the speaker anticipates the needs of the listener in recovering presuppositions.

- **Use different verbs to affect what event model the listener/reader builds—and with which attitude.** A group of volunteers, say, has removed lead from an older home and

Table 5.2 Stress Assignment for Disambiguation

John called Mary a virgin, and	*then* (**1**)
	she (**2**)
	insulted (**3**)
	him (**4**)

primary stress	presupposition about the relationship between being called a virgin and being insulted
1	none; *then* establishes chronology of events
2 and/or 4	yes; her insult is reciprocal
3	none; her insult is unexpected after what John had said (or else she insulted him rather than doing something else, such as giving a dismissive eye roll).

communicates the sanitation to three different audiences. Each audience is to be affected differently, hence different types of verbs are used:

- Owner (stative): To the owner of the home, the volunteers merely wish to report that the house is safe, without drawing attention to their volunteerism. They choose linking verbs and verbs with stative aspect that merely describe what is: *the house is safe, the lead dust is gone, the old paint is covered, the house has new water pipes*, etc.

- Insurance company (resultative): For the insurance company, they want to emphasize the current condition of the house as a result of completed actions without drawing too much attention to the qualifications of the volunteers. They take advantage of the resultative feature of the verb ending used for perfective aspect and passive voice: *the house has been rendered safe, all lead dust has been removed, the old paint was sealed under two coats of new paint, water pipes were replaced with new ones.*

- Newspaper (agentive): For a human-interest story in a newsletter or newspaper, they choose action verbs specific enough to evoke "mirror-neuron" simulation responses in the reader in hopes of attracting more volunteers for future projects via a 'me-too' effect: *we scrubbed everything, swept up dust from the floors, brushed new paint over walls and window frames, sawed and hacked through old water pipes and ripped them out and crimped together new PVC water supply lines.*

Identical information presented with different verbs calls up different mental representations (states, results, events), eliciting a different attitude in each audience, as intended.

Clearly, cooperation between speaker and listener already guides a lot of the parsing of syntactic structures. The so-called 'decoding' is not just automatic, but also intentional and deterministic, hence creative: The act of parsing already anticipates desired results by

stative
A verb aspect that merely indicates a condition. Linking verbs have that feature (A *is/seems* B), and so do any verbs that describe an existing condition.

perfective
Verbs that follow the pattern have + V + {-en / -ed} such as in *he has seen the light*. The verb suffix is sometimes referred to as the 'past participle ending,' but past/non-past is decided in the auxiliary *has* vs. *had*. The perfective aspect says that the action has been completed and that there is a currently relevant state as a result. The same ending is used in the passive voice (e.g. *he was seen*), and the resultative aspect carries over to passive verbs.

using cues from the speaker and from the speech situation. And that is before we even get to the level of literal interpretation.

Level 2: Literal Interpretation: Negotiated Sentence Meaning

A parser works automatically to determine what an utterance 'is' ('what is said,' in Grice's terms) even as it already anticipates what the utterance 'stands for' at the next higher level of interpretation (cf. Ariel 2008:263, 266). Once the listener, for example, has understood a speaker to say *I have nothing to wear for tonight*, the literal interpretation is that the speaker is wanting attire for that evening's event. What the listener understands the speaker to be doing in using that sentence (a directive?, expressive?, commissive?—see Chapter 4 for a review of those terms) belongs to a higher level of interpretation. That is the level of interpreting what the speaker means or implicates.

Of course, if even the syntactic structure of a sentence is subject to cooperation (between grammar and parser), then Grice's distinctions between speaker meaning, sentence meaning, and felicity (the recipient 'gets' it and reacts with the hoped-for perlocutionary act) are theoretical. In practice, those levels are not autonomous, but interactive. There is no easy way to determine 'what is said' without interpreting within/towards a context (cf. Sperber and Wilson, p. 98 above). This is a notorious problem studied in forensic linguistics. A famous example is the Second Amendment ('A well regulated Militia, being necessary to the security of a free State, the right of the people to keep and bear Arms, shall not be infringed'). Its wording ties the right of *the* people (collectively)—not just *people* (individuals)—to the necessity of having an orderly militia to defend the state; it is also read as granting a right to every private citizen to own fire arms.

'Legalese' is the attempt to write in such a way as to make sure that the wording is 'Clear, Correct, Concise, and Complete' (the "4 'C's"), hence sufficiently self-explanatory to preclude any future negotiation (asking, or second-guessing, what the author 'meant'). In the words of John Gibbons, the ideal is that 'the text is fixed and frozen' (1994/2013:22), and there is no possibility to (re-)negotiate the intended meaning with the author. The literal 'sentence meaning' perfectly overlaps with speaker meaning—no hidden premises to discover, no implicatures to negotiate. But what if the parser does not recover the same structure that was in the writer's head when the sentence was written down, i.e. what if the syntax is 'ambiguous'? Sanford Schane (2006:41) provides a hypothetical example:

> A state legislature has established a curfew. The law states that 'old men and women must not be out in public after 8 o'clock at night.' A young woman is arrested for violating the curfew. She claims that the law does not apply to her, that it affects only old women, and hence that she has been unlawfully arrested. The arresting officer maintains that the law does apply to her, that it is applicable to all women, and therefore the arrest of the young woman is valid.

felicity
The condition where the intended audience of a speech act understands its intent (e.g. understands a commitment as sincere and feasible). For a discussion of speech act and conversational principles, refer back to Chapter 4.

In Anglo-American law, Schane hastens to add, the woman would go free on account of the *rule of lenity* (essentially: If penal statutes are ambiguous, plaintiffs and government forfeit). The salient point is that we need a rule of lenity even in legal language. Removing language from its cooperative space would indeed make it 'fixed and frozen,' but unfortunately those words best describe proverbs—or dead languages.

Even the meaning of a word like *chicken* turns out to be subject to negotiation (as described in Schane 2006: Chapter 1). In the case of Frigaliment Importing Co. vs. BNS International Sales Corp., the meaning of *chicken* actually became the subject of a lawsuit. The Swiss company had ordered frozen eviscerated chickens from the New York wholesaler BNS, in two sizes: 1½ to 2 lbs., and 2½ to 3 lbs. When the shipment arrived, all the larger chickens turned out to be stewing chickens rather than broilers and fryers. The Swiss company sued, arguing that the seller had not delivered what they ordered. So, what is $CHICKEN_h$?

Here is the concept in the buyer's mind: In German, including Swiss German, compounding (recall p. 24) makes clear what the chicken is meant for. If the bird is specifically meant for stewing, it is called a *Suppenhuhn* (literally, a 'soup chicken')—too fat for broiling. That is the specific ('marked') term. The generic (unmarked) term is *Huhn*, and any *Huhn* that is not specifically meant to go into soup is by default a *Brathuhn* (frying chicken). Chickens ending up in soup is rather the exception in Europe—the way of preparing it is in an oven or on a rotisserie. Thus, the Swiss, not having explicitly ordered stewing chickens, expected *lean* birds in the 2½-to-3-lbs. category. BNS International argued that a chicken is a chicken (*gallus gallus*, if you prefer it in Latin), using the definition scratched out by the Department of Agriculture. But the Swiss argued that they had not ordered *chicken* the bird but *chicken* the product. An *eviscerated* chicken falls under the definition of 'manufactured product' by the Interstate Commerce Commission (ICC), hence the Department of Agriculture's definition would *not* apply. Upon examining the contract, which was written in English, the judge found that the use of the English word *chicken* had not made it sufficiently clear to the American vendor *not* to send stewers. Judgment for the defendant: The need for *lean* yields to the need for *lenience*, and the Swiss got stuck with the bill.

The legal stew over the definition of *chicken* illustrates that the term 'literal meaning,' if taken to mean 'perfectly precise meaning,' is wishful thinking—literally.[2] The wish is that language could be somehow isolated from its high-entropy cooperative nature and fixated into non-negotiable clarity. The wish is that a sentence perfectly "encodes" a mental model. For reasons explored in Chapter 1 and above (p. 103), speakers cannot use languages to convey or interpret mental models faithfully (you will notice that we have a chapter down below on clarity as essentially 'managed confusion').

---

2 We will have a detailed look at the collaborative nature of definitions in Chapter 7.

The 'search for the perfect language' (Eco 1995) is ultimately futile—because we already have it, except that the 'perfection' lies in cooperation.

Level 3: Extended Interpretation: Negotiated Implicatures

Speaker and hearer *must* cooperate if the mental model of the recipient is to mirror at least some of the mental model of the speaker: The words on their own are underdetermined (contain too little of the information that made the speaker select them). Interpretation is the art of adducing information: knowledge of the other (mind reading), of conventions, of the situation at hand, of the current or historical real world.

Negotiators use channels. On the syntactic level, the speaker's grammar anticipates the needs of the listener's parser and aligns accordingly. On the level of sentence meaning, speaker and listener cooperate to resolve ambiguities. The level of extended interpretation allows the linguistic sphere to reach into the social sphere. At that level, we negotiate identity and inclusion, navigate the intricate paths of politeness and protect 'face'—both our own and that of our conversation partner. That said, all channels broadcast simultaneously.

3.1 Linguistically Negotiated Identity

| Social identity is negotiated through language—spontaneously and long-term. |

Chapter 1 mentioned that individual languages can be associated with genetic groups (Longobardi et al. 2015), suggesting a biological connection between language and group identity. There are other identities expressed through speech. On a daily basis, a speaker may adopt a number of different 'lects' or modes of speaking, depending on who the conversation partners are and what is being talked about (see Table 5.3). With each lect, the speaker adopts a linguistic persona, presents (or accommodates to) a situational identity. In the real world, 'literal sentence meaning' takes a backseat to social negotiations.

Assume, for example, that the first conversation partner of the day is an intimate within her or his initial years of language acquisition (a 'baby,' if we forego the linguistic jargon). The adult instinctively falls into the style of 'child-directed speech' (known in older literature as 'motherese,' but it turned out not to be particularly gender specific). The adult's intonation contours become more exaggerated; pronunciation is hyper-enunciated; the sentences are simple; the tempo is slower; and the topics are context-embedded (focusing on the here-and-now). Then the boss calls on the telephone with a request to advise on an urgent technical problem; when the issue cannot be resolved over the phone, another request follows to show up for work early today. Surely the linguistic persona changes for that new speech situation: The register will be formal, probably somewhat reserved, and certainly filled with

Table 5.3 Lects and Their Domains

Domain	Lect
geographic region or ethnic speech community	dialect
social status (lower, middle, upper class)	sociolect
privilege/prestige	acrolect
status of partner (inferior, equal, intimate, superior)	register
conventions of presentation/stance taking/genre	style
insider group	slang
field of knowledge	jargon
individual's signature way of talking	idiolect

technical jargon. Once that phone call is over, some minor frustration about having morning playtime cut short might be shared with a spouse or partner. Again, the linguistic persona changes. A taxi might be called, and the taxi driver, who does not present as a native speaker of English, initiates a friendly banter. As in child-directed talk, the native speaker's speech slows down, the sentences become simple, but intonation is normal. Maybe the voice is a bit louder. This is known as 'foreigner-directed talk.' Not quite one hour, already four different linguistic personas before the workday has even started. Meanwhile, maybe, the baby is being read to at home and listens to Patricia's McKissack's *Flossie and the Fox*, in which a sassy young girl's dialect is pitched—with devastating success—against the fox's acrolect.

Table 5.3 also contains the term 'idiolect,' and that is a bit more stable across the different spontaneous linguistic personas one adopts over the course of a day. A speaker may have a regional accent, maybe not pronounce /r/ after a vowel as in 'cah' for *car*. Or the speaker may use words in a way that suggests a regional affiliation, e.g. calling all soft drinks *coke* or addressing others as *y'all* or *guys* (male or female). Or the speaker's voice may sound gravelly at the end of sentences ('vocal fry'), or maybe the intonation goes up at the end of every sentence whether it is a question or not ('uptalking'). To the degree that the speaker holds on to those individual traits across various lects, identity persists in speech.

Just as they adjust to other lects, speakers also react to idiolects. After just a minute or two, *equal* partners who feel comfortable talking to one another start picking up some of the other's idiosyncratic features, and they incorporate them into their own speech. Someone who has never used uptalking before may cautiously and subtly start to use that feature—careful not to come across as imitating or parodying. This is known as 'accommodation'; it is spontaneous, signals acceptance and inclusion, and evaporates soon after the conversation ends. If it involves entire communities, something else is going on.

Accommodation between entire communities usually reflects *unequal* power relations. The *less* influential group tends to align with linguistic features of the more influential (powerful, prestigious, affluent ...) group. Dialectologists have been aware of this phenomenon for a number of years now. The relations may be regional, as when rural communities interact with urban ones, or they may be cultural. A very dynamic scenario of accommodation is currently unfolding as a result of the massive trend towards urbanization in mainland China (cf. Xu 2015).

Note that each of the adopted lects affects word choice, sentence structure, intonation, pronunciation, sometimes even morphology. Again, as has been observed in so many domains of mental processing, those are adjustments on the fly. 'What is said' is not solely content driven. The anticipated social needs at the highest level of interpretation exert their influence downwards. A widely circulated (hopefully fictitious) anecdote illustrates how the medium fits not only the message but also the audience (Eisenberg 1994):

> There was once a plumber of foreign extraction who wrote to the Bureau of Standards in Washington, D.C., that he had found hydrochloric acid was fine for cleaning drains, and that it was harmless. Washington replied: 'The efficacy of hydrochloric acid is indisputable, but the corrosive residue is incompatible with metallic permanence.' The plumber wrote back that he was mighty glad the Bureau agreed with him. The Bureau replied with a note of alarm: 'We cannot assume responsibility for the production of toxic and noxious residues with hydrochloric acid and suggest you use an alternative procedure.' The plumber wrote he was happy to learn that the Bureau still agreed with him. Whereupon, Washington exploded: 'Don't use hydrochloric acid, it eats the hell out of pipes!!'

3.2 Linguistically Negotiated Politeness: Saving Face

> Indirection allows face saving—such as the ability to deny a request by renegotiating a speech act.

There is safety in being direct. But sometimes, there is safety in *not* being direct. Indirection affords escape hatches. Assume that the sentence *I have nothing to wear for tonight* was meant as an indirect request to consent to the expense of purchasing an outfit to wear that night, but phrased in such a way that the listener does not have an obligation to consent. Possible answers, thus: *Why don't we go right now and buy something appropriate? / Oh, I am sure we'll find Something in your wardrobe— you have such elegant taste.* The original statement licenses either response: Neither party has to lose face (as would be the case with denying / being denied a direct request).

subjunctive
A grammatical 'mood' of the verb phrase to signal hypothetical speech, as opposed to indicative mood (for assertives) or imperative mood (for commands / directives). The subjunctive mood appears to be falling out of everyday use in English.

There are two linguistic avenues for signaling politeness. One is grammatical. Japanese verbs in particular have special endings for formal register ('honorific' inflections). English still retains the otherwise defunct subjunctive to avoid directness: *Were you ever to sell your station wagon, would you let me know?* places the request into the realm of the hypothetical (the speaker does not even insert him- or herself as a buyer). *Please sell me your station wagon* is overly direct (even with *please* added in), which makes turning down the request potentially equally direct. The exchange could end up feeling impolite. Even more pathways for graceful extrication open up if the request is not stated as such, but by implicature: *I have been looking for a classic station wagon like this one for years now—they are so hard to find, especially in such good condition.* If the listener responds with an offer to sell, then the speaker's indirect request is thereby made explicit: The request is now on the 'conversational scorecard' (Lewis 1979). If the listener responds by thanking the speaker for the compliment (that the car is in good condition), then only the indirect expressive (along with the direct assertives) is brought into the open. The speaker puts it 'out there,' gauges how the listener chooses to take it, and then 'agrees' that he/she had meant it that way in the first place. Shifty, but in a cooperative, face-saving way.

Evasiveness is a virtue, not just for oracles: Polite language is an intricate negotiation of 'face.' There are two kinds of 'face' languages negotiate: positive face (prestige or acceptance) and negative face (imposition). Daily life requires a fine balance between imposing and catering, as is illustrated in the following parable:

> On a cold winter's day, a group of porcupines huddled together to stay warm and keep from freezing. But soon they felt one another's quills and moved apart. When the need for warmth brought them closer together again, their quills again forced them apart. They were driven back and forth at the mercy of their discomforts until they found the distance from one another that provided both a maximum of warmth and a minimum of pain. In human beings, the emptiness and monotony of the isolated self produces a need for society. This brings people together, but their many offensive qualities and intolerable faults drive them apart again. The optimum distance that they finally find that permits them to coexist is embodied in politeness and good manners. Because of this distance between us, we can only partially satisfy our need for warmth, but at the same time, we are spared the stab of one another's quills.
>
> (Arthur Schopenhauer 1974)

The set points for what counts as a 'face threatening act' are cultural. Some social contexts allow a considerable amount of directness in making and responding to requests, for instance. *My car had to be towed—could you give me a ride back home?—Sorry, I can't* is acceptable in some settings (e.g. among equals), but disturbingly ill-mannered in others.

To take away the personal edge, politeness conventions tend to be ritualized. We ritualize politeness in scripts (knocking on the door before entering), gestures (in some cultures, using *both* hands to transfer a document or business card from one person to another), morphology (using a *plural* second-person pronoun—English used to make the distinction between *you* and *thou* for just such a purpose), syntax (using the word order of 'question' to make a request), word choice (*please*), etc. Ritual (and ritualized language) provides safety across idiolects, dialects, sociolects, and so on. It assists clarity of intention in electronic communication (e-mail, texting) when much of the author's bandwidth of expression (facial expression, body language, intonation, stress assignment) is lost. Why else would we need emoticons?

Coming Together: Harnessing the Cooperative Nature of Language

> External language (speech) can change internal Language.

Various kinds of experts study how the cooperative imperative in languages can be exploited. Leaving the destructive potential of such techniques to the next chapter, we will focus here on the use of language in conflict resolution.

There are situations where nothing will end a conflict except death or language. Chapter 1 has argued why this should be so: Human beings are hyper-cooperative because they focus on the survival of the group. They can cooperate within their group (to come to one another's aid) or across groups (e.g. to form alliances against yet another group in an effort to create, secure, or conquer resources). A skilled negotiator seeks to change frames of mind so as to redefine groups from being competing enemies to becoming allies defending shared needs.

The late Marshall Rosenberg (2006) worked as a successful mediator in conflict zones across the globe. In an interview, he related the story of how he sat down with two tribes who had been engaged in bloody conflict for years. His technique was to redirect the language of assigning blame and pathology to the other ('You people are murderers!') to the language of human needs ('Are you saying your needs for safety aren't being met?'). He then directed the opposing party to restate those needs ('Would the chief on this side please say what you heard this chief said his needs were?'). When the other side reacted with countercharges ('Then why did you kill my son?'), he redirected the focus back to needs. Once the second chief, even just grudgingly, condescended to repeat what the first chief said, something had shifted: 'We're out of this intellectual analysis justifying position, and we're connecting at the level of human needs.' Rosenberg's technique redraws the frame from cooperating-to-defend (aggression) towards cooperating-over-needs that are revealed to be mutual (welfare). Nonviolent negotiators are trained to use language to manage conflict mediation not unlike how parliamentarians are able to use Robert's Rules of Order:

- **Differentiating observation from evaluation**, being able to carefully observe what is happening free of evaluation, and to specify behaviors and conditions that are affecting us;

- **Differentiating feeling from thinking**, being able to identify and express internal feeling states in a way that does not imply judgment, criticism, or blame/punishment;
- **Connecting with the universal human needs/values** (e.g. sustenance, trust, understanding) that are being met or not met in relation to what is happening and how we are feeling; and
- **Requesting what we would like** in a way that clearly and specifically states what we do want (rather than what we don't want), and that is truly a request and not a demand (i.e. attempting to motivate, however subtly, out of fear, guilt, shame, obligation, etc. rather than out of willingness and compassionate giving). ('Non-violent Communication Skills' n.d.)

A skilled mediator is able to frame a shared story (needs that are not met) in such a way that neither side loses face.

Hearing the story and saving face are at the heart of most conflict negotiations. They are quintessential also in resolving hostage situations. A hostage situation can be essentially a forum, in which case hostage negotiators try to frame the narrative. They model calm language, to prevent escalation and to allow the hostage taker the space to tell his or her story. They redraw the focus from what happened, from the deadline before a hostage is to be harmed or killed, and from the us-vs.-them mentality towards cooperation towards what can still be done to meet everyone's needs for preserving face and safety (Miller 2007):

> William, I want you to know that, even though the guy got shot *[passive tense: it wasn't completely your fault]* in the foot *[not a critical wound]* at the beginning of this thing *[everybody was confused]*, all kinds of unexpected things *[you didn't intend to cause harm]* can happen in a panic situation. But you've done a good job of keeping things cool from that point on *[you're still in control, but in a positive way]*, and no one else has been hurt *[you're now part of the solution, not the problem]*. That counts for a lot, and everybody here knows it *[there's still hope of avoiding dire consequences]*. Let's see if we can keep things peaceful for now so we can all come out of this safely, okay? *[we want you to be safe, too, not just the hostages]*

Since human beings shift their linguistic personas with each shifting group alliance over the course of the day (family, bosses, foreigners, clients ...), it is entirely possible to refocus the perception of what grouping is currently relevant—just as it is possible to morph someone's original story (adversarial) into a new one (need sharing).

Our languages are extensions of Language. That means external languages are vehicles to reach into internal Language. Mediators, hostage negotiators, orators, advertisers, motivational speakers, preachers, marriage counsellors, teachers ..., their job is to use words cooperatively to effect changes—temporary or permanent—in other peoples' brains. Language is so powerful that it can create social emotions, such as shame or pride, which measure the individual against the community based on culture-specific norms (Ahmed 2014, Kokkola 2017). Unfortunately, as we see in the next chapter, that kind of power can be used for evil.

(Im)pertinent Questions

- Find the Wikipedia entry on 'plausible deniability' and discuss whether such a legal concept is in the spirit of a classical tenet of Roman law, *in dubio pro reo* (if in doubt, find for the defendant), and the concept of lenity (p. 111).
- A newly forming field of research is 'narrative medicine.' Imagine all the ways in which training doctors in narrative behavior could benefit patients.
- We sometimes use expressions like 'words cannot express.' Under what conditions does cooperation through the use of words often 'fail' us?
- Artificial Intelligence is exploring the 'uncanny valley,' when a robot or 3D computer animation looks and talks *almost* like a real human being. Pixar, for example, was surprised by the negative reactions to their hyper-realistic depiction of Billy, a human baby, in *Tin Toy* (https://youtu.be/ffIZSAZRzDA). What makes a near-perfect human replica 'creepy'?
- www.voxghostwriting.com/ claims it provided the ghostwriter for Bill Clinton and James Patterson's *The President Is Missing*. Is using a ghostwriter so different from hiring one to write a term paper?

References

Ahmed, Sara. 2014. *The cultural politics of emotion*. 2nd ed. Edinburgh: Edinburgh University Press.

Ariel, Mira. 2008. *Pragmatics and grammar*. Cambridge Textbooks in Linguistics. Cambridge, New York: Cambridge University Press.

Chomsky, Noam A. 2000. *New horizons in the study of language and mind*. Cambridge: Cambridge University Press.

Eco, Umberto. 1995. *The search for the perfect language*. Malden, MA: Blackwell.

Eisenberg, Abne. 1994. Obfuscated meaning. *Dynamic Chiropractic* 12(12) (June 3). Online: www.dynamicchiropractic.com/mpacms/dc/article.php?id=41287.

Fleming, Margaret B. 1983. Women as purveyors of the English curriculum: Speculations of the genesis and destiny of Miss Fidditch.
The English Journal 72(2).30–33.

Fowler, H. Ramsey, and Jane E. Aaron. 2006. *The Little, Brown
handbook*. 10th ed. New York: Longman.

Gibbons, John. 1994/2013. *Language and the law*. London,
New York: Routledge.

Grice, Paul. 1975. Logic and conversation. Reprinted in *Studies in the
way of words*, ed. by H. P. Grice, 22–40. Cambridge, MA: Harvard
University Press, 1989.

Hahne, Anja, and Angela D. Friederici. 1999. Electrophysiological
evidence for two steps in syntactic analysis: Early automatic and
late controlled processes. *Journal of Cognitive Neuroscience*
11(2).194–205.

Help us diagram this sentence by Donald Trump! 2015. Slate
Magazine (July 31). Online: www.slate.com/blogs/lexicon_
valley/2015/07/31/donald_trump_this_run_on_sentence_from_
a_speech_in_sun_city_south_carolina.html.

Jackendoff, Ray. 1969. Some rules of semantic interpretation for
English. MIT Doctoral Dissertation, Cambridge, MA.

Kokkola, Lydia. 2017. Envisaging 'our' nation: Politicized affects
in minority language literature. *Children's Literature in Education*
(November 1). DOI: 10.1007/s10583-017-9340-8.

Lakoff, George. 1971. The role of deduction in grammar. *Studies
in linguistic semantics*, ed. by Charles J. Fillmore and Terence
D. Langendoen, 62–70. New York: Holt, Rinehart, and Winston.
Online: https://escholarship.org/uc/item/9v4164pm.

Lewis, David. 1979. Scorekeeping in a language game. Journal of
Philosophical Logic 8(3).339–59.

Longobardi, Giuseppe; Silvia Ghirotto; Cristina Guardiano;
Francesca Tassi; Andrea Benazzo; Andrea Ceolin; and Guido
Barbujani. 2015. Across language families: Genome diversity
mirrors linguistic variation within Europe. *American Journal of
Physical Anthropology* (June). DOI: 10.1002/ajpa.22758.

Miller, Laurence. 2007. Hostage negotiations: Psychological strategies for resolving crises. Online: www.policeone.com/standoff/
articles/hostage-negotiations-psychological-strategies-for-
resolving-crises-QHgRY29vtb38310m/.

Non-violent communication skills. n.d. The Center for Nonviolent
Communication. Online: https://web.archive.org/web/201902031
82657/.

Pinker, Steven. 1994. *The language instinct: How the mind creates
language*. New York: William Morrow.

Rosenberg, Marshall. 2006. Nonviolent communication Part 1.
Online: https://youtu.be/-dpk5Z7GIFs.

Schane, Sanford. 2006. *Language and the law*. London, New York:
Continuum.

Schopenhauer, Arthur. 1974. *Parerga and paralipomena: Short
philosophical essays*, trans. by E. F. J. Payne, vol. 2. Oxford:
Clarendon Press.

Street, James A., and Ewa Dąbrowska. 2010. More individual differences in language attainment: How much do adult native speakers of English know about passives and quantifiers? *Lingua* 120.2080–94.

Xu, Daming. 2015. Speech community and linguistic urbanization. *Globalizing sociolinguistics: Challenging and expanding theory*, ed. by Dick Smakman and Patrick Heinrich, 95–106. London, New York: Routledge.

6 The Language of Violence

POINT BY POINT

- Large-scale atrocity, violence, and oppression require, in addition to other background conditions, linguistic preparation.
- In the case of genocide and politicide, linguistic preparation involves the quantity, content, and context of certain types of language.
- Such linguistic preparation weakens attitudinal dispositions for moral respect and restraint; develops and strengthens the audience's attitudinal dispositions to dislike, fear, resent, hate, and be disgusted by the target victims; and thereby strengthens the audience's behavioral dispositions to behave violently toward them.
- In the case of widespread sexual assault, linguistic preparation involves pervasive social narratives and scripts about male and female sexual roles ('Men are to be in charge,' 'Women naturally desire to submit to men's sexual dominance,' etc.).
- In such contexts, problematic linguistic dispositions are formed and maintained. One of the most problematic is that of silencing, the disposition to prevent especially women from using certain words and phrases such as 'No!,' 'Stop!,' and 'I was assaulted' with their usual collectively accepted uses and meanings.
- Victims, especially women, are left with little effective linguistic power before, during, and after an assault.

> Atrocity, violence, and oppression require linguistic preparation.

Language, as we saw in the last chapter, can be used to bring humanity closer together; there is a language of cooperation. Language, as we will see in this chapter, can be used to rip us apart; sadly, there is a language of violence. For oppression, violence, and atrocity require linguistic preparation. Our examples, difficult as they are to discuss, will be of genocide, politicide, and sexual assault, including sexual assault on college campuses. At the heart of these atrocities are human dispositions.

genocide
'Acts committed with intent to destroy, in whole or in part, a national, ethnical, racial, or religious group.'

Genocide and Politicide

'Genocide' is defined by Article II of the United Nations (UN) Genocide Convention as 'acts committed with intent to destroy, in whole or in part, a national, ethnical, racial, or religious group' (Convention 1948). Paradigm instruments of genocide include:

- killing members of the group;
- causing serious bodily or mental harm to members of the group;
- deliberately inflicting on the group conditions of life calculated to bring about its physical destruction in whole or in part;
- imposing measures intended to prevent births within the group; and
- forcibly transferring children of the group to another group.

Since genocide requires intent, and since determining intent is difficult, estimates vary about the number of victims of genocide. However, most researchers agree that the "low" number is 20 million. Since 1915, the number of people around the world that have been killed by acts of genocide is at least 20 million, including:

8 million	Jews
7 million	Ukrainians
1.5 million	Cambodians
1.5 million	Armenians
800 thousand	Rwandans
750 thousand	Serbs, and
300 thousand	Bosnian Muslims.

politicide
Acts committed with intent to destroy, in whole or in part, groups of political rivals.

These numbers do not include those slaughtered in China, North Korea, or Darfur, nor do they include those slaughtered in a related type of atrocity known as 'politicide,' the intentional destruction of groups of political rivals, such as the millions killed in Stalin's Soviet Union.

How do genocide and politicide happen? How are they *allowed* to happen? In detail, these questions are difficult to answer, because they depend on the specific histories of the rival groups. The proximate causes of the Jewish genocide in World War II differ from those of Rwandan Tutsi genocide in the mid-1990s. But at a certain level of generality, the conditions that prepare genocide and politicide are not complex. Indeed, much of their preparation is linguistic.

Ten Stages of Genocide

To help drive home the point that genocide and politicide require linguistic preparation, consider Gregory Stanton's well-known model, 'The Ten Stages of Genocide' (2013). Though the stages are presented as linear, several often occur simultaneously and recursively. And the first seven stages are linguistic.

1. *Classification.* All cultures categorize people according to race, ethnicity, language, religion, sex, gender, and nationality. But categorization can become lethal when cultures begin to categorize these groups in the higher-order groups *us* and *them*. This is the source of *the other*. It is us and *them*: It is us and *those Muslims, those Jews,* or *those Christians*; us and *those illegal aliens* or *those communists*; us and *those poor people* or *those rich people*.

2. *Symbolization.* After we classify, we assign names ('Muslim,' 'Jew,' 'Christian,' 'immigrant,' 'poor,' 'rich') and other symbols, such as colors (black, brown, yellow, white) and dress (headdresses, turbans, burkas, baggy jeans, business suits). Like classification, symbolization does not necessarily lead to violence, unless these are also accompanied by dehumanization (Stage 4) and its resulting hate. In the latter case, the dominant group can force symbols and slurs upon members of a group: yellow star for Jews, blue scarf for people from the Eastern Region of Khmer Rouge, Cambodia; 'Jesus-freaks,' 'fanatics,' 'freeloaders,' 'the 1%.'

3. *Discrimination* (Stigmatization). The dominant group stigmatizes the more vulnerable and uses the powers of the state—its laws, customs, and other products of political power—to deny their rights. *They* cannot vote, go to school, run a business, buy insurance, receive medical care, drive a car, leave their homes after 10 pm. *They* may even be denied citizenship.

4. *Dehumanization.* The dominant group represents *them* as less than fully human, or not human at all. *They* are cave men, apes, vermin, roaches, dogs, insects, diseases, scum. At this stage, hate propaganda and hate talk are often used to vilify the vulnerable groups.

5. *Organization.* The dominant group begins to plan its genocide and to train and arm special units for the job. Often, smaller militias or terrorist groups are used so the state can plausibly deny its involvement.

6. *Polarization.* Extremists drive a greater wedge between the groups. They may broadcast vicious propaganda and create laws forbidding intermarriage and even mere social interaction. Moderates from within the dominant group are labeled 'unprincipled' and 'traitors' to the cause and sometimes are rounded up as 'enemies of the state' or 'enemies of the people.'

7. *Preparation.* Leaders plan the "Final Solution" to the "problem." They prepare the public by invoking fear of the other ('if we don't destroy *them*, they will destroy/invade/contaminate *us*') and euphemisms, such as 'ethnic cleansing,' 'purification,' and 'counter-terrorism,' to disguise intentions driven by hate. They prepare their armies by building arms reserves and, now, train all of their military units to complete "the mission."

8. *Persecution* (Extreme Victimization). Victims are separated. Their property is seized. They are segregated to ghettoes,

internment camps, concentration camps, 're-education' camps, and famine-stricken areas. They may be sterilized. Mass killings—genocidal massacres—begin.

9. *Extermination.* Genocidal massacres become rampant. Often, revenge killings occur in turn, leading to a downward spiral of bi-lateral genocide.

10. *Denial.* State leaders deny the mass killings, destroy documents and other evidence—for example, they may dig up mass graves and burn bodies—blame the victims, and intimidate witnesses.

Although Stanton describes these as ten stages of genocide, he is clear that these also describe ten stages of politicide. More will be said below about the elements of these stages, but what is important to notice for now is that the first seven stages—classification, symbolization, discrimination, dehumanization, organization, polarization, and preparation—are thoroughly linguistic. Genocide and politicide require relentless linguistic preparation.

Stanton is justifiably focused on the sociology, politics, and ethics of state-sponsored genocide and politicide, so his ten-stage model does not explicitly focus on the connections between language and violence. For example, Stanton's model fails to *explain* how language is used to prepare genocide and politicide; it represents only that it does. How, precisely, does dehumanization lead people so disposed to cooperate to instead be so violent? Much recent work has filled this gap. Before examining some of that recent work, it will be helpful to say a little about the nature of dispositions.

Dispositions

dispositions
Tendencies, or patterns, to which something is inclined in certain contexts.

Dispositions are tendencies, or patterns, to which something is inclined in certain contexts. Glass vases, to take a standard example, are disposed to break upon hitting a hard floor. In animals, many dispositions work automatically, or subconsciously. For example, animals are typically disposed to emit noises when in agony; to fight, flee, or freeze when in sudden danger; and to comply with the dictates of powerful members of their group. In addition to behavioral dispositions, human beings have attitudinal dispositions, such as dispositions to feel joy when something wonderful happens to someone they love, to become angry when powerful people bully the vulnerable, to feel guilty when doing something they believe to be wrong, and to feel ashamed when found out. Human beings also have cognitive dispositions, such as the disposition to believe what is said by someone of whom they approve, to disbelieve what is said by someone of whom they disapprove, and to think that most reasons are good which support a conclusion they wish to be true. Many human and non-human animal dispositions can be weakened or, in some cases, overridden, as any person can attest who begins to wear contact lenses, who begins to think 'maybe it's okay' for *this* particular person to be bullied, or who begins to doubt one's parents or religious leaders. Thus, dispositions strongly regulate, although they do not determine, what we do (behavior), how we feel (attitude), and what we understand (belief).

Dispositions are powerful and, although often complex, they are not mysterious. Rather, as C. L. Stevenson suggested long ago, such dispositions or powers should be understood much as we understand the purchasing 'power' of a dollar or the stimulating 'power' of coffee, that is, as a complex network of causal relations (1944:46).

Consider Stevenson's latter example, the dispositional 'power' of coffee. Such a power can be understood generally as a complex causal network consisting of: (i) stimuli, such as the amount of coffee ingested, and (ii) responses, such as the resulting changes in one's energy, attention, anxiety, or irritation. These stimuli and responses are mediated by (iii) the state of the thing affected—Stevenson called these 'attendant circumstances'—which in this example is the state of the person drinking the coffee, such as the drinker's fatigue when ingesting the coffee, the absorption rate of her stomach, and the constitution of her nervous system, and by (iv) the content and context of the stimuli—Stevenson called these the 'bases' of the disposition—which in this example would include the chemical composition of the coffee and the soil and temperature conditions in which it was grown. Thus, the dispositional 'power' of coffee to effect its typical responses is a function of the quantity and chemical *content* of the stimuli and the *context*, or conditions, in which it was grown and ingested. Notably, the context includes the coffee-drinker's important dispositions and other features (attendant circumstances). More generally: The dispositional power of a stimulus to effect its typical responses is a function of the quantity and content of the stimulus and the context, or conditions, in which it is produced—and one who specifies these and the correlations among them 'has said all about the disposition that there is to say' (1944:51). Although Stevenson here exaggerates—recent theories of dispositions typically offer much useful detail about the nature of dispositions (Fara 2009)—most such recent work similarly attempts to dispel any mystery surrounding the nature of dispositions.

The following are several typical human dispositions, including linguistic dispositions, which previous chapters have identified and explained and which will play an important role in the remainder of this chapter. Human beings are typically disposed to:

- discern and distinguish in objects fine-grained and higher-order properties (Chapter 2);
- categorize and symbolize accordingly (Chapters 1 and 2);
- sympathize with, cooperate with, and, indeed, collectively intend to help those in their in-group (Chapters 1 and 2);
- be more indifferent towards and, sometimes, harm those in an 'out-group' (Chapter 1);
- become aggressive when facing a mortal threat (Chapter 1);
- think narratively by using scripts and jumping to conclusions (Chapter 3);

dispositional power
The dispositional power of a stimulus to affect its typical responses in a thing is a function of the quantity and content of the stimulus and the context, or conditions, in which it is produced—which includes the state of the thing stimulated.

- attribute intentions, beliefs, and attitudes to others (Chapters 1 and 2);
- use languages to do things; that is, to describe, express, direct, commit, and create (Chapter 4);
- perform such speech acts, and interpret them as being performed, indirectly (Chapter 4);
- speak to and interpret others by exploiting conversational principles, such as the maxims of quantity, quality, relevance, and manner, and by exploiting social-political principles, such as 'Be polite,' 'Save face,' 'Accommodate speech patterns,' and 'Respect social distance' (Chapters 4 and 5);
- assign blame, especially to others (Chapter 5).

dispositional power of violent language
The dispositional power of violent language to effect genocide and politicide is a function of the quantity and content of such language and the context, or conditions, in which it is used—which includes important dispositions and other features of the target audience.

We are now in a better position to understand the sense in which the atrocities of genocide and politicide require linguistic preparation. For genocide and politicide are typically effected by the dispositional power of violent language. And the dispositional power of violent language to effect genocide and politicide is a function of the quantity and content of such language and the context, or conditions, in which it is used. Notably, the context includes important dispositions and other features of the target audience, including those dispositions just listed.

Content and Context of Genocidal Language

The most illuminating, research-based framework that we have found concerning the content and context of violent language is that produced independently and refined jointly by Jonathan Leader Maynard and Susan Benesch (2016). We will focus first on the content of violent language, then on the context in which it is used.

The content of violent language, using Maynard and Benesch's framework, dehumanizes, attributes guilt, constructs threats, destroys alternatives, valorizes violence, and biases the future. Violent language thus shapes the attitudes, beliefs, and behaviors of the target audience by rendering violence toward the target victims as not just acceptable and permissible, but necessary, inevitable, virtuous, and even glorious. Ultimately, such content (in the right context) erodes the audience's dispositions for moral restraint; develops and strengthens the audience's dispositions to dislike, fear, resent, hate, and be disgusted by the target victims; and thereby strengthens the audience's dispositions to behave violently toward them.

Dehumanization. Dehumanization aims to make violence against the target victims acceptable by deeming and directly describing them as something other than fully human. For example, such language might represent the target victims as uncivilized ('cave men,' 'hoards,' 'savages'), sub- or inhuman ('animals,' 'apes,' 'cockroaches,' 'vermin,' 'dogs,' 'yellow ants,' 'parasites,' 'diseases,' 'infestation'), or else superhumanly evil ('devils,' 'Satan,' 'demons') (Maynard and Benesch 2016:80). In so obviously flouting Grice's maxim of quality, sources of such violent language indirectly describe the targeted victims as too beastly, demonic, irrational, or unclean to be human and thereby indirectly express vile attitudes toward the targeted victims. The perlocutionary effect—or, at least, the desired perlocutionary effect—is to diminish the moral significance of the targeted victims, the moral significance of duties owed to them, and the moral significance of their deaths. Indeed, sources almost always follow such dehumanization by calling on their audiences to 'purify,' 'cleanse,' 'exorcise,' or otherwise 'exterminate' the 'toxins,' 'beasts,' and 'demons.' Thus, dehumanization can affect the target audience at the conscious and unconscious levels:

> Dehumanization can consciously defeat normative concerns about violence by allow[ing] perpetrators to believe that the targets of violence lack moral protections. Like guilt attribution and threat construction, dehumanization moves out-group members into a social category in which conventional moral restraints on how people can be treated do not seem to apply. They are now 'outside the universe of [moral] protection,' as Helen Fein [1979:4–9] has described it. But dehumanization can also work at a much less conscious level—perceptually eroding affective moral concern for certain categories of person, and encouraging emotional responses of revulsion or antipathy.
> (Leader Maynard and Benesch 2016:80–81)

Guilt attribution. Even if members of a target audience come to accept violence against the target victims—even if they are *for* it—they might still wonder whether such violence is morally permissible. Guilt attribution aims to erode such doubt by representing the target victims as active members of a group that has committed atrocious acts against the audience. In directly describing the target victims as guilty, sources of such violent language indirectly assert that the target victims have demonstrated that they are not really one of *us*, indirectly assert that the target victims have forfeited any claim to moral protection, and indirectly declare that it is permissible to 'punish the guilty.' Violence toward the target group is thereby 'justified.' As with dehumanization, such content (in the right context) erodes the audience's dispositions for moral restraint, develops and strengthens the audience's dispositions to dislike, fear, resent, hate, and be disgusted by the target victims, and thereby strengthens the audience's dispositions to behave violently toward them.

Threat construction. That an action is morally permissible does not, of course, mean that it is morally obligatory. One might be morally permitted to donate to a particular charity or to discipline their child for wrongdoing without thereby being morally obliged to do so. Thus, even if members of a target audience think that violence against the target victims is acceptable and even morally permissible, they might still be sufficiently disposed to eschew such violence. Threat construction aims to render such violence morally obligatory by directly representing the target victims as a mortal threat. That the target victims are represented as threatening implies that they are guilty not just of past deeds but of future deeds. That the threat is represented as mortal conversationally implicates that violence toward the target victims is nearly necessary and, therefore, nearly morally obligatory on grounds of self-defense—or, at least, on the grounds of defending *us*. Dispositions for moral restraint continue to weaken; dispositions to fear, resent, hate, and be disgusted by the target victims solidify; and dispositions to behave violently toward them strengthen.

Destruction of alternatives. Weakened as they may be, the audience's dispositions for moral restraint might still carry the day. Thus, the language of violence continues its assault on those dispositions by representing atrocity toward the target victims as the only remaining alternative and, thereby, conversationally implicating that such violence is inevitable. Write Leader Maynard and Benesch:

> In its most grandiose form, violence might be presented as a historical necessity, as an ineradicable feature of 'racial struggle,' 'class conflict,' 'human progress,' 'the nature of war' and so forth. The Holocaust, Communist mass killings, and colonial genocides against native peoples were all prominently justified by their perpetrators as simply mandated by iron laws of nature and historical change.
>   Irrespective of the method, the destruction of alternatives serves to 'deagentify' the violence: making it appear to be the product of irresistible inhuman forces rather than conscious choices by policymakers and perpetrators, and thereby promoting moral disengagement from their acts.
>
> (2016:83)

By directly asserting that violence against the target victims is a product of unstoppable, mysterious forces, sources of violent speech indirectly assert that the audience simply has no alternative but to engage in such violence.

Dehumanization, guilt attribution, threat construction, and destruction of alternatives primarily aim to weaken dispositions to moral restraint. Virtue-talk and future bias primarily aim to strengthen dispositions to violence by representing such violence as virtuous and even glorious.

Virtue-talk. Virtue-talk represents violence as virtuous by associating it with praiseworthy characteristics, such as courage, honor, patriotism, duty, toughness, even manliness and by representing resistance with blameworthy characteristics, such as cowardice, shame, treason, weakness, even 'failure as a man.' Sometimes virtue-talk comes in the form of what Stevenson called 'persuasive definition' (1944:139) in which sources aim to modify existing societal or cultural norms. For example, virtue-talk might valorize viciousness, ferocity, brutality, and ruthlessness, while denigrating compassion, care, and fairness. Consider several examples offered by Leader Maynard and Benesch (2016:84–85): (a) 'every man should be trained to be a fanatical hater' (Nazi SS general); (b) 'he behaves correctly who, by setting aside all possible impulses of personal feeling, proceeds ruthlessly and mercilessly' (Nazi police department training manual); (c) 'stop having mercy on the Batutsi' (The Hutu Ten Commandments); (d) 'since their goal is to exterminate and enslave us, we must not feel any mercy to them' (Rwandan radio broadcast); (e) '[we applaud] seething hatred and blood rancour against national and class enemies' (Khmer Rouge); (f) 'I would still my doubts the way I had learned to … the concepts of conscience, honour, humaneness we dismissed as idealistic prejudices, "intellectual" or "bourgeois" and, hence, perverse' (Bolshevik).

Since to save face most human beings are disposed to do what their culture or society deems virtuous and to avoid doing what is deemed dishonorable, such violent content (in the right context) has the perlocutionary effect of strengthening an audience's dispositions to violence.

Future bias. Likewise for future bias, whereby the content of violent language glorifies the consequences of such violence as noble, extensive, enduring, and certain, while the negative consequences are diminished and, often, ignored. Here is Boris Pasternak, author of *Doctor Zhivago*, in a 1935 letter to Olga Freidenberg, glorifying the consequences of Soviet politicide, while ignoring its ruthlessness and brutality to the victims:

> The fact is, the longer I live the more firmly I believe in what is being done, despite everything. Much of it strikes one as being savage [yet] the people have never before looked so far ahead, and with such a sense of self-esteem, and with such fine motives, and for such vital and clear-headed reasons.
> (Figes 2008:190 and cited in Leader Maynard and
> Benesch 2016:86).

Often, such glorification is rooted in ideological purification: 'the assuredly improved future of a racially pure nation, a theologically-correct caliphate, a "final solution" to a correctly diagnosed security threat' (Leader Maynard and Benesch 2016:86).

Once again, such violent content (in the right context) has the perlocutionary effect of strengthening an audience's dispositions to violence.

Let's turn from the content of violent language to the context in which it is used. In Leader Maynard and Benesch's framework, the most impactful contextual features of violent language are its source, audience, socio-political history, and means of dissemination.

Source. Like members of most other animal species, human beings are disposed to comply with the dictates of powerful members of the groups to which they belong. Thus, the extent to which violent language prepares the way for genocide often depends on the influence of its source. The most powerful sources are those whom the target audience views as its political, military, religious, or even business leaders (or a combination thereof); those whom the target audience views as having achieved status, such as the status of public figure or of epistemic authority; and those whom the audience views as otherwise charismatic.

Audience. Of course, the violent words of a source will have more power over an audience disposed to behave aggressively. That is why violent language is almost always directed to young men and to those who perceive grave danger either to their way of life or, especially, to their own mortality.

Socio-historical background. Of course, whether a target audience perceives grave danger and, consequently, is more disposed to be affected by violent language also depends on the particular socio-historical background of the target audience and victims. For example, a target audience in regions or societies that have scarce basic resources, a history of land disputes, dysfunctional judicial systems, or past episodes of violence are typically more disposed to be affected by violent language.

Means of dissemination. Finally, a target audience is more likely to be affected by violent language where there is little countervailing content. That is why the violent language will more likely affect a target audience when that language is disseminated by a single source, such as a single radio station, a single newspaper, or a media monopoly, or when a target audience *chooses* to listen only to a single source (or multiple sources with a shared viewpoint).

Leader Maynard and Benesch's framework and an awareness of the nature and power of dispositions thus discern a recipe for genocide and politicide: Mix the language of dehumanization, guilt attribution, threat construction, destruction of alternatives, virtue-talk, and future bias; place it in the mouth of powerful leaders and the ears of a threatened, aggressive audience; boil and let simmer within a socio-political history of strife and a controlled media. The result is at least 20 million.

Sexual Assault

Sexual assault, as defined by the US Department of Justice (2016), is 'any type of sexual contact or behavior that occurs without the explicit consent of the recipient.' Paradigm examples of sexual contact or behavior that fall under this definition include:

- completed forced penetration,
- attempted forced penetration,

- completed penetration of someone unable to give consent,
- unwanted sexual contact, such as unwanted kissing, grabbing, or fondling,
- child molestation,
- incest.

Methodologies used to determine the prevalence, incidences, and rates of sexual assault and used to compare these across racial, ethnic, gender, and other groups differ significantly. Consequently, so too do the statistics. The consequence in the United States, sadly, has been to turn sexual assault statistics, especially statistics of sexual assault on US college campuses, into heated political controversy. Two highly publicized cases of false reporting of sexual assault at Duke University and at the University of Virginia added fuel to the blaze.

The most methodologically sound study we know is the National Intimate Partner Sexual Violence Survey conducted by the US Center for Disease Control and Prevention (Breiding et al. 2014). The survey, last conducted in 2011 and reported in 2014, reveals that 19.3 percent of women in the US—nearly one out of five—will in their lifetimes be victims of rape or attempted rape (i.e. completed or attempted forced penetration) and that, in 2011 alone, 1.9 million women were victims of rape or attempted rape—roughly one victim every 16.5 seconds. That study might be contested by some on the grounds that (a) roughly two-thirds of those whom the study counts as victims result from alcohol- and drug-related incidences in which victims are unable to give consent, but that (b) it is possible those surveyed fail to understand that the relevant questions ask specifically about their ability to consent (Kessler 2015). In other words, perhaps those being surveyed think they are being asked only whether they "had sex" after drinking alcohol or taking drugs.

In such a large study, it is a near certainty that at least some respondents failed to understand that certain questions focused on the key issue of consent. But it is also a near certainty that it wasn't two-thirds. Researchers point to reliability measures in place to ensure that respondents understand the questions asked (Kessler 2015) and, really, the questions appear to give prominent place to the issue of consent. For example, here is the introductory text to this set of questions (Breiding et al. 2014):

> Sometimes sex happens when a person is unable to consent to it or stop it from happening because they were drunk, high, drugged, or passed out from alcohol, drugs, or medications. This can include times when they voluntarily consumed alcohol or drugs or they were given drugs or alcohol without their knowledge or consent. Please remember that even if someone uses alcohol or drugs, what happens to them is not their fault.

When you were drunk, high, drugged, or passed out and unable to consent, how many people have ever ....

Here, the issue of one's ability to consent seems front and center.

It is obviously important to agree on a clear picture of the prevalence of rape, attempted rape, and other types of sexual violence if we are to help prevent it and support victims. But for our purposes here, this political-statistical tree blocks the view of the moral forest. For even if alcohol- or drug-related incidences of sexual assault are set aside, these numbers remain: 10 percent, and 700 thousand. At least 10 percent of women—one of every ten—will in their lifetimes be victims of rape or attempted rape, and in 2011 alone, at least 700 thousand women were victims of rape or attempted rape—one every 45 seconds.

Again—wishing only for the moment to sidestep the political battle over exact numbers, and not in the least to diminish the trauma caused to all individuals by such violence—these numbers do not include alcohol- or drug-related incidences of rape or attempted rape, forcible grabbing or other forms of unwanted sexual contact, sexual coercion by non-physical pressure such as threat of losing one's job, stalking, any other form of sexual violence or intimidation, or any form of sexual violence against men. Here are several other sobering numbers:

- 1 out of 5—the number of women who are sexually assaulted on US college campuses by the time they graduate (Krebs et al. 2007);
- 1 out of 20—the number of men who are sexually assaulted on US college campuses by the time they graduate (Krebs et al. 2007);
- 25—the number of students in a typical 200-student lecture hall who are sexually assaulted on US college campuses by the time they graduate;
- 67 percent—percentage of sexual assault incidences in US that go unreported to police (Sinozich and Langton 2014);
- 80 percent—percentage of sexual assault incidences on US college campuses that go unreported to police (Sinozich and Langton 2014).

The obvious question is how these numbers can be so high. The truthful answer is that there are a large number of contributing factors, especially factors that affect sexual assault of children and factors that affect a perpetrator's sense of power. Isolating only several factors threatens to trivialize complex, socially consequential phenomena. While acknowledging that risk, and since this is a book about language, mind, and power, the remainder of this chapter will continue to focus, as when discussing genocide and politicide, on three important factors related to linguistic preparation: dispositions, content, and context.

Linguistic Dispositions, Content, and Context

> Linguistic
> disposition
> + content +
> social context
> ≈ What we
> say, how we
> say it, and
> what we
> understand.

This section homes in on specific types of dispositions that we will call *linguistic dispositions*. Given certain content and context, our linguistic dispositions strongly regulate, though they do not determine, what we say, how we say it, and how we understand what is said.

Previous chapters have already provided several examples of linguistic dispositions and how they affect linguistic behavior. They include dispositions to speak to and interpret others by exploiting conversational principles, such as the maxims of quantity, quality, relevance, and manner, and by exploiting social-political principles, such as 'Be polite,' 'Save face,' 'Accommodate speech patterns,' and 'Respect social distance' (Chapters 4 and 5).

To explore more deeply the notion of linguistic dispositions, recall the phenomenon of declarative illocution (Chapter 4). Paradigm declaratives, such as naming a ship the *Queen Elizabeth* or adjourning a court of law require formal arrangements, such as rules, laws, and special words ('I do solemnly swear ...'). These are the formal background conditions—the formal content and social context—required to bring about a new social reality. The social reality that they bring about—that a particular ship is so-named, that a particular court is adjourned—requires that a critical mass of language users recognize and accept the differential power relations of those involved. It is the mayor who can name a ship, the judge who can adjourn the court. If we did not acknowledge and accept these power differentials, the ship would not be so named and the court would not be so adjourned. The social reality that is thereby constructed and perpetuated requires collective intentionality (Chapter 2). It requires a critical mass of language users who are disposed to collectively recognize, accept, and have the will to maintain what seems magically done simply by making certain noises (or marks, or finger movements, etc.).

In fact, according to Pierre Bourdieu, *all* successful illocutions require analogous, though non-formal, features. Present in every actual use of language, according to Bourdieu, is a social power structure that requires collective recognition, acceptance, and the will to maintain what speakers do with those words. For example, consider the linguistic disposition to respect social distance, which in part regulates how strongly a speaker directs someone to do something, that is, whether a speaker is likely to direct someone quite directly ('Close the window'), indirectly ('Aren't you cold?'), or extremely indirectly ('I wonder if, by any chance, you might be cold?'). Which of these sentences is collectively acceptable for a speaker to use and, thereby, how strongly it is collectively acceptable for a speaker to do things with these words typically depends on the collectively perceived status, or power, differential between speaker and hearer. It is more collectively acceptable for speakers to direct someone more directly when they are collectively perceived to have more status or power (say, with their children), to do so indirectly when collectively perceived to have relatively similar status or power (say, with peers), and to do so extremely indirectly when collectively perceived to have less status or power (say, one's boss, professor, or priest). 'By virtue of the [linguistic units] spoken, the speakers who use them, and the groups defined by possession of the corresponding competence,' Bourdieu writes, 'the whole social structure is present in each interaction' (1991/1980:67).

Linguistic dispositions, content, and social context regulate what we say, how we say it, and how we understand it. Which brings us back to sexual violence, in this case male–female sexual violence. By focusing on male–female sexual violence, we do not wish to diminish the traumatic impact of female–female, male–male, female–male, or any other type of sexual violence. But the numbers show that the prevalence and incidences of male–female sexual violence are exponentially higher (Truman and Langton 2014). In part, this is because the social context in the many parts of the world, including the United States, include widespread social narratives and scripts (Chapter 2) about male and female sexual roles. Some of the more extreme narratives are:

- men are to be in charge;
- women are to serve men;
- women are thus to remain chaste and pure as a gift to whomever man she is given or by whomever eventually takes charge of her;
- women naturally desire to submit (and, in any case, are to submit) to men's sexual dominance, even to the sexual dominance of multiple men;
- as a "reward" for doing so, and only when doing so, women will finally get to experience their most intense, other-worldly sexual ecstasy;
- such intense sexual pleasure is therefore a gift for which a woman should be ever-grateful and for which she should thank the man who takes her.

In social contexts that include such widespread narratives and scripts, certain dispositions are formed and maintained, including certain linguistic dispositions. One of the most problematic of these linguistic dispositions is that of *ceasing* to recognize, accept, and maintain what is usually magically done when someone says 'No!,' 'Stop,' or 'I was assaulted.'

Silencing

Recall that speaking typically consists of locution, perlocution, and illocution. Correspondingly, a speaker can be silenced if they are prevented from uttering certain words, if the speaker's intention in uttering those words is frustrated, or if the speaker is prevented from using those words with their usual illocutionary point. Rae Langton calls these, respectively, 'simple silence,' 'perlocutionary frustration,' and 'illocutionary disablement' (1993). A speaker can also be effectively silenced if an audience simply refuses to take a speaker's words seriously or sincerely, a type of silencing that we will call 'illocutionary diminishment.' Each type of silencing can contribute to oppression and violence, including sexual oppression and violence.

Simple silence occurs when someone simply does not utter words they may wish to use. Paradigm examples are those in which someone is prevented from saying something by threat or intimidation or by an enforced non-disclosure "agreement." Other instances may include those in which someone fails to say something because they feel they will not be believed or taken seriously. Thus, simple silence may on occasion contribute to sexual violence because the victim fears for her safety, even for her life, if she says anything to the perpetrator at all. More insidiously, simple silence contributes to the cycle of sexual violence, especially by serial offenders, when it appears in the form of chronic under-reporting of incidences to authorities, a result of victims often feeling ashamed, that the violence was "no big deal," that the aftermath with police and the legal system will be too overwhelming, or that they will not be believed. According to the US Justice Department, 67 percent of all sexual assaults remain unreported (Sinozich and Langton 2014).

Perlocutionary frustration occurs when a speaker's perlocutionary intention goes unfulfilled. A person tells another that *Star Wars* is playing at the theater intending to suggest that they go, but the other person doesn't hear; a person tells another to close the window, intending that the window be closed, but the other doesn't care; etc. Sexual violence often occurs even when victims say 'No' intending the perpetrators to heed their refusal, or when victims say 'Stop' intending the perpetrators to stop, or when victims say 'Get off me!' intending the perpetrator to cease the unwanted contact, but the perpetrators—even while accepting that the victims are refusing—simply do not care.

Illocutionary disablement is far more subtle. In this type of silencing, a person uses words that ordinarily enable someone in their language community to perform a certain type of illocution—but not in *this* case. To use several of Langton's examples, consider that until quite recently in the US, two people of the same sex could exchange marriage vows and be pronounced married by someone officially permitted to perform marriage ceremonies and, yet, not actually be married. That is because a critical mass of language users failed to collectively accept that the words 'I pronounce you married' constituted *in this case* an act of marriage. No new social reality thereby came into existence. Likewise, in some countries, including until recently in the US, women and people of color could not vote.

A woman or person of color could write on or make a checkmark on an official ballot during an official election and, yet, not actually vote. That is because a critical mass of language users failed to collectively accept that the use of those words or symbols constituted *in this case* an act of voting. In some parts of the world, a man can utter the equivalent of 'divorced, divorced, divorced' and thereby make it the case that he and his wife are now divorced, yet a woman cannot do the same. That is because a critical mass of language users collectively accept that a man, but not a woman, can use these words to perform the illocution of divorce.

Illocutionary disablement can contribute to sexual violence by disabling a victim from using words to perform an illocution which those words are typically used to perform. Whereas using 'No' is often collectively accepted as an act of refusal; whereas using 'Stop' is often collectively accepted as a directive to stop; whereas using 'Get off me' is often collectively accepted as a directive to stop forcing physical contact upon the speaker: In some sexual situations, even using these words with their usual content is no longer collectively accepted by a critical mass of language users as having their usual illocutionary force. To drive this point home, consider that until only within the last generation, it was considered inconceivable— because considered literally incoherent—for a husband to rape his wife. Saying 'No,' 'Stop,' 'Get off me' was simply not accepted as an act of refusal or as a directive to stop or desist. The insidious consequence of such illocutionary disablement is to leave women with no effective linguistic means to refuse, but only with means to consent.

Illocutionary diminishment occurs when a speaker's audience takes the speaker to be performing a certain type of direct illocution insincerely. Paradigm examples are obvious cases of sarcasm ('That's a nice tie'), metaphor ('Juliet is the sun'), or lying. Illocutionary diminishment often contributes to sexual violence when the perpetrator does not take the victim to be speaking sincerely. Often, that is because of the social narratives that 'girls are taught to say no,' 'women really (naturally) want to be taken,' 'it's something women have to say so they don't appear slutty' (that is, so that they can save face). As with illocutionary disablement, the insidious consequence of illocutionary diminishment is to leave women with no linguistic means to refuse, but only with means to consent.

The combined result of widespread sexual narratives and scripts, its resulting dispositions, and the four types of silencing often leave a woman in a sexual context with little physical power, little social power, and little linguistic power to use words with their typical illocutionary forces and perlocutionary effects. Though she does her part by using the right words, we fail to do our part: offering recognition, collective acceptance, and the will to maintain what is otherwise typically magically done in using those words. On the "low" side, the result is 1 in 10.

(Im)pertinent Questions

- What are some recent examples from your own country or region of genocidal and politicidal language? Are you worried that such examples are preparing the way for genocide or politicide in your area of the world? Why or why not? Do you, like many in Nazi Germany, think that 'It couldn't happen here?' If so, how is your region or country different?

- What are some other important examples of silencing (of any kind)?

- This chapter has focused on the language of large-scale violence, but that shouldn't blind us to the more ubiquitous language of smaller-scale violence and harm. For an ugly, obvious example, consider racial or ethnic slurs. It's clear that uses of these, in some way, express contempt for a particular group of people. But how, exactly, do they do so? For example, is contempt expressed by a direct expressive illocution? Is contempt implicated? If implicated, how so?

- For a more subtle example, Simon Blackburn has argued that describing an adult woman as 'cute' is harmful (2013). How so? What are all of the ways a term of admiration or praise could be harmful?

- In an important article, Lynn Tirrell explains how other superficially nonharmful language can become 'toxic' and begins to explore ways to inoculate individuals, even an entire language community, from those toxins (2017). One cause of toxicity is to let stand unchallenged a speaker's linguistic introduction of certain negative feelings, attitudes, descriptions, assumptions, or behaviors so that they become part of the conversational common ground in ensuing linguistic exchanges; in this way, such negative feelings, attitudes, descriptions, assumptions, and behaviors become the new normal. If so, then one way to inoculate oneself or one's community from such linguistic violence is to challenge immediately the introduction of those feelings, attitudes, descriptions, assumptions, and behaviors into one's linguistic exchanges. How strongly, if at all, do you object when a friend, leader, or someone of whom you otherwise approve introduces such harms? Do you do so firmly? Do you tend to offer a disapproving smile? Do you tend to let it slide, chalking it up to his 'upbringing' or 'era in which he was raised' or 'just his poor way of expressing himself' or to her 'poor attempt at humor'? Do you sometimes actually compliment him or her or otherwise cheer on the introduction of those harms into the individual or community-wide conversation?

References

Blackburn, Simon. 2013. Disentangling disentangling. *Thick concepts*, ed. by Simon Kirchin, 121–35. Oxford: Oxford University Press.

Bourdieu, Pierre. 1991/1980. Price formation and the anticipation of profits. *Language and symbolic power*, by Pierre Bourdieu, 66–89. Cambridge, MA: Harvard University Press.

Breiding, Matthew J.; Sharon G. Smith; Kathleen C. Basile; Mikel L. Walters; Jieru Chen; and Melissa T. Merrick. 2014. Prevalence and characteristics of sexual violence, stalking, and intimate partner violence victimization: National intimate partner and sexual violence survey, United States, 2011. *Centers for Disease Control and Prevention Surveillance Summaries* 63(8). Online: www.cdc.gov/mmwr/pdf/ss/ss6308.pdf.

Fara, Michael. 2009. Dispositions. *The Stanford encyclopedia of philosophy* (Summer Edition), ed. by Edward N. Zalta. Online: http://plato.stanford.edu/archives/sum2009/entries/dispositions/.

Fein, Helen. 1979. *Accounting for genocide: National responses and Jewish victimization during the Holocaust*. New York: Free Press.

Figis, Orlando. 2008. *The whisperers: Private life in Stalin's Russia*. New York: Picador.

Kessler, Glenn. 2015. Obama's claim that one in five American women has been a victim of rape or attempted rape. *The Washington Post* (February 12). Online: www.washingtonpost.com/news/fact-checker/wp/2015/02/12/obamas-claim-that-one-in-five-american-women-have-been-raped.

Krebs, Christopher P.; Christine H. Lindquist; Tara D. Warner; Bonnie S. Fisher; and Sandra L. Martin. 2007. The campus sexual assault (CSA) study. National Institute of Justice Grant No. 2004-WG-BX-0010. Online: www.ncjrs.gov/pdffiles1/nij/grants/221153.pdf.

Langton, Rae. 1993. Speech acts and unspeakable acts. *Philosophy and Public Affairs* 22(4).293–330.

Leader Maynard, Jonathan, and Susan Benesch. 2016. Dangerous speech and dangerous ideology: An integrated model for monitoring and prevention. *Genocide Studies and Prevention: An International Journal* 9(3).70–95. DOI: 10.5038/1911-9933.9.3.1317.

Sinozich, Sofi, and Lynn Langton. 2014. *Rape and sexual assault victimization among college-age females, 1995–2013*. NCJ 248471. Bureau of Justice Statistics. Online: www.bjs.gov/content/pub/pdf/rsavcaf9513.pdf.

Stanton, Gregory H. 2013. The ten stages of genocide. Originally presented as a briefing paper, 'The Eight Stages of Genocide' at the U. S. State Department in 1996. Online: https://d0dbb2cb-698c-4513-aa47-eba3a335e06f.filesusr.com/ugd/df1038_ad3aa6da6c7548cba3683c2ce61043f0.pdf.

Stevenson, C. L. 1944. *Ethics and language*. New Haven, CT: Yale University Press.

Tirrell, Lynn. 2017. Toxic speech: Toward an epidemiology of discursive harm. *Philosophical Topics* 45(2).139–61.

Truman, Jennifer L., and Lynn Langton. 2014. *Criminal victimization, 2013*. NCJ 247648. Bureau of Justice Statistics. Online: www.bjs.gov/ content/pub/pdf/cv13.pdf.

United States Department of Justice. 2016. Sexual assault. Online: www.justice.gov/ovw/sexual-assault.

7   Clarity from Managed Confusion

POINT BY POINT

- Lossiness of transmission and the co-creativeness of understanding make direct transfer of information impossible; clarity is achieved from cooperatively managing confusion.
- Cooperation is built into all levels of language performance, from phonology to syntax to discourse.
- Whether just chatting or writing a definition, speakers/writers align information with the audience's needs (information management).
- Speakers/writers also distribute the audience's cognitive load. We select the cognitive faculties of parsing, logic, predicting, and event modeling to illustrate this point with four pieces of literature.
- Cooperation between author and reader implies a cognitive esthetics of literature. Author and reader embrace in a collaborative dance (and the author leads).
- Using language to communicate allows intimate access into each others' minds. We are open books.

Cooperation towards Understanding

> Clarity is a psychological term. It is achieved through cooperation between reader and writer.

One can beat compliance into children, but not clarity. In 1762, Jean-Jacques Rousseau demonstrated the difference. His book *Émile, ou de l'éducation* describes in loving detail how a child can be led to clarity: through managed confusion and cooperation. Rousseau refused any pedagogy that relied on fear of secular and religious authority. Naturally, the book was burned the year it appeared.

In *Émile*, Rousseau (1762) assumes the persona of a private tutor, who accompanies the boy from childhood. Here he demonstrates his managed-confusion technique by *not* teaching the child to read:

Sometimes Émile receives notes of invitation from his father or mother, his relations or friends; he is invited to a dinner, a walk, a boating expedition, to see some public entertainment. These notes are short, clear, plain, and well written. Some one must read them to him, and he cannot always find anybody when wanted; no more consideration is shown to him than he himself showed to you yesterday. Time passes, the chance is lost. The note is read to him at last, but it is too late. Oh! if only he had known how to read! He receives other notes, so short, so interesting, he would like to try to read them. Sometimes he gets help, sometimes none. He does his best, and at last he makes out half the note; it is something about going to-morrow to drink cream—Where? With whom? He cannot tell—how hard he tries to make out the rest![1]

It is a paradox: Clarity arises from the art of managing confusion. Information is not simply handed down. We will look at literary techniques of such negotiated information management. We will next see the measure of all such entropy-induced negotiation: shared clarity as alignment with audience needs. To illustrate the point, we will examine a genre whose very purpose is clarity: definitions. Finally, we will marvel at the level of sophistication at which some of the finest writers are managing the readers' resources in the service of their literary themes—linguistic parsing, logic, predictive processing, and event modeling.

The Need for Managed Confusion

> Linguistic cooperation is mutual management of confusion.

Managed confusion is a concept explored by Art Graesser at the University of Memphis' Institute for Intelligent Systems. Graesser and his team are developing intelligent tutoring packages that adjust to the user's emotions and knowledge by tracking dialogue patterns, speech intonation, facial expressions, and body posture. The states of mind most conducive to learning—which the 'auto-tutor' is intentionally programmed to bring about—are 'regulated confusion' and

---

1 In the original French: 'Émile reçoit quelquefois de son père, de sa mère, de ses parents, de ses amis, des billets d'invitation pour un dîner, pour une promenade, pour une partie sur l'eau, pour voir quelque fête publique. Ces billets sont courts, clairs, nets, bien écrits. Il faut trouver quelqu'un qui les lui lise; ce quelqu'un ou ne se trouve pas toujours à point nommé, ou rend à l'enfant le peu de complaisance que l'enfant eut pour lui la veille. Ainsi l'occasion, le moment se passe. On lui lit enfin le billet, mais il n'est plus temps. Ah! si l'on eût su lire soi-même! On en reçoit d'autres: ils sont si courts! le sujet en est si intéressant! on voudrait essayer de les déchiffrer; on trouve tantôt de l'aide et tantôt des refus. On s'évertue, on déchiffre enfin la moitié d'un billet: il s'agit d'aller demain manger de la crème... on ne sait où ni avec qui ... Combien on fait d'efforts pour lire le reste!' (1762:81) The English translation is by Barbara Foxley, www.gutenberg.org/cache/epub/5427/pg5427-images.html.

'cognitive disequilibrium.' In those states, a learner, or a reader, is optimally engaged.

*Un*regulated (chaotic) confusion would signal lack of cooperation on the side of the author. The perception is that the author simply does not care how clear the writing would be for someone else. There is a place for this, as in a diary that was not written for any other purpose than to hold on to private experiences, or in some of the more surrealist writings of Gertrude Stein. On the other hand, the attempt to *eliminate* all confusion aims at rendering cooperative co-creation on the side of the reader/learner unnecessary—as in 'legalese' (Chapter 5) or the infantilizing linguistic domination that many of us (well, at least both of us) remember from old school books.

A successful author is generally not disinterested in how the reader thinks: As in all human linguistic interaction, successful communication is the positive outcome of cooperation.[2] A successful author knows how to make the lossiness of transmission into the reader's playground: Readers successfully co-create a story from 'the well-organized absence of information' (Stanton 2012). There are specific linguistic techniques that a writer can use to achieve and maintain the kind of cooperation in quality, quantity, relation, and manner described in Chapter 5.

Publishers and literary marketers are at work trying to fine-tune those techniques, because applying them increases their financial return. As early as 2012, Alexandra Alter wrote an exposé for the *Wall Street Journal* outlining how electronic e-book devices (Kindle, Nook, iPad, etc.) feed information to Amazon and Barnes & Noble about how fast and how completely texts are read, how long individual sessions are, which passages readers most highlight and what comments they write, which books they read in a single session, and whether a reader immediately bought a sequel. One company, Sourcebooks, had taken to releasing early online editions of books, optimizing them based on user feedback and data, and incorporating those insights into the final printed version (Alter 2012). London-based jellybooks offers an app for EPUB3 files; in exchange for free e-books, the user shares *individualized* data about how the book is read and even what the user posts about it (in blogs, on Facebook, etc.; Rhomberg 2015). For an author, it would certainly be 'interesting,' as best-selling author Scott Turow put it, to 'hitch the equivalent of a polygraph to my readers and know how they are responding word by word' (Neary 2013). But though writing is indeed 'a sort of collaborative dance,' in the words of novelist Jonathan Evison, 'I'm still trying to be the leader' (ibid.).

The importance of managed confusion is also not lost on Artificial Intelligence research and development. Computers will soon learn to negotiate clarity with users. Currently, a personal assistant such

---

2 Again, there are writers like Gertrude Stein who are not writing to cooperate. Asked whether she wrote for a specific audience, she responded that 'if you have an audience the being an audience is their business, they are the audience you are the writer, let each attend to their own business' (1939:41).

as Cortana, Siri, or Google Now still primarily works by responding to *specifics*. One of the original architects of Siri, Adam Cheyes, explains that the original 'Siri' scans for information and comes back with scripted replies—some of the more snappy ones authored by a team of comedy writers employed by Apple (Pogue 2015:31). Siri's software is, 'in essence, a passel of if / then statements' (ibid.). Thus, Cheyes elaborates, Siri can answer 'Where does my sister live?' and 'What is the weather in Boston?,' but not 'What is the weather where my sister lives?' The next generation of personal assistants will not give up on such a question but attempt to integrate information. Viv Labs is developing Viv, an assistant that generates its own programs dynamically to make cross-connections between information it has and information it seeks (online), to answer *non-specific* queries such as 'I want to pick up a great bottle of wine on the way to my brother's house—something that goes well with lasagna' (ibid.).[3] That way, it can negotiate for clarity with the user more intelligently than just displaying an error message. It can, to a degree, cooperate. A developer environment for dynamic program generation within 'capsules' of knowledge already exists for Samsung's Bixby platform.

If computers were to approximate the linguistic information management of humans, they would need to integrate not just different pieces of information, but also recognize when the information is the same. To reprise Jackendoff's example from Chapter 5, a computer would need to know that the category *bastard* is applied to the specific individual *Charlie* in the sentence *I wanted Charlie to help me, but the bastard wouldn't do it* (1969:57). Even resolving what antecedent goes with what pronoun is already a challenge for computers. A human speaker of English has no difficulty deciding whether *Kylie* or *Kim* is the binder of the pronoun *her* in the sentence *Kylie told Kanye that Kim had hurt her*. A computer would need some knowledge not only of what gender goes with which name but also of 'binding relations' (for example, if the pronoun were *herself* instead of *her*, the binder would be local and *Kim* is the antecedent, not *Kylie*).

binding
A pronoun takes its reference from an antecedent that is said to 'bind' it. Exploring the rules and limitations of such relations is part or a syntactic area of research called 'Binding Theory.'

An example from Henry James, at the end of Chapter 3, illustrated how an author can break a reader's flow to hinder predictive processing and, at the slower pace, provide time for more creative associations. A writer can also manage towards the other end of confusion: speeding up the reader to prioritize easy, predictive processing; that would typically be done to prevent reflection (because the reader's ideas could be critical). The advertising industry, for example, knows how to write and test for maximum reading speed. Typically, only about 28 percent of a page in a magazine is read,

---

3 The holy grail of Artificial Intelligence is for computers to script real-world knowledge. Doug Lenat's 'Project Cyc' (www.cyc.com) has been amassing a gigantic database of such 'common-sense' scripts since 1984, part of which is now available as OpenCyc. Common-sense knowledge of the real world can greatly improve the quality of the next generation of personal assistants built on platforms such as Viv to better manage confusion arising from non-specific queries.

so efforts are invested in creating copy that draws customers in and holds their attention long enough to create a story or positive feeling towards a product, or at the least create a breadcrumb (one of many half-conscious perceptions that together add up to a familiarity effect). Here is a sampling of linguistic techniques for guiding a reader's parsing and understanding.

Linguistic Information Management Strategies

Keeping Track of Proforms

> Proforms speed up comprehension by creating cohesion and coherence.

English has a system of proforms that is rarely described in full detail in grammar books (which tend to focus exclusively on 'pronouns'). In the following paragraph, note how some function words connect to earlier or later words or phrases, establishing cohesion:

> When **our** grandfather died, **my** brother and I discovered that **he** hid food under **his** pillow. **We** had no idea **it** was **there**. **We since** learned that many Holocaust survivors **do that**.

> [When **our**$_b$ grandfather$_g$ died]$_a$ [**my** brother and I]$_b$ discovered$_x$ that **he**$_g$ [hid food$_f$ (under **his**$_g$ pillow)$_p$]$_h$. **We**$_b$ [had no idea]$_x$ **it**$_f$ was **there**$_p$. **We**$_b$ [**since**$_a$] learned that many [Holocaust survivors]$_g$ [**do that**]$_h$.

phoricity
The property of a word to point to other words. Forward-pointing words are *cataphoric*, whereas words referring back to previous words are *anaphoric*. In contrast, words that point to items in the speech situation are **deictic**. Deixis can involve time ('an hour from now'), person (saying 'you' while having eye contact with someone), or space ('Look there!').

Some of the proforms are forward pointing ('cataphoric'). The possessive determiner *our*, which has the lexical function of pronoun, anticipates *my brother and I*. Similarly, *my* reaches forward to *I*. The pronoun *he*, in contrast, points backwards (i.e. it is 'anaphoric') to *our grandfather* (as does *his*); the pronoun *we* goes back to the noun phrase *my brother and I*; and the pronoun *it* stands for the earlier *food*. Also anaphoric are the proforms *there* (which has the prepositional phrase *under his pillow* as its antecedent), *since* (connecting back to the clause *when our grandfather died*), and *do that* (pointing to the verb phrase *hide food under his pillow*).

Each of these proforms (pro-NP, pro-PP, pro-clause, and pro-VP) does double duty. A proform refreshes an item in short-term memory, and it makes the text cohesive by signaling that no new topic is being introduced.

NP = noun phrase
PP = prepositional phrase
VP = verb phrase
clause = subject + predicate with tense

A classifying noun phrase can be anaphoric as well, so the noun phrase *many Holocaust survivors* is construed with *our grandfather*. Associating the individual with a group, the language signals that no

new person is being introduced, while at the same time saying something new about that person—brilliant information management!
Note, too, that something similar is going on in the way *had no idea*
relates back to *discovered*.

Not all texts are tightly controlled in their use of proforms, in part
because not all writers are good writers. As discussed in Chapter 5
(p. 105), a text can *fail* to cooperate with the recipient by violating
quantity, allowing too many words to intervene between a proform
and its antecedent:

> Pete Rose amassed an unequaled record as a hitter, using his bat
> to do things no one else has ever done. Even after his betting
> scandal and even though he was banned from baseball, it₂ still
> stands out today.

There are too many grammatical candidates that could each be the
antecedent for pro-NP *it* (*baseball, betting scandal, bat, hitter*). If the
reader is nonetheless able to make the connection to *an unequaled
record as a hitter* anyway, one of two paralinguistic repairs might
have kicked in: (a) on a written page, it is possible to go back and
scan the preceding text, or (b) the reader has constructed some kind
of event model in which the 'unequaled record' was a tracked topic
of interest.

How cognitive event models assist in linguistic proform resolution deserves a second look, especially because the effect, just like
proforms, receives scant mention in linguistics. A skilled writer will
keep a mental inventory of what should be in a reader's event model,
and control it like a computer game designer controls which items an
avatar is currently carrying on a video quest. Compare the following
two passages constructed by Art Glenberg et al. (1987):

> Warren spent the afternoon shopping at the store. He set down
> his bag and went to look at some scarves. He had been shopping
> all day. He thought it was getting too heavy to carry.
>
> Warren spent the afternoon shopping at the store. He picked
> up his bag and went to look at some scarves. He had been
> shopping all day. He thought it was getting too heavy to carry.

Note that the (grammatically too remote) antecedent of *it* ('his bag')
is more easily associated in the second text than it is in the first. In the
first text, Warren had *discarded* his bag; it thus no longer serves any
plot of the mental event model co-constructed in the reader's mind.
One should note, then: If the antecedent is linguistically remote *and*
the object referred to is not expected to be tracked in the event model
as 'salient' within the narrative, then an author should not refer to the
constituent with a proform.

How many words may precede a proform before its antecedent
becomes *linguistically* 'remote' may also be audience dependent.
A typical adult can easily track four lexical heads of phrases and two
topics at a time, a total of six items to which to connect a proform.

A child's workspace may be more limited. Julie Sedivy (2014:401) suggests that a children's book author may deliberately minimize the amount of words between a proform and its antecedent. In the following passage from *Thank you, Amelia Bedelia* (1993), author Peggy Parish repeats the literal-minded protagonist's name more often than a writer for an adult audience would:

> 'Jelly! Roll!' exclaimed Amelia Bedelia. 'I have never heard tell of jelly rolling.' But Amelia Bedelia got out a jar of jelly. Amelia Bedelia tried again and again. But she just could not get that jelly to roll.
>   Amelia Bedelia washed her hands. She got out a mixing bowl. Amelia Bedelia began to mix a little of this and a pinch of that.

Adults prefer proforms to repetitions. Repetitions, especially of names and grammatical objects, measurably slow down the reader (Gordon et al. 1993), an effect dubbed the 'repeated-name penalty' (Sedivy 2014:395). Again, one of the primary functions of proforms is to refresh information already in short-term memory, thus signaling that no new information is being introduced, a possibility that needs to be unconsciously ruled out every time a full noun phrase is used. Proforms can definitely speed things up by reducing decision making, thus cognitive load.

Just as writers use rhythm, word choice, and syntax to manipulate reading speed, so can they use proforms to speed up or slow down the reader. Two passages shall illustrate the point. The first, 'Reminiscences of Childhood' by Dylan Thomas (n.d.), is a narrated dream sequence:

> And when they do not believe me, I flap my arms and slowly leave the ground, only a few inches at first, then gaining air until I fly waving my cap level with the upper windows of the school, peering in until the mistress at the piano screams and the metronome falls to the ground and stops, and there is no more time.

Dylan Thomas, a perfectionist who challenged himself to capture the difference between *flocks* and *phlox* in his pronunciation (Jones 1977:74), left nothing to chance when it came to his craft and revised even pieces already published (this is his 1945 version of 'Reminiscences,' following the 1943 version). Here he captures a dream sequence in the same cadence in which children tell a story (cf. p. 72 above), with a bubbly flow of 'and then ..., and then ....' Thus, proforms are used sparingly—he is not interested in that kind of cohesion: *my* refers back to *I*, *then* connects to *leave the ground*, the preposition *in* means *the upper windows of the school*. However, there are some clever lexical connectors from 'given' to what was previously introduced as 'new' information: *a few inches* picks up *leave the ground*, the verb *fly* echoes *gaining air*, and *there is no more time* is the consequence of the stopped *metronome*. But those noun phrases are not repetitions of earlier noun phrases; they are resultative. Relying on given-new chaining over proform cohesion gives this passage a forward momentum suitable for an action sequence. The reader's curiosity is directed towards figuring out 'what happens next?'

Israeli author Ephraim Kishon pursues a different strategy in the following passage from 'Lovely Rain, Isn't It' in *The Seasick Whale* (1965):

> If the kind reader is ever, by mistake, invited into an English home, he should take care not to show his surprise when the head of the family pulls off his left shoe before lunch and fills it with sand. This is a pious act in remembrance of the fact that at the siege of Mount Tabor in 1193, King Richard's boots filled with sand. (There is a factory in Scotland manufacturing this special shoe-sand under the brand name 'Scotch-Sand.') Such is the force of tradition in Britain.
>
> But that's not all. No self-respecting biscuit tin would be seen without an inscription somewhat along these lines: 'Our factory received its letters patent at the hands of His Majesty King Charles, during the siege of Glasgow, when His Majesty relieved the rigours of the campaign with our crisp biscuits.' The other side of the tin features King Charles' smugly satisfied face, obviously after a square meal of biscuits, and not long before the unhappy monarch was beheaded.

The passage, in the capable translation of Yohanan Goldman, is tightly controlled for cohesion with proforms. One (*such*) sums up the entire first paragraph and is itself connected to by *that* in the next paragraph. Another (*this*) is simultaneously anaphoric (referring back to *fills it with sand*) and cataphoric (anticipating *a pious act*). It does not get any more tightly cohesive than that. The lexical references do not form given-new chains so much as given-given chains (note how the words *sand / shoe sand / Scotch-Sand* and *biscuits / square meal* are repeated). They are corroborative reiterations: Kishon is not aiming for forward momentum; he belabors. And that hammering home is quite intentional: Kishon's books thrive on a particular kind of humor where an initially outrageous situation is developed in such legalistic and impeccable detail that the ludicrous becomes absurdly plausible. Kishon is making a case. For that, he needs cohesion and coherence.

Ordering Constituents

Even English, with its strict word order, needs to reshuffle for information management.

English word order is quite strict. We understand how words function (e.g. as subject) given where in the sentence they appear (before the verb). That was not always so. As recently as a thousand years ago, English had a different grammar, one that allowed a much more flexible word order. The difference was that beyond

number
Inflections for singular and plural. English started out with three numbers (singular, dual, plural) and ended up with just the regular plural inflection -s.

gender
Inflections for male, female, and neuter, now entirely gone from English.

person
Inflections for typically three persons (I/we, you, he/she/it/they); only the third-person agreement ending -s remains in English; the last person suffix to drop out was second-person -st (e.g. *O good Horatio, I'll take the ghost's word for a thousand pound. Didst perceive?* Hamlet iii).

Case
Inflections for subject (nominative), object (accusative, dative), possessive (genitive), etc. In modern English, only pronouns show the last vestiges of Case (e.g. *who/whom*).

loss of inflections
The close language contact between Danish and English during the time when the Scandinavian empire extended into England (ninth and tenth centuries) resulted in a process by which both languages eventually lost most of their inflections.

assigning each function (subject, predicate, object, modifier) a place in the sentence, English also had word endings to indicate their functions. There were endings for such things as number, gender, person, and Case. With such a system, a subject would either be in its default position or could appear *elsewhere* in a sentence because its function was clearly identified by its ending. Thus, if an author was working on a poem and the subject of the clause fit better into the next line because it would disrupt his alliterations in the current one, he could 'scramble' his syntax and change the word order to make it happen. The following lines are difficult to parse for those familiar only with Modern English:

Þa ſtoð on ſtæðe, ſtiðlice clýpoðe

Þa *st*od on *st*æðe, *st*iðlice clypode
Then stood on shore, [and] sternly called,

Picinᵹa aꞃ, poꞃðum mælðe

*W*icinga ar, *w*ordum mælde
of-the-Vikings one, with-words announced-himself

The subject is *ar*, 'one.'

Language change is rarely consistent, though, and modern English still holds on to some of the scrambling that characterized Old English even if its grammar, now that the tell-tale endings are gone, does not easily support it. Hence, things can get tricky when we do not follow a default word order, and misunderstandings can occur. Consider what can happen when we scramble modifiers without the benefit of inflections to make the relations clear:

No one can shoot anything on this property except the owner.
    After years of being lost under a pile of dust, Walter P. Stanley, III … found all the old records of the Bangor Lions Club.
        (picture caption in the Welsh *Bangor Daily News*, January 20, 1978)

While it *is* grammatically possible to place *except the owner* at the end of the sentence (by 'extraposition'), that placement, in modern English, opens up the interpretation that the prepositional phrase modifies the direct object *anything*, putting the 'owner' on the endangered list. Case markings—as still exist in German today—would make clear whether *except the owner* is to be construed with the subject of *shoot* or with the object. In English, only the canonic ('un-scrambled' default) word order is unambiguous: 'No one except the owner can shoot anything on this property.' In the second sentence, the placement of *after years of being lost under a pile of dust* would allow the comical reading that the modifier pertains to Walter P. Stanley. All relations are unambiguous, though, if we revise to: 'For years, they were lost under a pile of dust. Now, Walter P. Stanley, III has found all the old records of the Bangor Lions Club.'

Placing constituents of a sentence in such a manner that the reader's subconscious parser does not have to revisit early committed structures obviously has a positive effect on reading speed. Not only does such proactive writing reduce cognitive load, it also engenders cooperative trust, in that the reader comes to take for granted that the writer mastered the language—not the other way around. Cooperative trust and the feeling of safety in predictive processing meet the reader's need in information management.

Information Management: Chaining Given and New

This book certainly does not shy away from paradoxes, does it: On the one hand, English relies on a strict ordering of constituents to show how they relate to each other (as subjects, predicates, objects, modifiers, etc.). On the other hand, templates (extraposition, clefting, topicalization, etc.—see Chapter 5) sidestep that strict ordering. Templates allow us to arrange constituents not by their default grammatical positions but by their saliency—to signal progression from 'given' to 'new.' English *can* have it both ways as long as the templates are familiar and thus permit recovery of the default order and relations.

Information management applies not only within sentences, but across them. By picking up, at the beginning of a sentence, 'known' information that was 'new' at the end of the previous sentence, the logical connections become intuitively clear—another smooth speeder-upper in guiding the reader towards clarity:

> One day, Standingdeer was staring at the list of 85 symbols, known as a syllabary, that represent all of the [*syllables used to make Cherokee words*].
>
> [*They*] were broken into two columns, and it occurred to him that sounds from each column could be combined to create a smaller number of [*26 sounds*].
>
> [*The use of these sounds*] seemed to all follow a definite pattern, unlike the larger list, which had to be memorized verbatim.
>
> (Maguire 2015)

Given-new chains promote dynamic reading flow as we follow Standingdeer's discovery. Given-given chains, on the other hand, concentrate focus on a topic. Chaining the 'given' parts together is done by having the beginning of each sentence refer back to the beginning of the previous sentence:

> [*He*] never heard Cherokee at home and learned only English in school.
>
> [*He*] says [*his grandparents and uncles*] know how to speak it, but it wasn't passed down.
>
> [*In those days, elders*] thought it more important that younger generations learn English well so that they would be ready for college and jobs.
>
> (Maguire 2015)

Focusing on local *cohesion* should, of course, not distract from the goal of overall *coherence*. One could imagine a passage that is cohesive from one sentence to the next but incoherent as a whole:

> Last year, we went to Paris. That's one expensive city! Cities aren't usually my thing anyway, I like hiking. Hiking has some real benefits for your health. Health insurance is gone up again too, you know, especially the co-pay. It's all coming out of my salary. Which hasn't been raised for five years, you know.

This text links new to given all right, but there is no rhyme or reason why: I traipses from one association to the next. The technical linguistic term is 'blathering.'

Ordering parts of sentences to relate constituents to one another clearly, to make sentences cohesive, to make texts coherent, and to ensure sustained cooperation between reader and writer is often a job for specialists called copy editors. These experts can fine tune an early digital release of a book before it goes into print, make sure that a *Time* or *Newsweek* article can be read between two subway stations (or the entire issue in a single train commute), and that the readers are at their least critical—because they are happily cooperating under an easy cognitive load. Copy editors are confusion managers: They know how to assist the readers' information processing by making sure the text is cohesive and coherent, by arranging constituents for information progression, and by chaining new and given information across sentences.

Clarity as Alignment with Audience Needs: The Example of Definitions

Definitions reflect negotiated interests— unless they aim for unilateral control.

The linguistic techniques outlined above make a text cohesive. Cohesion is really another word for cooperation: The writer arranges and presents information in such a way that the reader can track sameness and difference, relations and progressions, event models and word inventories. This is really how clarity is achieved: The writer anticipates the reader's needs (linguistic and cognitive) and presents the text accordingly. We shall test this model of linguistic cooperation against a genre that is all about clarity: definitions. Here, too, clarity turns out to be defined on audience needs. Simply comparing definitions across various dictionaries already reveals a variety of approaches to such cooperation. Some dictionaries, for example, play it safe and include pictures and illustrations; others, like the traditional *Oxford English Dictionary*, eschew them and rely entirely on words.

Defining a word with other words is a matter of negotiating interests. Some definitions are meant to preserve a status quo on behalf of some institution of power: a state's definition of *marriage* or of *waste* (does leaving water bottles for dehydrated immigrants in a wildlife refuge at the Mexican border constitute littering?—Williams 2010) a government's definition of *privacy* or *militant*, an insurance company's audacious definition of *acts of God*, a teacher's definition of *late*. Others challenge authority, such as many on the website urbandictionary.com. Legal or counterculture definitions have a unilateral power agenda; cooperative definitions are bilateral and interactive.

How should a dictionary define a word like *yellow*? If dictionaries are cooperative, then the approach depends on the intended reader. For academic audiences, the following analytical definition might be appropriate:

> *yellow* A color of 570–590 nm in wavelength and 535–505 THz in frequency; the third color in a rainbow after red and orange.

The definition presumes that the user knows what 'wavelength' means and what the sequence of colors in a rainbow is. Essentially, the reader is expected to know what 'yellow' is, if only not to misread its position on the spectrum (the third color *after* 'red and orange' could be blue: red-and-orange, $yellow_1$, $green_2$ $blue_3$, …). In a popular dictionary with global distribution, such a technical approach may not be the best one. In that case, one could try to think of objects that are typically yellow and that are common and well-known across the globe, such as egg yolks or the sun:

> *yellow* The color of gold, egg yolks, ripe lemons, and taxi cabs.

This is known as a definition by synthesis. Just as in the analytical definition for an academic audience, the main concern is the knowledge base of the reader. It may still leave some readers wondering where in the world taxicabs are yellow (or what a taxicab is).

To find a definition that works best for a particular audience and subject matter, we can choose among the following kinds of approaches:

stipulative	Specifies how a term is used within a given context, e.g. 'We use the term *intimate* for a conversation partner who is a family member, spouse, lover, or very close friend.'
lexical	Defines a word with other words based on: common usage, e.g. 'A *soccer mom* is a typically suburban mother who accompanies her children to their soccer games and is considered as part of a significant voting bloc or demographic group.' synonyms, e.g. '*Polestar*—the *North Star* towards which the axis of the earth points.' grammatical function, e.g. '*and*—used as a function word to indicate connection or addition esp. of items within the same class or type; used to join sentence elements of the same grammatical rank of function.'

analysis, e.g. '*yellow*—a color of 570–590 nm in wavelength and 535–505 THz in frequency; the third color in a rainbow after red and orange.'

synthesis, e.g. '*yellow*—the color of gold, egg yolks, ripe lemons, and taxi cabs.'

cause, e.g. '*jaundice*—yellowish pigmentation of the skin, tissues, and body fluids caused by the deposition of bile pigments.'

function, e.g. '*chair*—a piece of furniture with a raised surface used to sit on, commonly for use by one person.'

circularity, e.g. '*odor*—a smell, scent, aroma' (with other entries for *scent* and *aroma* using the same words).

theoretical	Positions the term within the context of a well-established belief or theory and associates it with a cluster of relevant properties, e.g. '*water*—the liquid that descends from the clouds as rain, forms streams, lakes and seas, and is a major constituent of all living matter and that when pure is an odorless, tasteless, very slightly compressible liquid oxide of hydrogen H_2O which appears bluish in thick layers, freezes at 0°C and boils at 100°C, has a maximum density at 4°C and a high specific heat, is feebly ionized to hydrogen and hydroxyl ions, and is a poor conductor of electricity and a good solvent.'
operational	Defines a term by how it is arrived at, e.g. '*smoot*—the unit of length (five feet and seven inches) equivalent of the body height of Oliver Smoot, MIT class of 1962, the (now retired) chair of the American National Standards Institute. In October 1958, Smoot's body was used to measure the length of Boston's Massachusetts Avenue Bridge by MIT fraternity Lambda Chi Alpha (it measures 364.4 smoots and one ear).'
persuasive	Defines a term in a way so as to influence attitudes, e.g. '*faith*—belief without evidence in what is told by one who speaks without knowledge, of things without parallel.' (Ambrose Bierce, *The Devil's Dictionary*)

These definition types can and should certainly be combined.

To illustrate how definitions are customized, imagine how the word *onion* would need to be defined if it were to be used in a brochure that advocates its cultivation in an area that traditionally does not grow onions but could sustain farming them. One would probably combine approaches as follows:

synthesis (category)	food, vegetable
analysis	fleshy, concentric layers, roots on bottom and leaves on top that protrude above ground
operation	use chopped or sliced to add to dishes, grow in cool climates in fertile and well-drained soil
persuasion	adds flavor and nutrition (gain frame), has been cultivated for thousands of years (bandwagon frame)

The resulting description should appeal to potential farmers:

> The **onion** is a vegetable that has been grown as food for thousands of years. It has fleshy, concentric layers and grows under the earth, with green stalks that protrude above. Chopped or sliced, it adds flavor and nutrition to dishes. It is grown in cool climates and requires fertile, well-drained soil.

A description written for botanists would be different. The botanist would not have to be introduced to what an onion is, but rather would need specific criteria for what is required for membership in that species of the genus *allum*.

The point of this excursion into definitions is to illustrate the point that clarity, including scientific clarity, does not occur 'objectively,' in a vacuum. The 'rule of lenity' (p. 111) proves that even legal language cannot be 'objectively clear' from one person to the next. Clarity requires cooperation. Language users depend on cooperation, though cooperation is not only innate but additionally also an acquired skill (e.g. in 'attentive listening' training). With the ability to imagine what goes on in someone else's mind (= Theory of Mind), authors and copy editors can improve the clarity of writing by creating cohesion with proforms and lexical references, and coherence by facilitating the creation of a clear mental model. Authors keep track of what the readers would likely hold in those mental models. They can proactively manage information, ordering by saliency within and across sentences. They align their writing with the assumed needs and knowledge of their readers. Clarity is not unilateral or egocentric or even static; it is the result of mutual engagement in managed confusion.

Based on this understanding of cooperation between writer and reader, let us do something iconoclastic and turn to (well, on, actually) literary criticism.

Masters of Managed Confusion: Famous Authors

Literary theory tends to ignore co-creation—the merging of readers' and authors' stories.

Academic literary scholars are traditionally stand-offish on the topic of mind melds between writers and readers. Literary researchers see better science in looking at 'the text' without 'making assumptions' about the author. Alternatively, they concentrate on the reader's responses to the text. Stanley Fish (1980) famously emphasized that there are as many 'texts' as there are readers. Either way, however, literary criticism would not attempt to describe how readers connect to *authors*.

But connect they do. It is not an unscientific question to ask how the author's text interacts with the reader's. Hugh Crago (2014) asked exactly that question. He argued that enthralled readers connect their mental lives to something that comes to them from outside—they merge to someone else's story. In doing so, they necessarily connect to its author. One should add that they can also connect to other readers: Stories are meant to be shared or jointly experienced—else we would not have book clubs or readings, go to see works performed, or read out loud to our loved ones.

By deciding *not* to investigate how author and reader connect, literary critics frame their research in terms of the **literary techniques** (foreshadowing, irony, imagery, etc.) or 'affective stylistics' (Fish 1980). How those literary qualities come about is off topic because literary critics are (rightfully) suspicious about authors' comments about their own works. Too readily, authors' self-reports fall into two categories, neither useful for study. Some authors showcase their inspiration (genius) and report the writing experience as if it had originated outside of them, as did Coleridge with his famous account of how he got to write 'Kublai Kahn' (he explained its unevenness by claiming that it came to him under the influence of laudanum, a self-medicated opiate, and that he was interrupted when he wrote down his vision). Other authors, in contrast, emphasize their craftsmanship. Writing is art, and art is technique and hard work, certainly *not* the result of feeling and inspiration:

> Nobody but a beginner imagines that he who creates must feel. Every real and genuine artist smiles at such naïve blunders as that. A melancholy enough smile, perhaps, but still a smile. For what an artist talks about is never the main point; it is the raw material, in and for itself indifferent, out of which, with bland and serene mastery, he creates the work of art. If you care too much about what you have to say, if your heart is too much in it, you can be pretty sure of making a mess. You get pathetic, you wax sentimental; something dull and doddering, without roots or outlines, with no sense of humour—something tiresome and banal grows under your hand, and you get nothing out of it but apathy in your audience, and disappointment and misery in yourself.
>
> (Thomas Mann, *Tonio Kröger* 2009/1903)

Really? An author 'indifferent' to the story that begs to be written? If so, why would any reader care to merge to it? We have already explored how the human mind processes and connects to story; in the remainder of this chapter, we will look at how (perfectly describable) **linguistic techniques** of cooperation open and sustain a narrative connection between writer and reader. They do so by managing and distributing the cognitive load of the reader.

Language, Logic, Predictability, and Event Model

cognitive load
The concentration of mental effort on one task to a degree that it can potentially interfere with another.

Good authors know how to distribute their readers' cognitive loads across four domains.

Linguistic techniques and literary techniques are complementary. Both impose a cognitive load, and the writer can stack that load either way (that is, if the writer thinks of the reader as cooperating and co-creating). A light cognitive load (i.e. fast reading) translates into automatic, predictive, uncritical processing. Understanding

Table 7.1 Domain-specific Operating Systems of the Mind/Brain

Domain	Language faculty
predication (pattern detection, rules establishing relations)	linguistic faculty
proposition (relations between arguments that apply in principal rather than in detail)	logic
prediction (anticipation of likely result without regard to details of the sequence)	telic processing
plot (subplots towards plot, mental inventory)	event model

the role of language itself in the service of literary objectives effectively turns authors into applied linguists. Trained or self-trained, it very much appears that the best of them are. In addition to what the reader's parsing load is, the writer also keeps in mind how predictable the writing is, whether the reader can follow the logic, and what the reader's event model likely contains at any given time. The author chooses how to distribute those loads for the reader.

There are at least four separate types of processing (Table 7.1) that together constitute the *Language* faculty.

- The **linguistic component** contains the productive grammar of all languages and a set of strategies for co-creating structure that we called the parser. It also contains all the knowledge of the various levels of pattern knowledge and combinatorial rules from phonology up to discourse. It computes in **predications** (attributing something to something): A predicate says something about a subject, a modifier something about a noun phrase or verb phrase, a complement something about a subject or object, etc.
- **Logic** sees sameness in relations that are expressed differently in language. Since, as we saw in Chapter 5, there are different linguistic structures for expressing the same content, this is the system that can see relations at a more general level. For example, its symbolic system allows us to compare two concepts against a third, as in metaphors (cf. Pietarinen 2008, based on Peirce 1998). The point of calling a dictator a butcher, for instance, is to compare them on their professional control over defenseless beings that will come to harm without any boundaries set by remorse or shame. The system that reveals these higher-order content-free logical relations computes in **propositions**.
- **Predictability** is not concerned with detailed predications or content-free propositions, but with short-circuiting scripts to jump to their anticipated result. **Telic processing** (see Chapter 3) allows adjustments on the fly and hunches that permit us to abandon a thought because it does not appear promising. Deterministic thinking is an extension of ancient skills mentioned in Chapter 1 (ballistic movement, stone tool knapping).

- **Event models** keep a dynamic representation of what should be kept in memory to follow a narrative. It contains, as we saw in Art Glenberg's example above (p. 145), inventories of details relevant to the unfolding action, to which the linguistic system has access for proform resolution. Its computations are yet different because it computes in **plots** and its constituting subplots.

Let us pretend that we read the four pieces of literature discussed below on an electronic device and that at the completion of each piece we are presented with sliders to rate how challenging language, logic, predictability, and creating an adequate event model were. The ratings are relative to each other and should add up to 1, with a minimal score of 0.1 and a maximum score of 0.7 for each rubric.[4] Let us first compare two texts of almost identical length, Ernest Hemingway's 'Hills Like White Elephants' (1459 words) and Dylan Thomas' 'The International Eisteddfod' (1468 words).

'Hills Like White Elephants' by Ernest Hemingway

Language=0.1, Logic=0.1, Predictability=0.3, Event model=0.5

Hemingway's short story describes a painfully awkward conversation between a man and a woman. They never name the elephant (her imminent abortion). The reader feels obliged to empathize with her resigned deference about going through with the procedure and with his tone-deaf attempts to save negative face. The strained euphemisms damage more than they repair ('They just let the air in'). The bleakness of their conversation matches the landscape around them (which includes blanched hills like white elephants)—and so do the author's linguistic choices. The words are simple, monosyllabic, repetitive:

> 'We want two *Anis del Toro*.'
> 'With water?'
> 'Do you want it with water?'
> 'I don't know,' the girl said. 'Is it good with water?'
> 'It's all right.'
> 'You want them with water?' asked the woman.
> 'Yes, with water.'
>
> (Hemingway 1987)

Hemingway's sentence rhythms trail off. Note below how the clauses of the introductory sentences end with three directly adjacent syllables that are all stressed:

> The hills across the valley of the Ebro were lóng ánd whíte. On this side there was no shade ánd nó trées and the station was between two lines of rails ín thé sún. Close against the side of

---

4 The ratings below the following titles are our (the authors') subjective ratings, *not the results of an actual survey.*

the station there was the warm shadow of the building and a curtain, made of strings of bámbóo béads, hung across the open door into the bar, to kéep óut flíes.

Chatter, chatter, chatter, bláh-bláh-bláh: bland and serene mastery. The language is as bland as is the logic of the piece: Two people talk at each other while waiting for a train. Hemingway keeps demands on linguistic and logical processing minimal.

Creating an adequate event model, however, is quite another matter. The details here seem unconnected. Hemingway's skeletal wording compels the reader to wire-frame a mental scenery, grasping at every little detail from the sparse setting in the way we cast furtive glances in an embarrassing conversation where random details are better than the discourse. We see 'a curtain, made of strings of bamboo beads, hung across the open door into the bar, to keep out flies.' It becomes a detail in one's mental model without a clear connection to a plot/event (a) because *something* needs to be imagined, and this is something, and (b) because it is thankfully irrelevant—*anything* is better than the topic at hand. It is, indeed, possible to read this short story and not understand what is going on, which explains the second-highest score, for demands on predicting. Where is the narrative headed? The major cognitive challenge is to co-create an event model with telic subplots; however, just what overarching plot those subplots (such as ordering *Anis del Toro*) are working towards remains obscure. The reader comes to share a sense of foreboding that belies the façade of putting up a good front.

'The International Eisteddfod' by Dylan Thomas

Language=0.7, Logic=0.1, Predictability=0.1, Event model=0.1

Dylan Thomas distributes processing loads quite differently from Hemingway. The narrator's persona walks, wide-eyed, through an art festival so exotically diverse and so bewildering and bursting with sensations and impressions that it feels like (actually, *is*) sensory overload just reading about it:

> Here, over the bridge, come three Javanese, winged, breastplated, helmeted, carrying gongs and steel bubbles. Kilted, sporraned, tartan'd, daggered Scotsmen reel and strathspey up a side-street, piping hot. Burgundian girls, wearing, on their heads, bird-cages made of velvet, suddenly whisk on the pavement into a coloured dance. A viking goes into a pub. In black felt feathered hats and short leather trousers, enormous Austrians, with thighs big as Welshmen's bodies, but much browner, yodel to fiddles and split the rain with their smiles. Frilled, ribboned, sashed, fezzed, and white-turbaned, in baggy-blue sharavari and squashed red boots, Ukrainians with Manchester accents gopak up the hill. Everything is strange in Llangollen.

(Thomas 1978)

The language here is so challenging that it is difficult to read out loud. The words are as unpredictable as the performers and their outfits. There are startling compounds like *baggy-blue* and unlikely word combinations such as *bird cages made of velvet* and *split the rain with their smiles*. A frequency count reveals that Dylan Thomas packs twice as many different words into his text as Hemingway uses for his (remember that both texts have the same length).

Whereas Dylan Thomas' vocabulary and morphology are as diverse and exuberant as his syntax is complex and varied, Hemingway uses bare-bones morphology and repeats words, sometimes in a row ('Would you please please please please please please stop talking?'), making us agree that indeed this too, too sullied talk should end. And just like Hemingway, Dylan Thomas uses rhythm to reflect his purpose. A lilting iambic flow ('frénzied flúte and fíddle whíp them úp') bonks against a spondee ('into jét-bláck blíss'), where primary stresses directly adjacent break the momentum (Dylan Thomas' favorite speedbump). It's the same three stressed syllables as at the end of Hemingway's clauses above, but here they do not expectedly trail off into rhythmic ellipses but jar unannounced. The helter-skelter rhythms mimic a random visual slideshow; the jumbled prose that defies a smooth reading mirrors the narrator's slow progress through the throng. A complex sentence like 'Burgundian girls, wearing, on their heads, bird-cages made of velvet, suddenly whisk on the pavement into a coloured dance' is followed by a one-liner that could be the opening line of a bawdy joke: 'A viking goes into a pub.' And then, unprompted, a single sound drifts up: 'The *f*renzied *f*lute and *f*iddle whip them up … as they *f*rolic like undertakers.' In the slow progress, every moment of reading brings linguistic surprise.

Dylan Thomas, like Hemingway, compels the reader to visualize. However, his mental images are not sparse but kaleidoscopic, and more often than not the reader just has to make up things on the spur of the moment when the meaning of words like *sharavari* and *gopak* are too obscure to bring up anything familiar. Both authors make cognitive demands on the reader. Hemingway presents easy language but not much that can be automatically and predictively processed and plotted. Dylan Thomas presents both unfamiliar language and unfamiliar scenes. The impressionist vignettes quickly signal that there is not much in the way of logic that needs to be deduced. Details in the event model persist only from one episode to the next, like tweets, after which they can be overwritten.

spondee
The interruption of an iambic meter, where an unstressed syllable alternates with a stressed one, with two stressed syllables in a row—essentially a deliberate violation of the meter. One of the most famous examples occurs at the end of Dylan Thomas' 1951 poem 'Do Not Go Gentle Into That Good Night': 'And you, my father, there on the sád héight, / Cúrse, bléss me now with your fíerce téars, I pray.'

Murder on the Orient Express **by Agatha Christie**

Language=0.1, Logic=0.3, Predictability=0.3, Event model=0.3

Agatha Christie's masterpiece balances cognitive demands quite evenly. In the passage below, logic, predictability, and event model compete for attention evenly, so as a trade-off, the parsing demands are kept light. In the novel, Hercule Poirot must solve a murder on board a train that is stuck in the snow, without a track of footprints leading away from the crime scene. Details compete for importance as several individuals could be the perpetrator—and, as it turns out, are: It was a revenge killing in which the conspirators (protecting each other in their testimonies) took turns stabbing their nemesis.

> M. Bouc was handling the button that Mrs. Hubbard had left behind her. 'This button. I cannot understand it. Does it mean that after all, Pierre Michel is involved in some way?' he asked. He paused, then continued, as Poirot did not reply. 'What have you to say, my friend?' 'That button, it suggests possibilities,' said Poirot thoughtfully. 'Let us interview next the Swedish lady before we discuss the evidence that we have heard.'
> …
> 'Have you a scarlet silk kimono, Mademoiselle?' 'No, indeed. I have a good comfortable dressing-gown of Jaeger material.' 'And the lady with you, Miss Debenham? What colour is her dressing-gown?'
>
> (Christie 2017)

The competing demands of confusion management—prediction, logic, and event-model subplots—are actually thematized in the book. Poirot characteristically remarks upon the conflict between his intuitive gut-level predictions and the exacting standards of logic that his little grey cells demand. 'Monsieur Bouc' pretends to cooperate with Poirot but draws attention to details that are *not* relevant to the solution of the crime to lure the master crime solver off track. Even the English language is at times at odds with the Belgian detective, but not with his thought processes. Logic triumphs over red herring.

Oh Say Can You Say **by Dr. Seuss**

Language=0.7, Logic=0.1, Predictability=0.1, Event model=0.1

A subgenre of children's literature whose existence is puzzling at first thought is nonsense literature, especially nonsense rhymes. But if the child knows that the content is deliberately illogical for hilarity, delights in the magically unpredictable, and is relieved from tracking subplots in event models in search for a logical solution, then the entire focus of the text can be on the language:

> Briggs pats pink pigs.
> Briggs pats big pigs.
> (Don't ask me why. It doesn't matter.)
> Pete Briggs is a pink pig, big pig patter.
> Pete Briggs pats his big pink pigs all day.
> (Don't ask me why. I cannot say.)
> Then Pete puts his patted pigs away
> in his Pete Briggs' Pink Pigs Big Pigs Pigpen.
>
> (Seuss 1979)

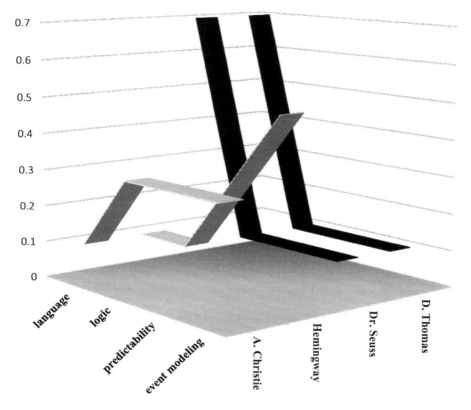

Figure 7.1 Cognitive-load Distributions by Four Authors

Twice, the child is told point blank not to pursue logic: It doesn't matter. The *only* thing that matters here is the language, as is actually quite appropriate for a children's book. The book appears in the 'I Can Read It All by Myself' series, but just in case an adult is reading these words to a child, the book contains an impertinent tongue-in-cheek challenge to his or her positive face (as an adult who has mastered speech): 'Are you having trouble / in saying this stuff? It's really quite easy for me.'

If we plot the demands on the reader across the four texts, we see something quite amazing: Dylan Thomas patterns with Dr. Seuss.

This match between Dylan Thomas and Theodor Geisel may not be all that accidental given those two authors: Compulsive linguistic perfectionism is a signature characteristic for both writers. However, both knew when to draw attention to the language and when to the story (cf. *Yertle the Turtle* by Geisel and *A Child's Christmas in Wales* by Dylan Thomas for a very different distribution of processing loads).

A Collaborative Dance, but the Author Leads

The cooperative approach to writing taken in this chapter is not one typically taken in academic teaching. The modern emphasis of college composition classes is rather on discovery and on finding one's voice—a somewhat autistic approach to writing. Literary theory treats the investigation of an author's intentions as an 'intentional fallacy,' analyzing the text for its internal qualities to the exclusion of its collaborative qualities. They all have excellent things to teach, of course, but when in a group of blind men each palpitate a part of an elephant, they each have a deficient conception of the total animal.

Writing (like storytelling) connects minds, immediately or over a distance. One should not underestimate the power of those connections. German literary criticism knows the term 'Werther-Effekt,' named for the (anecdotally attested) epidemic of suicides following Goethe's 1774 publication of *The Sorrows of Young Werther*. Psychiatrists, on the other hand, can use bibliotherapy to help avert suicide. Chapter 6 described the recipes for using language to destroy humans, and Chapter 5 described language as the ultimate tool of altruistic cooperation. The *art* of writing/speaking, like the art of attentive reading/listening, comes from trained skill and deliberation in mind reading and in leading the collaborative dance.

There are two major benefits of superior language command, and they may well have evolutionary benefits.

The first benefit is that a superior writer like Dylan Thomas or a superior storyteller like Garrison Keillor command respect and have prestige. Ruth Berger (2008:179) assumes that humans find speakers who master all the templates described in Chapter 5 attractive:

> Peacock feathers, long hair, and overly complex grammar have one thing in common: They are not really practical. For others, however—rivals, potential sexual partners—they serve as an indicator whether someone is an especially 'fit' representative of the respective species. We trust that a brilliant commander of long sentences and sophisticated vocabulary will be successful in life.

As shiny long hair and symmetrically patterned peacock feathers are indicators of physical health (so Berger), excellence in linguistic performance is an indicator of mental health and discipline. This benefit of the doubt may account for the charisma we ascribe to successful political candidates with grammar glamour[5] and the peculiar trust we put in the testimonials from well-spoken actors and actresses from the silver screen.

The second benefit is the near-telekinetic power of language, which turns us into open books. Knowing the kinds of linguistic

---

5   The word *glamour* is originally a Scots variant of the word *grammar*. In the Middle Ages, grammar was one of the core areas of the university curriculum and stood for learnedness, including also knowledge of the occult, so the word *glamour* meant 'enchantment, magic.' For a decline in syntactic complexity as an early indicator of Alzheimer's, see Iacono et al. 2009.

tools of cooperation, such as the templates listed in Chapter 5, adds informational bandwidth—vital, given the lossiness described in Chapter 1. Sophisticated knowledge of language as described in these past chapters improves access to minds, which needs to be managed responsibly. Let us take a step back and take a comprehensive view of the implications in our conclusion.

(Im)pertinent Questions

- This is a two-part question:
  1. What makes people perceive a speaker as 'charismatic'?
  2. A study by Kowronski et al. (1998) showed that a speaker criticizing others for specific traits (being 'nasty' or a 'liar') plants in the listeners the unconscious belief that the speaker also has those traits ('spontaneous trait transference'). How can a speaker criticize and name-call others and yet be perceived as charismatic?
- Great apes (like chimpanzees) use hand gestures to communicate. Gestures are immune to mimicry because their originators are instantly verified. What do human gestures contribute to speech and trust?
- How does the act of labeling ('This is a coffee mug') reflect communal judgment? Is *everything* we label tied to communal judgment?
- How would you define a 'conversational narcissist'?

References

Alter, Alexandra. 2012. Your e-book is reading you. *The Wall Street Journal* (July 19). Online: www.wsj.com/articles/SB10001424052702304870304577490950051438304.

Berger, Ruth. 2008. *Warum der Mensch spricht: Eine Naturgeschichte der Sprache.* Frankfurt: Eichborn.

Christie, Agatha. 2017. *Murder on the Orient Express: A Hercule Poirot mystery.* New York: William Morrow, HarperCollins.

Crago, Hugh. 2014. *Entranced by story: Brain, tale and teller from infancy to old age.* New York: Routledge.

Fish, Stanley E. 1980. *Is there a text in this class? The authority of interpretive communities.* Cambridge, MA: Harvard University Press.

Glenberg, Art M.; M. Meyer; and K. Lindem. 1987. Mental models contribute to foregrounding during text comprehension. *Journal of Memory and Language* 26.69–83.

Gordon, Peter C.; Barbara J. Grosz; and Laura A. Gilliom. 1993. Pronouns, names, and the centering of attention in discourse. *Cognitive Science* 17.311–47.

Hemingway, Ernest. 1987. Hills like white elephants. *The complete short stories of Ernest Hemingway: The Finca Vigía edition*, 211–14. New York: Scribner Paperback Fiction, Simon & Schuster.

Iacono, Diego; William R. Markesbery; Myron D. Gross; O. Pletnikova; G. Rudow; Peter Zandi; and Juan Cesar Troncoso. 2009. The Nun Study: Clinically silent AD, neuronal hypertrophy, and linguistic skills in early life. *Neurology* 73(9) (September 1).665–73.

Jackendoff, Ray. 1969. Some rules of semantic interpretation for English. MIT Doctoral Dissertation, Cambridge, MA.

Jones, Daniel. 1977. *My friend Dylan Thomas*. New York: Charles Scribner's Sons.

Kishon, Ephraim. 1965. *The seasick whale*, trans. by Yohanan Goldman. Tel Aviv: Bronfman.

Kowronski, John J.; Donal E. Carlston; Lynda Mae; and Matthew T. Crawford. 1998. Spontaneous trait transference: Communicators take on the qualities they describe in others. *Journal of Personality and Social Psychology* 74(4).837–48.

Maguire, Marti. 2015. Cherokee native's goal: Saving a language even he learned late in life. *The Charlotte Observer* (November 29).14A.

Mann, Thomas. 2009/1903. *Tonio Kröger*. Online: https://literature save2.files.wordpress.com/2009/12/thomas-mann-tonio-kroger. pdf.

Neary, Lynn. 2013. E-readers track how we read, but is the data useful for authors? *All Things Considered* (January 28), NPR.

Parish, Peggy. 1993. *Thank you, Amelia Bedelia*. Madison, WI: Demco Media.

Peirce, Charles S. 1998. *The essential Peirce 2*. The Peirce Edition Project. Bloomington: Indiana University Press.

Pietarinen, Ahti-Veikko. 2008. An iconic logic of metaphors. *Proceedings of the International Conference on Computational Science (ICCS)* (Seoul, July 27–29). Online: https://fliphtml5. com/sqxl/khpe.

Pogue, David. 2015. Super Siri. *Scientific American* 313(3):31.

Rhomberg, Andrew. 2015. Should authors and publishers spy on readers? *Digital Book World* (January 9).

Rousseau, Jean-Jacques. 1762. *Émile, ou de l'éducation*, ed. by Jean-Marie Tremblay. Chicoutimi: Université du Québec à Chicoutimi. Online: http://classiques.uqac.ca/classiques/Rousseau_jj/emile/ emile_de_education_1_3.pdf.

Sedivy, Julie. 2014. *Language in mind: An introduction to psycho-linguistics*. Sunderland, MA: Sinauer.

Seuss, Dr. [Theodor Seuss Geisel]. 1979. *Oh say can you say?* Beginner Books. New York: Random House.

Stanton, Andrew. 2012. The clues to a great story. TED Talk. Online:www.ted.com/talks/andrew_stanton_the_clues_to_a_ great_story?language=en. http://www.ted.com/talks/andrew_%20 stanton_%20the_%20clues_%20to_%20a_%20great_%20story? language=en.

Stein, Gertrude. 1939. Response. The situation in American writing: Seven questions. *Partisan Review* 6(4) (Summer):25–51.

Thomas, Dylan. 1978. The International Eisteddfod. *Quite early one morning*, 58–62. Everyman's Library. London: Dent, New York: Dutton.

Thomas, Dylan. n.d. Reminiscences of childhood. Second version. *Dylan Thomas: Selected writings*, ed. by J. P. Harries, 3–8. London: Heinemann Educational Books. Online: https://youtu.be/ Ce_qzuBPQpc (read by the author).

Williams, Carol J. 2010. Conviction in migrant-water case overturned. *L.A. Times* (September 3).AA3.

Conclusion

The power of language and the language of power: Linguistic discrimination is real.

Throughout this book, we explained why language is so powerful and described some of the most important ways in which it is used to create and maintain relations of power. That is, we set out to explain the power of language so we could explain the language of power. With the force of explanation now behind us, we would like in this conclusion to once again renew and broaden the call for linguistic equality in the sense of sufficient opportunities for immersion, knowledge, and understanding. We would also like to return to the notion of linguistic equality in the sense of linguistic discrimination and rights and the need for moral vigilance. We will do so by describing several other pressing linguistic harms: gatekeeping, wealth disparity, screen time, contaminated language, uncooperative language, and inadequate legal and institutional protections.

Power structures, of course, exist among social animals as well, without language. They are created by social alliances and, ultimately, physical violence. Humans, on the other hand, can *talk* themselves into an existing power structure (e.g. by using frames to appeal to voters) or into creating one (e.g. by creating a vision attracting a following large enough to build a megachurch). Since human violence is so easily fatal (we are fragile, but many have firearms), there is incentive in keeping conflicts verbal as long as possible, and to try to resolve them verbally. We saw that when humans eventually do use physical violence, that violence is usually verbal at first. Examples range from widespread sexual assault (where narratives and scripts help to shape linguistic dispositions) to organized violence against a population (where language 'others,' stigmatizes, dehumanizes, legitimizes discrimination, institutionalizes disenfranchisement, and finally encourages and licenses spontaneous or organized physical violence such as vandalism and shootings).

We traced both the power of language and our trusting defenselessness against that power back to evolutionary pressures. Animals sustain social communities through communication (those two words define each other), and they are vulnerable to 'fake news' in the form of mimicry. They may follow a false chemical trail to their doom, or respond to the distress call of a juvenile that turns out to have come from a cat, or lose food to a bird whose alarm calls were hitherto trustworthy. Animals started to turn to combinatorial calls, triggering a cognitive arms race towards encryption of which humans are the clear winners—at least when measured in terms of collaborative achievements (good and bad).

It takes considerable intelligence to learn and imitate the combinatorial signals of a different group or species, but the rewards are considerable. Bottle-nosed and spotted dolphins off Bermuda, for example, have different vocalization patterns, but they have been filmed settling conflicts acoustically and with body language, and even to babysit each others' calves (Elliser and Herzing 2016).

Alpha chimps build alliances based mostly on 'display' and on fighting prowess, asserting their first pick of food and females. They do share some of their food to ingratiate group members and to call in favors when needed (reciprocal altruism). Alpha(bet) humans derive their privileges from linguistic alliances and in-groups. A powerful human does not have to be physically strong enough to win fist fights (actually, we tend to see brawns and brains rather as opposites— even Dr. Bruce Banner loses about 100 IQ points when he turns into the Incredible Hulk). Typically, humans *convince* others rather than pummel them into alliance, thus harnessing their collective power. Such alliances, too, are usually legitimized with a quantum of reciprocal altruism (philanthropy, charity, foundations, etc.).

A shared language puts humans in synch with each other on several levels. Our brains tune into each other's rhythms of speaking, anticipate what we are going to hear, and prime the semantic fields we think we will need to follow the conversation. That is effectively mind reading—one of the ways in which we boost the informational bandwidth of speech (which, again, by virtue of its entropy conveys a sparse amount of information, given how many signals it burns through). Language users rely on creative and empathic cooperation when they negotiate meaning, and their cooperation is built on trust. With trust, a speech community can have consensus and shared intentions, agree on the meanings of their words (e.g. whether something is a creek or a brook, a pond or a lake, a cup or a bowl, or when to use the pronouns *he*, *she*, or *they*). This kind of distributed cognition is so advanced among humans that our words refer to real-world objects and events only via our shared or negotiated concepts of them. We even have social emotions such as pride or shame, which exist primarily in distributed cognition (as we observe ourselves by taking the other's perspective).

Shared concepts and social emotions naturally differ across in-groups. A nurse in Taiwan, for example, will be evaluated on a concept of 'caring' based on how one would tend to a sick family member; the same nurse would not be evaluated on that model in a US hospital, where 'caring' is a health *management* regimen that assumes active participation of the patient (Davis, Thiede, and Smith 2013). In-groups also compare and rank themselves vis-à-vis other in-groups, often with a 'deficit view' towards those they perceive

distributed cognition
Neural networks extending across brains, so to speak, linking a speech community's collective knowledge and judgments, biases, social emotions (pride in success, shame in failure ...), and creativity. Human brains do not mature in isolation but fail to thrive if cut off from distributed cognition.

social emotion
An emotion that does not originate within the individual (as would joy/ sadness, anger/ fear, trust/distrust, surprise/anticipation) but within distributed cognition, reflecting the individual's standing within the in-group (notably pride/shame).

to have less power. A (now somewhat dated) joke illustrates such ranking. When Ozark Airlines still existed, the story went that when a flight approached Atlanta and asked for the local time, the air controller double checked what airline the pilot was flying for—because for a Delta flight, the answer would have been 'fourteen hundred hours,' for TWA it would have been 'two o'clock,' but for Ozark Airlines, the flight controllers would have explained that the big hand is on the 'twelve' and the little hand is on the 'two.' Ozark Airlines, in that joke, stands in for Appalachian speech communities who are often poor and treated as backwards and made fun of, based almost entirely on their 'Mountain Talk.'

The following concluding discussion concerns the mechanisms of linguistic discrimination and disenfranchisements and the need to address language disparities—why we need linguistic equality in the sense of sufficient opportunity for immersion, factual knowledge of its power, and understanding of why and how language has that power.

Standards and Shibboleths

> We construct artificial language varieties as gatekeepers.

Jeffrey Reaser (2019) quoted a teacher's response in a 'critical language pedagogy' workshop:

> My home language is extremely close to Standardized, Northern English. I have never felt chastised, victimized or unintelligent because of my language. This is a privilege that goes often unrecognized by individuals. This is a prejudice that I have not undergone, but am certainly aware of its effect on my students.

As another teacher in the same workshop pointed out, 'passive prejudice doesn't stay passive' (ibid.). What is a language's 'standard' version, and how do we get one?

And as can be inferred from the 'Mountain Talk' example above, the answer is 'power.' A segment with social (and thus also economic) capital protects its assets by creating an artificial linguistic in-group. Such a variety has no native speakers in the sense that actual dialects have native speakers; it is strictly a social construct. A large social linguistic stratum is unlikely to achieve consistency in pronunciation everywhere; writers and speakers of 'standard' American English create coherence for themselves instead by avoiding features that would unmistakably tie them to a specific language variety, 'markers' that thereby become 'non-standard.' Some of those markers may very well have been standard once; Bishop Robert Lowth's 1762 *A Short Introduction to English Grammar* names, among others, the split infinitive (*Star Trek*'s 'to boldly go' taking a seemingly deliberate swipe here) and the 'illogical' double negative (though no one really thinks that Marvin Gaye and Tammi Terrell's 'Ain't No Mountain High Enough' actually *delimits* the

Bishop Robert Lowth (1710–1787) Bishop of the Church of England and professor of poetry at Oxford University. His works on grammar became normative for English schools and indeed for editing standards, which also makes him the patron saint of prescriptive grammar.

lovers' commitment to reaching out for each other). Using just one 'non-standard' marker with consistency voids the speaker's membership in the self-declared community of 'standard speakers' and opens that person up to charges of being 'uneducated':

- expressing past reference with forms used for perfective aspect in written English ('I seen the ad in the paper');
- reducing consonant clusters in speech ('tas force' for 'task force');
- not using plural inflection where the content is clearly already plural ('three mile from here'),
- not using agreement inflection -*s* ('he talk a good game');
- using regionally or socially marked words such as *ain't*, *youse*, *y'all*, or *tryna* ('trying to'—Miller 2019).

Linguists call such flagged forms *shibboleths* after a story in Judges 12, where a dialectal difference in pronunciation was used to profile and kill Ephraimite refugees:

> The Gileadites held the fords of the Jordan against the Ephraimites. And when any fugitive from Ephraim said, 'Let me cross,' the men of Gilead would ask him, 'Are you an Ephraimite?'; if he said 'No,' they would say to him, 'Then say *shibboleth*'; but he would say 'sibboleth,' not being able to pronounce it correctly. Thereupon they would seize him and slay him by the fords of the Jordan. Forty-two thousand Ephraimites fell at that time.
>
> (*Jewish Study Bible* 2014:525)

socially constructed language varieties Language varieties constructed from prestige dialects and affected by speakers for the sole reason of being exclusive. Examples given here are 'standard American English,' 'Mid-Atlantic English,' the 'Queen's English,' and 'academic English.' A slang designed to exclude outsiders, as used by a gang or by truckers, would be another example, but slangs change fast to remain exclusive, whereas prestige constructs use power to be so.

Shibboleths are a cheap and popular tool for using language as a gatekeeper. Note that even the Hebrew Bible labels the variant pronunciation as incorrect. Today, we scan for shibboleths in cover letters, business proposals, portfolios, and prompted essays for college applications, and we continue to brand them 'incorrect' in many college usage handbooks for composition classes (Algeo 1977).

It is certainly telling that 'standard' varieties of European language are conventionalized from the dialects spoken where power was/is concentrated, mostly royal palaces: London, Paris, Hannover, Dresden, Madrid, Vienna …. In England, the privileged variety of English is actually referred to as 'the Queen's English' even today. In the US, the power center was not established by royalty but by radio: Announcers, anchors, newscasters for NBC institutionalized their 'network standard' by consciously avoiding all regional identifiers. Hollywood actors of the 'golden age' similarly affected a standard of speaking English that seemed half-way suspended between the US and English, but home to neither (hence called the 'Mid-Atlantic' accent). After World War II, US elite varieties started avoiding the English -*r*-dropping in words like *car* and brought back the postvocalic /r/.

Notice that Germany was referenced twice in the list of power centers above. To illustrate just how important language and power are to each other, one of the authors of this book witnessed the linguistic repercussions of German reunification in 1991. Hannover-derived 'High German' was the standard of the West, whereas Dresden-centered 'Saxon' was the power language of the socialist German Democratic Republic. The Federal Republic of Germany, an economic steam roller even then, soon asserted linguistic dominance. Varieties with even more ancient tradition, such as the 'Lower German' (Plattdeutsch) that is related to Frisian and spoken in the North of Germany, are not even a blip on that radar of linguistic power. A March 2018 speech by Johann Saathoff in German parliament demonstrated what it is like to be linguistically ghosted. Saathoff reacted to a legislative proposal by the right-wing (and anti-immigrant) party 'Alternative for Germany' to declare German the official language of Germany. He repeatedly switched to his native Plattdeutsch during his speech. His point: Whose German? And who benefits from impoverishing the linguistic landscape? The reaction was an uneasy mix of delighted applause and incredulous laughter in the Bundestag, and Saathoff drew a bemused request by its president, Norbert Lammert, for intelligibility on the floor (https://youtu.be/85FPjbTHAMQ).

Linguistic attitudes of a power elite can culminate in outlawing languages or language varieties and suppressing them. Such an effort appears to be underway in the Xinjian Uyghur Autonomous Region. Some estimated 1.5 million Uyghurs and Kazakhs are being held in internment camps—parents in Vocational Skills Education Training Centers and children (including infants—Hoja and Hoshur 2017) in Children's Rescue, Care and Protection Centers (Zenz 2019). Officially, this is so the parents can study and save up for their children's education, while the children are 'happily growing up under the loving care of the Party and the government' (ibid.). The driving rationale is to forestall the spread of radicalized Muslim teaching in the wake of sporadic terror attacks (Ramzy and Buckley 2019). The only permitted language in those detention centers, of course, is Mandarin Chinese (not native for most Uyghurs), taught mostly by ethnic Han teachers (Zaili 2019). Any use of Uyghur (or singing Uyghur songs—ibid.) results in draconian penalties both for the teachers and for the students (including the class leaders) (Zenz 2019, section 3.4).

The author of that study, Adrian Zenz, felt reminded of the 'colonial boarding schools used by the United States, Canada or Australia' (ibid., section 3.6). Those memories are still painfully fresh on the American continent, where efforts were institutionalized to eradicate Native American Languages. In North Carolina, efforts are now underway to recruit the fluency and knowledge of the few remaining Cherokee elders to accompany young children on their way back to their language—speakers who vividly recount being physically punished in school if they spoke Cherokee. Language policies aimed at eradication were/are similarly directed against Kurdish,

Taiwanese, Tagalog, Ukrainian, Lithuanian, Georgian, Azerbaijani, Korean, Cajun French, Galician, Basque, Catalan, and a long list of other languages—including even Esperanto, an *artificial* language, during World War II. Institutionalized linguistic discrimination and criminalization can be an indicator of fascism and a harbinger of persecution (cf. Chapter 6).

That said, attitudes about languages and language varieties are so deep seated (Preston 2013) that linguistic discrimination occurs with impunity and without question in everyday life. 'Othering' occurs even at institutions that have pledged and committed themselves to diversity. A memorable example of such conflictedness comes from Missy Watson and Rachael Shapiro (2018). When Watson worked on new course outcomes in first-year composition at CUNY to reflect current theory on linguistic diversity, she asked scholars at other universities to weigh in. For discussion, she offered the following outcome: 'Acknowledge your and others' range of linguistic differences as resources, and draw on those resources to develop rhetorical sensibility.' One of the responses, from Ligia Mihut at Barry University, was sobering: 'Students recognize the extent to which cultural standards, institutional practices, and values oppress, marginalize, alienate, or create/enhance privilege and power.' Is linguistic equality at an institute of higher learning even feasible?

Stephany Brett Dunstan (2013) documented in her dissertation that students from Appalachian English speech communities experience college quite differently from speakers who emulate the 'standard' more closely. Based solely on the way they speak, their intelligence was perceived as lower by professors and fellow students, affecting their sense of belonging, their class participation, and requiring extra efforts to have their academic contributions valued. Two educational missions are at odds here: On the one hand, schools teach (and aim to model) acceptance, diversity, and social sensitivity. That mission is suspended, however, when it comes to another central concern of education: to protect and perpetuate its own linguistic norms of 'academic English,' another artificial linguistic power construct. In the words of Asao Inoue, we compare 'student writing that use a local Standardized Edited American English (SEAE) with populations of people who do not use that discourse on a daily basis—judging apples by the standards of oranges' (2015:6).

Given the two contradictory missions of embracing and preventing linguistic diversity, academics are naturally conflicted. They will readily enough accept frames of diversity (everyone speaks a dialect, 'standard' is a social construct, all dialects are rule governed and systematic, etc.) but resist the implications. Such inflexibility in higher education has been a source of concern for linguists for many decades (cf. Thiede 1983). Nonetheless, many of us remain committed to the uphill battle of changing academic language attitudes. For instance, in 2012, Stephany Brett Dustan, Walt Wolfram, Andrey J. Jaeger, and Rebecca E. Crandall launched an 'Educating the Educators' initiative (2015) to call attention to linguistic discrimination in the 'university backyard.' To do this, they developed and piloted a 'campus-infusion model' at North Carolina State University with a multi-pronged approach targeting Student Affairs, Academic Affairs, Human Resources, Faculty Affairs, and the Office of Institutional Equity and Diversity (2015:274). Their approach addresses housing, convocation, courses and lectures, new employee and faculty orientation, and more, using 'diversity ambassadors' with online resources. Pre- and post-workshop surveys showed some positive shifts in language attitudes, at least intellectually. In practice, there has been little change.

Illiteracy and Aliteracy

Not reading is, ultimately, socially isolating.

Librarian of Congress Daniel Boorstin sounded the alarm in his 1984 report to Congress:

We must face and defeat the twin menaces of illiteracy and aliteracy—the inability to read and lack of the will to read—if our citizens are to remain free and qualified to govern themselves.

(Boorstin 1984:18)

He echoed the concerns of H. L. Mencken (see p. 74 above), but with added urgency: What most alarmed Boorstin in 1984 was the time that young people spent in front of screens and the impact that had on their literacy. John Hersey had prophetically warned as early as 1954 that television was going to be the 'enemy of reading' (1954:148), and Mary Winn certainly corroborated those fears with her seminal 1977 exposé *The Plug-in Drug*, updated and expanded in 2002: Over the years, there had been a negative correlation between screen time (nowadays also including smart phones and tablets in addition to computers and television) and SAT verbal scores, the ability to read deeply, and the motivation to read long works of literature. What are the implications? Mario Vargas Llosa, winner of the 2010 Nobel Prize for Literature, brings us back to Mencken's and Boorstin's simple point: People who do not read are more easily manipulated (Lier 2019).

The general consensus is that by not being 'much of a reader,' the aliterate are cut off from public discourse and thus kept, uncritically, 'in the dark.' Reading books should make all the difference, then—but a counter-argument can be, and has been, made. While literary scholars and intellectuals present books as the *delivery* vehicles of culture and critical thinking, Juliana Spahr polemicized: 'No one is more convinced than writers of literature that literature has a role to play in the political sphere, that it can provoke and resist' (2018:4). Her study of modern American literature led her to a different conclusion, that 'literature is a genre that is unusually manipulated and dependent' (2018:193), catering, in its constant need for scarce money, to universities' curricula and promotion criteria, literary societies, humanities grants, agents, government support, literary prizes, etc. A similar view was expressed, with impertinent directness, by Ursula K. Le Guin in her "acceptance" speech of the National Book Foundation's Medal for Distinguished Contribution to American Letters at the 65th National Book Awards on November 19, 2014. She said:

> I have had a long career and a good one, in good company. And here, at the end of it, I really don't want to watch American literature get sold down the river.
>
> (youtu.be/Et9Nf-rsALk)

The audience, which included high-ranking Amazon executives, knew quite well what 'river' the author was referring to. A few brave audience members applauded.

So if commercially optimized books are not necessarily the pedagogical enjoinders of critical thinking by virtue of their political messages, why are we here still emphasizing the importance of immersive reading? Because it is not just the *content* of the books, it is also the *activity* of reading and the immersive *experience* that make the difference. Vargas Llosa describes the socio-psychological impact of a culture of reading (Lier 2019):

> A society of many readers is more free and more critical. One effect of literature is to create critical people vis-à-vis those in power. A people that does not read is much easier to manipulate. The good readers are rebels, in a political, religious, and sexual sense. Literature is more than just entertainment. Of course, reading Shakespeare is entertaining, Cervantes, Goethe, Thomas Mann, that's wonderful. But we get more out of it than pleasure. The idea is that besides of our own lives, there are other lives, more intense, more enriched. That creates a kind of rebellion against reality in us. And that, in turn, is the engine of progress.

Visual Word Form Area
A brain region at the junction between the occipital lobe and the temporal lobe responsible for the recognition of objects and faces, which can take on reading as a superimposed function. Immersive readers make connections from the area to the anterior portions of the insula and of the cingulate cortex to link reading into a 'feeling network'—reflective 'deep reading' that is different from superficial reading for just content.

Maryanne Wolf (2016) summarizes the neurological differences between a literate and an illiterate/aliterate brain, observing that 'literate persons activate areas when they process language that were not activated before they were literate' (2016:59). Children who love to read and do so often and immersively form and strengthen new neural pathways that connect the 'Visual Word Form Area' to a brain circuit dubbed the 'feeling network.' Those children (as do adult bookworms) treat book characters as if they were real human beings, taking their perspectives, empathizing with them, interrogating them, and caring for them. Literature provides 'virtual gossip' (Vermeule 2010:xii) and thus, far from isolating the reader, has a socializing effect (Whalen et al. 2012).

Fiction, writes Keith Oatley, 'is a kind of simulation that runs on minds' (2008:1030). While it may seem as if the immersed reader is withdrawn from the world, quite the opposite is happening. Readers of fiction experience social events by proxy (Oatley compares the vividness of such vicarious social experiences to 'the mind's flight simulator'), and the effects carry over into the actual social realm. And herein lies the subversive power of reading: The cognitive demands on reading (cf. Chapter 7) are intense, whereas the screen relieves them. What Vargas Llosa laments as a 'culture of the screen' (Lier 2019) appears to have what we are tempted to call a 'domestication effect' on people (recall p. 30 above). Both the socializing power of reading and the social alienation caused by the screen can be demonstrated experimentally.

After reading a story that transported (q.v. p. 75 above) them, subjects in an experiment were more likely to offer to retrieve pencils the experimenter "accidentally" spilled on the ground, regardless of how they had scored on altruism before the test (Johnson 2012). To take advantage of the effect and to stimulate their ability to listen and to empathize, medical students and residents at the University of California, Irvine, College of Medicine have been made to read poetry (Shapiro and Rucker 2003). Indeed, a survey of how literature positively enhances social behavior was presented by Hammond (2019). Works of literature turn out to be the true social media.

Screen time, on the other hand, is harmful, and particularly so to babies. Patricia Kuhl's research (2010) shows that infants process language as meaningful *only* with an interacting adult—they may attune to speech that comes from a screen, but MEG imaging shows that they do not expect for it to convey anything, and the processing is confined to the auditory cortex alone. In contrast, interaction between adults and babies utilizes a broad bandwidth of information and requires massive networking between brain areas. In an interactive book reading session, for example, an infant in the reader's lap feels the vibration of the adult's voice, entrains with the rhythm of the language (which is why so many children's books are written in poetry), associates words and pictures, anticipates words that rhyme, interacts with the page (turning it, or moving flaps and parts), and is rewarded with joy and cuddles upon pointing to where the little mouse is on any of the pages of Margaret Wise Brown's *Goodnight Moon!* The richness of these many simultaneous modalities actually makes it easier to confirm what is salient (Thiede 2019); Lori Curtindale et al. refer to this reliance on multimodality as 'intersensory facilitation' (2019:285). None of this interaction can happen with a screen. Television as a babysitter thus slows down language acquisition by depriving infants of meaningful interactive language, and language deprivation presents clinically by 24 months (Radesky et al. 2016:825). The result is a 'Matthew Effect' ('For unto every one that hath shall be given, and he shall have abundance: but from him that hath not shall be taken even that which he hath'—Matthew 25:29). Children thriving on quality 'language nutrition' (a term coined by pediatricians; cf. Zauche et al. 2017) have an easier time fast-mapping and absorbing even more vocabulary—as language-starved children fall further behind.

Matthew Effect
In pediatrics, the term for children falling further and further behind while others progress exponentially. The term was coined to explain the long-term effect of the '30-million-word gap,' the cumulative amount of words underprivileged children will *not* have been exposed to compared to their 4-year-old peers, who grew up being read to and interacted with regularly.

Affluent parents know this and start reading to their children often before they are even born. They realize that to 'supercharge your baby' (Vance 2018), interactive book reading beats 'educational' toys, apps, and electronic games (Sosa 2016). The sad fact is, however, that almost half of the children in the United States grow up in poverty (AAP Council On Community Pediatrics 2016). Susan Neumann conducted a study in Philadelphia's low-income neighborhoods: 'We found a total of 33 books for children in a community of 10,000 children … 33 books in all of the neighborhood' (NPR 2014). In contrast, children in Philadelphia's affluent neighborhoods averaged 300 books per child. Similar disparities exist worldwide. A recent UNICEF survey of some 100,000 children in 35 countries (not including the US) found nearly half of them without children's books (Manu et al. 2019). However, the presence of at least one children's book (statistically) in low-income households already doubles that child's chances of being on track for literacy (ibid.).

Philanthropic initiatives to provide disadvantaged children with books to read have been implemented for some time, sporadically for decades, though they seem to be gaining traction. RIF (Reading is Fundamental), established in 1966, has collected and donated more than 415 million books since that time (www.rif.org/). More recently, Imagination Library, an initiative by singer/composer, actress, and entrepreneur Dolly Parton, has expanded its mission of sending a free book each month to children from Kentucky to the US and other English-speaking countries, moving a total volume exceeding 15 million books in 2017 alone (https://imaginationlibrary.com/). Other initiatives, such as First Book, are less well funded, but still award many books to children (1.5 million in the case of First Book: https://firstbook.org/). Pediatricians have taken to *prescribing* children's books as supplementary language nutrition, and they have established initiatives like 'Reach Out and Read' to promote a healthy language environment at home (https://reachoutandread.org/).

Parents at the local level can get involved as well. Many already volunteer to read to elementary school children, get involved with church programs addressing the needs of immigrant learners of English, support libraries and librarians at public and private schools. English professors nationwide organize literacy events such as a 'Seuss-a-thon' for very young children on Theodor Geisel's birthday. Public libraries and cities offer literacy camps, read-a-thons, family literacy nights, read-and-romps, and other creative and fun events involving books.

Clearly, there is increasing public realization that poverty and screens prevent children from becoming fully literate, and indeed there seems to be a sense of alarm at the magnitude of the resulting deficits and social disparities. Whereas the first time this sense of alarm occurred, it was framed in terms of *national security* (in 1957, after Russia beat the US to space with their sputnik satellite), this time the sentiment appears to be a grassroots fear that *democracy* is in danger.

Contaminated Language

> Language that comes in the guise of cooperation but is designed to deceive and makes the recipients act against their own best interest is as toxic as polluted air and water.

Human language relies on mind reading, which presumes trust. Just as attending a school or university presupposes that it is physically safe to do so, just as drinking tap water presupposes that the water is potable, so we expect that our conversation partners intend to meet the sincerity conditions of what they say. Sadly, this very book was completed after fatal shootings at the University of North Carolina at Charlotte, and we have seen tap water dispensed to an entire city in full knowledge that it was contaminated with lead (see p. 8 above). Some caution is in order about the quality of the language we consume on a daily basis as well.

A major erosion of trust occurs on, ironically enough, platforms that were originally developed as 'social' media. Messages that appear to come from what are supposed to be trusted sources (friends) may have been planted there by professional influencers, capable of affecting public opinion and even the outcome of a presidential election (Mueller 2019, Cleary 2019). The flood (and ephemeral shelf life) of information on social media—tweets are superseded by other tweets in moments—makes it difficult for the reader to construct a coherent narrative, even though those pieces of information and misinformation are framed to nourish and confirm some vague ideological premise or promise. Incoherence confounds critical thinking; what remains is affiliation to in-groups (modern 'tribalism').

While younger people draw much of their information from the Internet, older ones tend to trust local sources—local newspapers, radio stations, television stations. Those sources, too, can be deceptive. In 2017, the Federal Communications Commission of the United States relaxed restrictions to benefit the Sinclair Broadcast Group (Kang 2018). Sinclair now has a monopoly on local television stations (almost a contradiction in terms, and something the FCC should have actually *prevented*). The conglomerate can oblige the local stations it owns to include 'must-read' items (originally station promotions) in their news coverage, and those, in 2016, included positive coverage of one presidential candidate while focusing on health issues and the use of a private e-mail server of the other. Sinclair stations also feature 'Terrorism Desk Alerts' that label and stereotype immigrants and Muslims (Rosenberg 2018).

The systematic contamination of public discourse, exacerbated by labeling factual information as 'fake news,' has polarized society to the point that moderates are beginning to feel marginalized or threatened (cf. p. 123 above). In the world of dubious news and deceptive social media, we feel reminded of the trademark slogan of the three witches in Macbeth (Act 1, scene 1): 'Fair is Foul, Foul is Fair.' Indeed, in her commencement speech at Harvard University on May 30, 2019, German chancellor Angela Merkel implored the assembled graduates not to describe 'lies as truth and truth as lies,' and instead to 'take the time to stop, be still, pause' (Angerer 2019). Having grown up in the German Democratic Republic herself, Merkel has formative memories of growing up with contaminated language from state-run media: propaganda, deceptive frames, deliberate misinformation, and a constant feeling of imminent threat or betrayal.

To break this cycle of controlling and conforming, we too need to stop, be still, pause, to recognize and contain the control that electronic media have presumed to exert over our lives. On average, young persons in the US divide their attention over multiple screens, which puts them in a state of 'continuous partial attention.' A study by Time Inc. showed that they switch media sources an average of 27 times in an hour (Barren 2014). There is a hidden 'switch cost' associated with such divided attention in the form of increases in the levels of hormones normally associated with stress: cortisol and norepinephrine (adrenalin) (Levitin 2014). Those hormones put the brain into 'a heightened *fight or flight* mode for enormous amounts of our days' (Wolf 2016:147). Of course we are concerned about the obvious fact that such a mental state is not conducive to learning. Our larger concern here is that this kind of chronic mental state of latent alarm can be extended over entire in-groups with the techniques described in the previous paragraphs, leading to a form of collective learned helplessness that is normally seen in abusive relationships and cultures of poverty and powerlessness.

It is important to see in this context how traditional anchors of trustworthiness are being singled out for attack or infiltration. Historically responsible news outlets such as PBS, CNN, or *The New York Times* are framed as the 'enemy of the people.' The humanities, traditionally the self-appointed guardians of critical thinking, are losing status (and funding) to 'STEM' research. Altruistic reciprocity is derided as mere 'political correctness,' critical thinking as offensive to 'traditional' or 'parental' values (cf. p. 74 above). Universities are offered grants with political agendas, such as BB&T's 'Moral Foundation grants,' which until 2015 required any university that accepted it to teach works of Ayn Rand (even though the faculty were typically not informed of that provision); to create chaired faculty positions, library reading rooms, and 'capitalism centers' dedicated to Ayn Rand; and to hand students free copies of *Atlas Shrugged* and other works (Beets 2015).[1]

Since it is impossible to clean up (fact check, reframe) contaminated language once it has been consumed (having originated from origins we have traditionally trusted, such as friends, public personalities, and local sources), it is easier to create a counterculture than to repair

learned helplessness
In psychology, the term for accepting aversive (painful, fear-inducing) situations because of a resigned feeling that nothing can be done to avoid them.

Ayn Rand (1905–1982)
Russian-born author whose best-known works are the novels *The Fountainhead* and *Atlas Shrugged*. Rand specifically rejected altruism, advocating rational and ethical egoism instead. She rejected faith/religion in favor of 'objectivism,' which led her to argue that only reason leads to knowledge and that the best social arrangement is 'laissez-faire capitalism.'

---

1   In the interest of full disclosure: The Belk College of Business at our home university, the University of North Carolina at Charlotte, accepted such a grant in 2005.

the dominant one. Young people in particular are savvy enough to frame counter-narratives in the wake of school shootings, in response to the anticipated consequences of climate change they will inherit, and in calling out humanitarian and environmental crises such as mass detention of immigrants and the separation of their children. New values include being 'woke' as a stance against othering from a position of privilege.

Taking back the narrative would require, at the very minimum, the systematic inclusion of critical thinking skills in the curricula of schools and at universities (which is indeed happening in some states), promoting forensic (debating) and linguistic skills, and sponsoring programs aimed at conflict resolution such as international baccalaureates and Model United Nations. It would seem that the only way to avoid the influence of contaminated language is to claim and change the rules of the discourse.

At the level of higher education, technology offers possible venues for disseminating quality information. Rather than allowing publishers to own knowledge and charge ever-increasing amounts of money for accessing scientific work (the biggest amount of a university library budget no longer goes to books but to serials subscriptions, e-books, and databases), scientists began to deposit their work in open-access forums. When that, too, was co-opted by predatory open-access publishers charging exorbitant up-front fees from the authors, university libraries began monitoring and listing predatory publishers in databases of their own. In response to prohibitive costs associated with higher education, universities such as Harvard, MIT, University of California, Berkeley, University of Texas, Georgetown, and Boston University developed MOOCs (Massive Open Online Courses) and produced documentaries for Public Television (such as the North Carolina Language and Life Project, https://languageandlife.org/).

Uncooperative Language

> Some language is not aimed at negotiating clarity, but counts on the recipient's *inability* to understand it.

Besides language that pretends to cooperate but really aims to deceive, there is also language that is factually correct but does not even pretend to cooperate. Some of those instances of deliberately uncooperative language have become proverbial, such as the 'fine print' of a sales contract, the packaging slip for medications, or its spoken equivalent, the acoustically sped-up 'disclaimer' at the end of a television or radio ad. As was outlined in Chapter 7 in the discussion of definitions, clarity is a negotiation and results from aligning with the audience's needs. These documents are designed for a different audience: Their main raison d'être is protection from lawsuits.

A little-known but instructive example of how uncooperative language can have significant consequences is the trial of former governor of Illinois Rod R. Blagojevich following his near-unanimous impeachment in 2009 for abuse of power and corruption in office.

Prosecutors knew they had an obvious and airtight case, but the jury was unable to understand the material provided to them, which was highly technical with interconnected parts and terms that were clearly important (such as *conspiracy to commit extortion*) but whose definitions they could only guess at. The jury spent several days just trying to figure out how to break down their assignment into manageable tasks. One of them, Steve Wlodek, said: 'It was like, "Here's a manual, go fly the space shuttle"' (Davey and Saulny 2010). In hindsight, it does not surprise that the jury did not return a verdict anywhere close to what the prosecution had expected.

Shawn Burton (2018) gives an example of how an uncooperative legal document can be rephrased in comprehensive language without losing precision. This is how a contract's liability-limitation clause was made transparent by GE Aviation's digital services unit (the service provider's name having changed meanwhile from Austin to FES):

Before:

UNDER NO CIRCUMSTANCES SHALL COMPANY HAVE ANY LIABILITY, WHETHER IN CONTRACT, TORT (INCLUDING NEGLIGENCE), STRICT LIABILITY, OTHER LEGAL THEORY, OR BREACH OF WARRANTY FOR: (i) ANY LOST PROFITS; (ii) ANY LOSS OR REPLACEMENT OF DATA FILES LOST OR DAMAGED; (iii) CONSEQUENTIAL, SPECIAL, PUNITIVE, INCIDENTAL OR INDIRECT DAMAGES ARISING OUT OF THIS AGREEMENT, THE DELIVERY, USE, SUPPORT, OPERATION, OR FAILURE OF THE SYSTEM; OR (iv) CONSEQUENTIAL, SPECIAL, PUNITIVE, INCIDENTAL OR INDIRECT DAMAGES ARISING OUT OF THE INACCURACY OR LOSS OF ANY DATA GENERATED BY THE SYSTEM; EVEN IF COMPANY HAS BEEN ADVISED OF THE POSSIBILITY OF SUCH DAMAGES, PROVIDED THAT THE FOREGOING DISCLAIMER UNDER SUB-SECTION (iii) ABOVE DOES NOT APPLY TO THE EXTENT SUCH DAMAGES ARE BASED UPON THE USE OF THE SYSTEM AND ARE ARISING OUT OF AUSTIN'S WILLFUL MISCONDUCT OR GROSS NEGLIGENCE THAT RESULTS IN A BREACH OF SECTION 6 HERETO.

After:

Your and our total compensation obligation under this contract cannot exceed twenty-five percent of the amount FES has billed you in the last twelve months for the applicable service, and neither of us have any compensation, contribution or other obligation for consequential, punitive, incidental, indirect or exemplary losses (including, but not limited to, profit or revenue loss, capital costs, replacement costs and increased operating costs).

The idea that citizens should be able to understand the laws and contracts that govern them can be traced back to the English 1362 'Statute of Pleading,' which officially changed the legal language of the land from Anglo-Norman French to English because the people had 'no Knowledge nor Understanding of that which is said for them or against them by their Serjeants and other Pleaders.' In the US, President Carter signed an executive order for federal regulations to be 'as simple and clear as possible,' followed by legislation under the Clinton and Obama presidencies. The Obama-era Plain Writing Act became law on October 13, 2010. Federal law now requires key regulations, such as the Truth in Lending Act and the Fair Credit Reporting Act, to be generally intelligible. Whether all US states eventually implement similar provisions for clarity remains to be seen.

Why We Need Linguistic Equality

Unlike the Universal Declaration of Human Rights, the Universal Declaration of Linguistic Rights has never been ratified. In other words, the right to one's own language is not internationally a legally recognized human right. Even the human rights study most recently available to the authors, the 2019 Human Rights Measurement Initiative (HRMI) dataset, measures empowerment and safety from the state (both scoring surprisingly low in the United States) as well as overall quality of life, but does *not* include linguistic rights among its survey of 'economic and social rights' (https://rightstracker.org/en).

In spite of all the efforts and good intentions outlined above, linguistic discrimination is not illegal. 'This verbal class distinction by now should be antique,' sang Professor Henry Higgins in the movie *My Fair Lady*, but it remains, even in the United States. It is not uncommon to experience any of the following, simply based on one's public linguistic persona and way of speaking:

- being told over a phone that an apartment is no longer available;
- not being called back after what appeared to be a successful job interview;
- being told you do not talk the right way to be a school teacher, bank clerk, newscaster …;
- feeling left out as the audience of children's books, movies, performances, novels …;
- being accosted for speaking differently in a restaurant;
- arousing suspicion or derision.

There is no legal recourse against any of the representative examples listed above. Without laws guaranteeing the right to one's own language, a grassroots-level change in perception must change the narrative and eventually lead to linguistic equality (the way in which changing realities eventually resulted in the US federal recognition of same-sex marriage in June 2015).

Since, for all the reasons outlined in this book, linguistic in-groups naturally hold on to their linguistic attitudes, it is up to academics to change their frames. In sociolinguistics, this is known as 'linguistic gratuity,' ways in which linguists and academics who study language behavior give back to the community (Wolfram, Reaser, and Vaughn 2008). This is not to be done, of course, with caricaturizing documentaries on PBS of the more exotic features of local varieties, which are apt to backfire. Instead, we can exploit the fact that people are naturally curious about language and local history, tend to take pride in their region and state, and want to know about the historical importance of their (and each others') communities. Language can play a central role here. The Lumbee Indians of North Carolina, for example, having been denied full federal recognition and having lost their last native speaker of Lumbee prior to the Civil War, now take a large part of their tribal identity from their distinctive dialect of English (Hannel 2015:25). People's natural curiosity about language can become the starting point of education that can lead to a shift in perceptual frames. Venues of such efforts can include documentary films and videos, museum exhibits, audio CDs, books and booklets for popular audiences, school curricula, and university-level initiatives (cf. Wolfram, Reaser, and Vaughn 2008) such as produced by the North Carolina Language and Life Project. Seen in historical context, varieties perceived as 'bad speech' can come to be perceived as cultural heritage.

Language nourishes us. It builds brain structures in the young child and affords social health later on (empathy, altruistic bonding with in-groups, critical thinking, informed decision making, even the ability to delay gratification for long-term gains). Withholding or willfully contaminating language is thus nothing short of a human rights violation. People have a right to be nourished.

References

AAP Council on Community Pediatrics. 2016. Poverty and child health in the United States. *Pediatrics* 137(4).e20160339. DOI: 10.1542/peds.2016-0339.

Algeo, John. 1977. Grammatical usage: Modern shibboleths. *James B. McMillan: Essays in Linguistics by His Friends and Colleagues*, ed. by James C. Raymond and J. Willis Russel, 53–71. Tuscaloosa, AL: University of Alabama Press.

Angerer, Carlo. 2019. Angela Merkel stresses importance of breaking down walls in Harvard graduation speech. NBC News (May 30). Online: www.nbcnews.com/news/world/angela-merkel-stresses-importance-breaking-down-walls-harvard-graduation-speech-n1012216.

Barren, Naomi. 2014. *Words unseen: The fate of reading in a digital world.* London: Oxford University Press.

Beets, S. Douglas. 2015. BB&T, *Atlas Shrugged*, and the ethics of corporation influence on college curricula. *Journal of Academic Ethics* 13(4).311–44.

Boorstin, Daniel J. 1984. Letter of transmittal. *Books in our future: A report from the Librarian of Congress to the Congress*, 6–57. Washington, DC: Joint Committee on the Library of Congress of the United States. Online: http://files.eric.ed.gov/fulltext/ED253243.pdf.

Burton, Shawn. 2018. The case for plain-language contracts. *Harvard Business Review* (January–February). Online: http://hbr.org/2018/01/the-case-for-plain-language-contracts.

Cleary, Gillian. 2019. Twitterbots: Anatomy of a propaganda campaign. Symantec Blog / Threat Intelligence (June 5). Online: www.symantec.com/blogs/threat-intelligence/twitterbots-propaganda-disinformation.

Curtindale, Lori M.; Lorraine E. Bahrick; Robert Lickliter; and John Colombo. 2019. Effects of multimodal synchrony on infant attention and hear rate during events with social and nonsocial stimuli. *Journal of Experimental Child Psychology* 178.283–94. DOI: 10.1016/j.jecp.2018.10. 006.

Davey, Monica, and Susan Saulny. 2010. Jurors fault complexity of the Blagojevich trial. *The New York Times*, New York Edition (August 19).A1. Online: www.nytimes.com/2010/08/19/us/19jury.html.

Davis, Boyd; Ralf Thiede; and Mary K. Smith. 2013. Cross-cultural socialization into a common profession: Exploring how nursing students in Taiwan and in the U.S. narrate professional identity. *Crossroads* (University of Bialystok) 1.6–23.

Dunstan, Stephany Brett. 2013. The influence of speaking a dialect of Appalachian English on the college experience. PhD dissertation, North Carolina State University.

Dunstan, Stephany Brett; Walt Wolfram; Andrey J. Jaeger; and Rebecca E. Crandall. 2015. Educating the educated: Language diversity in the university backyard. *American Speech* 90(2).266–80. DOI: 10.1215/ 00031283-3130368.

Elliser, Cindy R., and Denise L. Herzing. 2016. Long-term interspecies association patterns of Atlantic bottlenose dolphins, *Tursiops truncatus*, and Atlantic spotted dolphins, *Stenella frontalis*, in the Bahamas. *Marine Mammal Science* 32(1) (January).38–56. DOI: 10.1111/mms.12242.

Hammond, Claudia. 2019. Does reading fiction make us better people? BBC (June 3). Online: www.bbc.com/future/story/20190523-does-reading-fiction-make-us-better-people?.

Hannel, Eric. 2015. *Reinterpreting a Native American identity: Examining the Lumbee through the Peoplehood Model*. Lanham, MD: Lexington.

Hersey, John. 1954. Why do students bog down on the first R? A local committee sheds light on a national problem: Reading. *LIFE* 36(21) (May 24).136–50.

Hoja, Gulchehra, and Shohret Hoshur. 2017. Children of detained Uyghurs face 'terrible' conditions in overcrowded XinJiang orphanages. Radio Free Asia (October 18), trans. by Mamatjan Juma and Alim Seytoff, written in English by Joshua

Lipes. Online: www.rfa.org/english/news/uyghur/children-10182017144425.html.

Inoue, Asao B. 2015. *Antiracist writing assessment ecologies: Teaching and assessing writing for a socially just future.* Anderson, SC: Oarlor Press; Fort Collins, CO: The WAC Clearing House.

Jewish Study Bible, The, ed. by Adele Berlin and Marc Zvi Brettler. 2014. 2nd ed. Jewish Publication Society. Oxford: Oxford University Press.

Johnson, Dan R. 2012. Transportation into a story increases empathy, prosocial behavior, and perceptual bias toward fearful expressions. *Personality and Individual Differences* 53(2) (January).150–55. DOI: 10.1016/j.paid.2011.10.005.

Kang, Cecilia. 2018. F.C.C. link to Sinclair is explored. *The New York Times* (February 16).B1. Online: www.nytimes.com/2018/02/15/technology/ fcc-sinclair-ajit-pai.html.

Kuhl, Patricia K. 2010. Brain mechanisms in early language acquisition. *Neuron* 67 (September 9).713–27.

Levitin, Daniel. 2014. *The organized mind: Thinking straight in the age of information overload.* New York: Viking Press.

Lier, Judith, 2019. Mario Vargas Llosa im Interview: Ein Volk, das nicht liest, ist leichter zu manipulieren. *Stern* (June 8). Online: www.stern.de/kultur/buecher/mario-vargas-llosa-im-interview---einvolk--das-nicht-liest--ist-leichter-zu-manipulieren--8737498.%20html.

Manu, Alexander; Fernanda Ewerling; Aluisio J. D. Barros; and Cesar G. Victora. 2019. Association between availability of children's books and the literacy-numeracy skills of children aged 36 to 59 months: Secondary analysis of the UNICEF multiple-indicator cluster surveys covering 35 countries. *Journal of Global Health* 9(1).1–11. DOI: 10.7189/jogh.09.010403.

Miller, Sarah. 2019. Tryna keep up with tryna: Grammaticalization in the digital age. Presented at the SouthEastern Conference on Linguistics LXXXVI (Boca Raton, FL, June 1).

Mueller, Robert S. III. 2019. *Report on the investigation into Russian interference in the 2016 Presidential Election,* vol. 1. Washington, DC: US Department of Justice. Online: www.justice.gov/storage/report.pdf.

NPR. 2014. Nonprofit fights illiteracy by getting books to kids who need them. Morning Edition (December 29). Online: www.npr.org/2014/12/29/373729964/first-book-gets-reading-material-into-the-hands-of-low-income-students.

Oatley, Keith. 2008. The mind's flight simulator. *The Psychologist* 21(12) (December).1030–32.

Preston, Dennis R. 2013. Language with an attitude. *The handbook of language variation and change,* ed. by J. K. Chambers and Natalie Schilling, 157–82. New York: John Wiley and Sons.

Radesky, Jenny S.; Judith Carta; and Megan Bair-Merritt. 2016. The 30 million-word gap: Relevance for pediatrics. *JAMA Pediatrics* 170(9) (September).825–26.

Ramzy, Austin, and Chris Buckley. 2019. The Xinjiang Papers: 'Absolutely no mercy': Leaked files expose how China organized mass detentions of Muslims. *The New York Times* (November 16). Online: www.nytimes.com/interactive/2019/11/16/world/asia/china-xinjiang-documents.html.

Reaser, Jeffrey. 2019. From deficit to difference to asset: Empowering students via critical language pedagogy. Presented at the SouthEastern Conference on Linguistics LXXXVI (Boca Raton, FL, May 30).

Rosenberg, Eli. 2018. Trump said Sinclair 'is far superior to CNN': What we know about the conservative media giant. *The Washington Post* (April 3).

Shapiro, Johanna, and Lloyd Rucker. 2003. Can poetry make better doctors? Teaching the Humanities and Arts to medical students and residents at the University of California, Irvine, College of Medicine. *Academic Medicine* 78(10) (October 1).953–57. Online: http://escholarship.org/uc/item/ 97m8q243.

Sosa, Anna V. 2016. Association of the type of toy used during play with the quantity and quality of parent–infant communication. *JAMA Pediatrics* 170(2) (February).132–37.

Spahr, Juliana. 2018. *Du Bois's telegram: Literary resistance and state containment.* Cambridge, MA and London: Harvard University Press.

Statute of Pleading. 1362. Online: http://languageandlaw.org/TEXTS/STATS/PLEADING.HTM.

Thiede, Ralf. 1983. A Black English/Standard English interim grammar in college composition: A case study. *Transactions of the Missouri Academy of Science* 17.171–80.

Thiede, Ralf. 2019. Synesthetic entrainment in interactive reading sessions of children's books. *Children's Literature Association Quarterly* 44(4) (December).381–400.

Vance, Erik. 2018. Can you super-charge your baby? *Scientific American* 318(6) (June).34–39.

Vermeule, Blakey. 2010. *Why Do We Care about Literary Characters?* Baltimore, MD: Johns Hopkins University Press.

Watson, Missy, and Rachael Shapiro. 2018. Clarifying the multiple dimensions of monolingualism: Keeping our sights on language politics. *Composition Forum* 38 (Spring). Online: http://compositionforum.com/issue/38/monolingualism.php.

Whalen, Douglas H.; Lisa Zunshine; and Michael Holquist. 2012. Theory of mind and embedding of perspective: A psychological test of a literary 'sweet spot.' *Scientific Study of Literature* 2(2).301–15. DOI: 10.1075/ssol.2.2.06wha.

Winn, Marie. 1977. *The plug-in drug: Television, children, and the family.* New York: Viking.

Winn, Marie. 2002. *The plug-in drug: Television, computers, and family life.* New York: Penguin Putnam.

Wolf, Maryanne, with Stephanie Gottwald. 2016. *Tales of literacy for the 21st century.* The Literary Agenda. Oxford and New York: Oxford University Press.

Wolfram, Walt; Jeffrey Reaser; and Charlotte Vaughn. 2008. Operationalizing linguistic gratuity: From principle to practice. *Language and Linguistics Compass* 2(6).1109–34. DOI: 10.1111/ j.1749-818x.2008.00092.x.

Zaili, Li [pseudonym]. 2019. 'Hanification': Uyghur children cut off from their roots. *Bitter Winter* (March 23). Online: http:// bitterwinter.org/uyghur-children-cut-off-from-their-roots.

Zauche, Lauren Head; Ashley E. Darcy Mahoney; Taylor A. Thul; Michael S. Zauche; Arianne B. Weldon; and Jennifer L. Stapel-Wax. 2017. The power of language nutrition for children's brain development, health, and future academic achievement. *Journal of Pediatric Health Care* 31(4) (July/August).493–503.

Zenz, Adrian. 2019. Break their roots: Evidence for China's parent–child separation campaign in Xinjiang. *The Journal of Political Risk* 7(7) (July 4). Online: www.jpolrisk.com/break-their-roots-evidence-for-chinas-parent-child-separation-campaign-inxinjiang.

Index

Alex the African Grey Parrot
44–6, 52
aliteracy *see* illiteracy and aliteracy
analogy *see* comparing
analysis 39, 42–5, 57, 63, 81;
conversational 99; discourse 99
aphasia 23; *see also* dysphasia
aphorism *see* comparing
apperception *see* scripts
assertive 25, 87–91, 96, 115;
see also speech acts
Austin, John L. 86–7

babbling 17–18
Bayesian modeling 66
Benesch, Susan 126; *see also*
violent language
Bourdieu, Pierre 133–4
brain 6, 11; evolution of 20–3;
v. mind 6; outcome-oriented
processing *see* Language;
overlaid functions 20–1, 30;
states and reflexes 39–40;
see also Broca's Area; Language;
metaphor, of brain as computer;
metaphor, of brain as narrating
device; Wernicke's Area
Broca's Area 21, 23, 27, 29
Burling, Robbins 51, 54–5

Chomsky, Noam 8, 103
Christie, Agatha 83, 158–9
clarity *see* managed confusion
collective intentionality 1, 12, 37,
50, 56–7, 81–2; for declarative
illocution 133; for implicature
99; and language use 57; and
meaning 57; and reality 133–4;
and storytelling 75–76; *see also*
language acquisition; silencing,

illocutionary disablement;
violence, and collective
intentionality
commissive 87–90, 96; *see also*
speech acts
communication systems:
combinatorial 16–20; evolution
of 17; and safety 16–20;
single-signal 16–18
comparing 12, 18, 38, 44–6, 58
concepts 12, 18, 31, 37, 38, 81;
abstract 44–5; apperception
63–4; complexity 38–9,
41–4; for conventionalizing
see conventions; distinct from
brain states 39–40; of events 41;
for imagining *see* imagining;
for imitating *see* imitation; of
objects 40–41; for planning
see planning; relational 44–5;
shared 166–7; synthesis 46; for
thinking 38
conflict resolution *see* language, of
conflict resolution
conventions 50–3; for culture
51–3; communicative 51–2; for
implicature *see* implicature; and
interpretation 112; and politeness
see politeness; semantic
52–3; *see also* imitation, for
conventions
cooperation 11, 12, 14, 19, 55; of
brain processes 27; for conflict
resolution *see* language, of
conflict resolution; because
of entropy 20–2, 102–103;
for linguistic processing 82,
103–16; for narrative *see*
scripts; of nonhuman animals
56; for processing implicatures

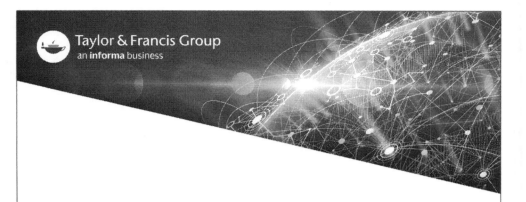